HUMOR

IN

BLUE

HUMOR
IN
BLUE

The book of your past may be forgotten and hidden by time; But you may relive the moments of humor if you allow your thoughts to rediscover its pages. *(Author)*

Rolf J. "Pröpper" Wysock Albert J. "Pröpper" Wysock

Library of Congress Control Number: 2019907872

PAPERBACK: 978-1-7333366-5-9
EBOOK: 978-1-7333366-6-6

Ordering Information:

For orders and inquiries, please contact:
1-888-404-1388
www.goldtouchpress.com
book.orders@goldtouchpress.com

Printed in the United States of America

DEDICATION

This book is dedicated to all the brave men and women who wore or are wearing the badge of honor. Especially to all the heroes, regardless of department, who were willing to answer society's call to serve and protect it and were brutally taken from us by the cowards of that society.

Yes, there is a "***Blue Line***". A select close-knit brother and sisterhood, bonded together by the badge of pride, integrity and guts. Its members are reluctant to share their special camaraderie with others who truly wouldn't understand their remarkable way of handling danger, hardship, and the unique creation of their humor; they simply prefer the company of each other. It is an exclusive and unusual world of justness, reliability, mutual sharing, respect, trust and dependency that the civilian sector wouldn't genuinely understand. Contrary to the oft accepted but erroneous belief that police officers hide behind the "Blue Line", its members are the first to demand punishment and expulsion of those who deliberately or knowingly violate the law, strict departmental rules or tarnish the noble profession. "**Regrettably, criminal intent only sees a uniform and not the person in it**." (Author)

ONCE A COP, ALWAYS A COP.

Once the badge goes on, it never comes off, whether they can see it or not.
It fuses to the soul through adversity, fear, and adrenaline, and no
Who as ever worn it with pride, integrity and guts, can
Ever sleep through the 'call of the wild'
That wafts through bedroom windows in the deep of night.

Author: Unknown

PREFACE

Before the intended theme of this book is introduced, it is absolutely critical to be emblematic and first address several extremely pressing issues that threaten the wellbeing of our society and the willingness of the public to believe a blatant lie and reject the obvious truth defies logic. Acts of kindness are only occasionally reported and quickly forgotten. Our interest is immediately perked when listening to reports of bad news, scandal and negative public opinion. By remaining strictly unbiased and approach the subject matter realistically it is ardently hoped and desired not to offend anyone and allow readers to be the judge. Thus it is difficult not to write satire.

Independent Press?

> "There is no such a thing in America a as an independent press, unless it is out in country towns. You are all slaves. You know it, and I know it. There is not one of you who dare to express an honest opinion. If you express it, you would know beforehand that it would never appear in print. I am paid \$150 for keeping honest opinions out of the paper I am connected with. Others of you are paid similar salaries for doing similar things. If I should allow honest opinions to be printed in one issue of my paper, I would be like Othello before twenty-four hours: my occupation would be gone. The man who would be so foolish as to write honest opinions would be out on the street hunting for another job. The business of a New York journalist is to distort the truth, to lie outright, to pervert, to vilify, to fawn at the feet of Mammon, and so sell his country and his race for his daily bread, or for what is about the same-his salary. You know this, and I know it; and what foolery to be toasting an 'Independent Press'! We are the tools and vassals of rich men behind the scenes. We are jumping-jacks. They pull the string

> and we dance. Our time, our talents, our lives, our possibilities, is all the property of other men. We are intellectual prostitutes."
>
> *(John Swinton, New York Times journalist, ca. 1883)*

There may be some truth to John Swinton's assessment. On February 10, 1946 the British Foreign Minister Ernest Bevin when attending the London Conference of Foreign Ministers had this to say: **"A newspaper has three things to do." "One is to amuse, another is to entertain, and the rest is to mislead."** We are at the edge and steadily marching towards impending chaos because we fail to apply common sense and possess dangerously low knowledge of history and hide behind rose-colored glasses. Unfortunately, too many members of Congress missed the 'wakeup call' in 1963 and didn't hear Congressman Albert Herlong Jr. of Florida citing the 45 long term Communist goals.

> **"Humor is humor and timeless; an enemy of Political Correctness. Grotesque imaging and vocalized extreme violence depicted as humor are products of the Far Left opposition."** (Author)

Starting with the recent tragic events suffered by POLICE, readers are urged to take personal bias off the table and recognize that there are two sides to every story. Quoting *Desiderius Erasmus (1465-1536) In Praise of Folly:* **"Therefore, if any singly complain they are particularly reflected upon, they do but betray their own guilt, at least their own cowardice…the ingenious reader will easily perceive I aimed at diversion rather than satire…":** In the analysis, simple logic and common sense are applied in interpretation of the facts; thus no apology is required.

Unfortunately, we have not only failed miserably to solve the malaise of the past but have also allowed Political Folly to fester as we entered the Twenty First Century. Those who refuse to accept reality hide their ignorance in a world of make believe. Crime is steadily becoming so prevalent and a daily occurrence, it is relatively safe to assume that well over half of our society is involved in some acts of a nefarious nature. Not necessarily hurtful or serious, but unlawful nevertheless. Minor infractions are routinely shrugged off and looked upon as less and less of an offense; perhaps even accepted as part of life by many. An endless list of reasons and excuses, offered in defense, often baffle the imagination that all too frequently defy rational – **Affluenza?** *More than 10,000 DUI (Driving under the Influence) victims die per year.

The Drunk Driver

His friends told him: "You've had too much!"
To heed their advice, he wouldn't do such.
He took just one more for the road.
By now he had more than his share of a load.
Drinking and driving to him were not new.
Many times he had driven after having more than a few.

Out of the bar he has to stumble.
For his keys he has to search and fumble.
With his vision blurred, he sees double.
To find the ignition, he has trouble.
He thinks he's ready now to drive;
Someone soon will not be alive.

His car is swerving from side to side;
No place for the innocent to run or hide.
Rounding a curve, he's over too far;
Head-on he crashes into another car.
The squealing of tires, then a horrible sound;
Death's grip once again has been unbound.

Among the twisted wreckage upon the ground,
Her torn and lifeless body is found.
She had in a box a new wedding gown;
Then the drunk came along and mowed her down.
What could have been a happy bride and groom,
Was turned into a nightmare's eerie gloom.
All that remains is a mute stone with her name.
For this terrible tragedy a drunk driver is to blame.

Cpl Rolf J. Wysock DSP T-6

Political Correctness has inundated our daily activities and seriously hinders the equitable adjudication of punishment by our legal system. Adding to the ridiculousness are judges who at times, sit on the fringe of lunacy. Those who know and speak the truth are routinely chastised and their voices ridiculed into silence by "Political Correctness". Today and throughout past history, individuals who dare to speak out publicly and expose the truth are excoriated; at times even suffer character assassination. **"Prejudices are what fools use for reason."** Voltaire (1694-1778) Of course it is much easier to indoctrinate and sway the gullible masses to believe that society is at fault and that the government is the solution; Lenin's experiment in 1917 failed. **"The narrow-minded and sociopaths are prone to convict an entire group for the misdeeds of a very few."** (Author)

> "Sometimes the law defends plunder and participants in it. Thus the beneficiaries are spared the shame and danger that their acts would otherwise involve…But how is this legal plunder to be identified? Quite simply. See if the law takes from some persons what belongs to them and gives it to the other persons to whom it doesn't belong. See if the law benefits one citizen at the expense of another by doing what the citizen himself cannot do without committing a crime. Then abolish the law without delay…No legal plunder; this is the principle of justice, peace, order, stability, harmony and logic."
>
> *Frederic Bastiat, The Law*

As Voltaire (1694-1778) so aptly put it, **"Work helps to preserve us from three evils – weariness, vice, and want."** Then who has been "deprived" of an opportunity to better themselves? Is it a lack of opportunity? **Really…**? What about proper parenting, self respect, moral values, taking responsibility for your actions, accepting fatherhood, obedience to law and order or no dependency on government handouts? "Equality", a term continuously referred to, is a Utopian dream and a mitigated failure waiting to be awakened by the "Alptraum", the nightmare of reality and discover that **everybody** is "**<u>NOT</u>"** a winner. **"Each player must accept the cards life deals him or her but once they are in hand, he or she alone must decide how to play the cards in order to win the game.** (Voltaire (1694-1778) Instead of encouraging individuals to do their very best, they are urged to simply accept that trying your best is sufficient. These mindless wonders may even suggest we recognize the fact that they tried; never mind how hard. The claim for equality demands that we don't make things too complicated, allow others to catch up and avoid running the risk of possibly embarrassing or alienating them! **"Allowing the lack of common sense to prevail and left unchecked gradually mutates into stupidity."** (Author)

> "Nonviolence is the answer to the political and moral questions of our time; the need for man to overcome oppression and violence without resorting to oppression and violence.
>
> "Man must evolve for all human conflict a method which rejects revenge, aggression and retaliation. The foundation of such a method is love."
>
> *Martin Luther King, Jr. (1929-1968),*
> *Acceptance speech of the Nobel Peace Prize*
> *[December 11,* 1964]

Those arrested for criminal acts blame and hate the police; despite overwhelming evidence proving otherwise. Sadly this blatant hypocrisy frequently explodes into a crescendo of hatred towards Law Enforcement and the brutal murder of totally innocent police officers; whose only crime was that they wore a uniform and enforced the law. Society, regardless of status, demands the right to be protected from crime by its government. How is society planning to do that? The answer is simple, the **POLICE**. The longer society pretends not to hear the distant thunder of the impending storm, the more devastating will be the destruction of common sense and logical reasoning. **"Those who refuse to accept legal proof that contradicts their beliefs, do so because it often challenges their intellectual qualities and exposes their prejudicial nature."** (Author)

Unfortunately unbiased reporting and revelation of the truth is something the Media are loath to reveal. Officials deceptively skirt the truth and conveniently avoid answering questions such as: "Why do law-abiding persons rarely have a conflict with police and instead prefer courts to settle a questionable issue?" "Why are the majority of all cases involving confrontations with police initiated by individuals of questionable character, criminal involvement or lengthy criminal records? Why is there acquiescence to their demand for Instant gratification through demented street justice; wrongfully challenging sanctioned interpretations of the Legal System? **"Those who know are ridiculed and chastised into silence."** (Author) Effective control of established legal authority has been diluted by a lack of education, self-respect, as well as an unwillingness or inability to rationalize. Quoting Oscar Wilde (1854-1900), **"There is no sin except stupidity."** According to Paul Tabori (1908-1974), **"Stupidity does hurt – only it seldom hurts the stupid."** It is virtually impossible to imagine the cost of stupidity; our prisons are full. Disturbingly, a large segment of our society deliberately refuses to accept these findings and recreate the police into the villains and the suspect into innocent victims. Police are there to help you but not to kiss your ass. "**Persons who fail to respect the rights of others failed to develop self-respect; and that starts at home."** (Author)

> "Don't you see that the whole aim of Newspeak is to narrow the range of thought? In the end we shall make thought-crime literally impossible, because there will be no words in which to express it. Every concept that can ever be needed will be expressed by exactly one word, with its meaning rigidly defined and all its subsidiary meanings rubbed out and forgotten....The process will still be continuing long after you and I are dead. Every year fewer and fewer words and the range of consciousness always a little smaller. Even now, of course, there's no reason or excuse for committing thought-crime. It's merely a question of self-discipline, reality-control. But in the end there won't be any need even for that....Has it ever occurred to you, Winston, that by the year 2050, at the very latest, not a single human being will be alive who could understand such conversation as we are having now?
>
> *(Orwell, 1984)*

Every stratum of our society is plagued by individuals who are quick to pass judgment. These misguided persons do not seem to realize, or even care that police officers are a product of the same society; theirs. Despite society's proclivity to commit crime we demand that police officers are held to a much higher standard of morality and values. Therefore, the following questions must be asked. Are Police Officers different? Do Police Officers act differently? Do Police Officers think differently? Are Police Officers more selective with whom they associate? Are they quicker and often better in judging human character? Are they by nature, more law abiding? As a retired and active duty Law Enforcement officers we can unequivocally say, that 90% of us will answer **"yes!"**

Police officers are not only legally bound to follow strict guidelines of the law but are also required to adhere to Departmental Rules and Regulations. It cannot be denied that in the past police officers were occasional partners of political corruption; especially in large cities. According to the most recent studies, Police corruption is generally put at about 1%; or 10 police officers in a department of 1,000 personnel. Because a police officer's transgression reflects upon the entire department, appropriate disciplinary action and corrective measures are frequently executed with a double-edged sword of Departmental Rules and Regulations and Civil Law. **"If you don't believe that you are a part of the best; then what are you doing to make it the best?" (Author)** Unlike the civilian sector, once you are fired from a police department - **You are finished in Law Enforcement**.

The loss of even one human life at the hands of another human being will long be remembered and often never forgotten by some. The horrible tragedy of a shooting, especially a mass shooting is immediately followed by hysterical uproar demanding – "Gun Control"; controlled by emotion and void of logical reason. In our desperate attempt searching for a solution and appease a grief stricken society we skirt reality and point the accusatory finger at the wrong person; the law abiding and legal gun owner. Cities like Chicago, Detroit etc. which not only have the strictest gun-laws in the nation but also the highest crime rate prove that the proposal of even stricter gun laws is not the answer; the **certainty of punishment** for violating them is. **"Fear follows crime and is its punishment."** Voltaire (1694-1778) It is not the gun that shoots; the finger pulls the trigger and fires the gun. We are told not to judge all Muslims by the many acts of a few, yet we judge all gun owners by the mindless actions of a few mentally disturbed individuals. You are **you**, and responsible for **your own** actions.

According to the most up-to-date research, police officers are very reluctant to shoot a suspect and wait until the last possible moment to engage; sadly sometimes too late. As a reward, they often suffer the pain of negative public sentiment that has been generated by mostly dubious, altered or totally prefabricated accusations.

> "Laws that forbid the carrying of arms…disarm only those who are neither inclined nor determined to commit crimes. Can it be supposed that those who have the courage to violate the most sacred laws of humanity… will respect the less important and arbitrary ones…Such laws make things worse for the assaulted and better for the assailants, they serve rather to encourage than to prevent homicides, for an unarmed man be attacked with greater confidence than an armed man."
>
> *Cesare Beccaria, 1809,*
> *On Crimes and Punishment, 1764*

Demands to adapt to a different and restricted lifestyle frequently placed on a police officer far exceed the expected norm of members of the general society. Honoring the oath of office and pride in the badge requires a much more cautious approach in selecting friends and associates; a proficiency in understanding human nature, an instant judge of character and the ability to pass sound judgment; a critical element in successful policing. Those who fail to develop the instinct and the ability to detect that something is amiss ahead of time, ought to consider another career.

Proposals ranging from l***owering entrance requirements, disregarding low test scores*** to ***overlooking criminal convictions*** in an effort to achieve political appeasement and reduce anti police violence, is an absolute absurdity and an affront to Law Enforcement.

Advances in technology, computerization and education are placing far greater demands and responsibility on today's police officers and their profession. A failure to measurably enhance the requirements for future police officers is paving the road to guaranteed disaster.

Although police academies in general do a commendable job preparing recruits for public service, they are not able to prepare rookie cops for the gruesome side of the profession; the possible psychological consequences. The unusual aspects of the job demand handling cases involving human tragedy place the profession into a category by itself. Police officers are expected to perform their duties responsibly and with professional composure; regardless of the trying circumstances that often challenge the limits of their mental acumen. Police officers frequently apply their own particular type of humor in an effort to maintain control of unexpected or unusual situations; when appropriate. Unfortunately some fail to develop the unique abilities to cope with the stress and tragedy they are confronted by. The overall purpose of this book is to show that there is also a humorous side to policing that is often misunderstood and perhaps even considered grotesque by others; yet police officers will be able to understand and relate to it.

For some police response is welcomed, while a larger segment resents the uniformed presence. Officers must keep in mind that any wrongful action taken by them will reflect on their entire department. People in general do not like to be told what to do. Physical confrontations with police are extremely disproportionately initiated by a suspect or group. The anti-police attitude is not developed from a few contacts with police but taught; that seed already germinated some time ago. Sadly, many members of our political leadership choose to ignore the flashing warning signs and instead cover them with the absurd lunacy of **"Political Correctness"**. Revised and distorted history is being written to fit into the present political agenda and is deviously disseminated to the bi-pedal Lemmings who are unaware of the fact that they are approaching the abyss of cultural demise. Cunningly coerced, the well orchestrated deceit is hailed as a success by the unlearned throng. **"We must remember not to judge any public servant**

by one act, and especially should we beware of attacking the men who are merely the occasions and not the cause of disaster." (Theodore Roosevelt)

In order to fully understand the harsh reality of the conflicting relationship between society and police that is facing us today, we must go to the source of the problem; our present generation. Reiterating what has already been stated; turmoil has become not only expected but also accepted by a large segment of society. Family unity, the corner-stone and foundation of a well-functioning and productive society, is no longer valued. Far too many of our young people come from broken, unstable or single parent homes. Many troubled youths seek solace by joining gangs or listen to noise that, for a lack of a better word, is grossly misidentified nonsense and an insult to music. The absence of mature family guidance sadly fails to teach that respect for authority starts with self-respect. A lack of discipline has encouraged wrongdoing without the worry of possible consequences or punishment for a wrongful act that discards respect for authority. Parents themselves commit crimes or cover for their childdren's wrongful acts. If a loophole in the law doesn't get someone out of a bind, there is always a litany of canned B.S. blaming it on something else. Whatever happened to personal responsibility? Why even bother when it wasn't really your fault. **"Those who blaspheme the name of all LAW ENFORCEMENT and violently oppose it are idiots and the disguised ilk of society."** (Author)

> "Human prejudice is universal. It depends upon human need-self respect. There are so many ways in which the human mind can evade facts; none in which it can discard the desire for self approval. We men and women must try to think well of ourselves. And in order to achieve this end we have to disguise the truth from ourselves in a thousand ways. We deny, we forget, we explain away our own faults; we exaggerate the faults of others."
>
> *Ranyard West's book, "Psychology and World Order"*

At a certain point in our life, however, we have to make a choice; either a life skirting the law or stay on the side of it. Is what Martin

Luther King, Jr. (1929-1968) so bravely fought for in vain? Was his profound message when accepting the Nobel Peace Prize [December 11, 1964] merely just a figure of speech?

> "Nonviolence is the answer to the political and moral questions of our time; the need for man to overcome oppression and violence without resorting to oppression and violence.
>
> Man must evolve for all human conflict a method which rejects revenge, aggression and retaliation. The foundation of such a method is love."

Either by design or genuinely unintended, Political Correctness has evolved into a road block that is exceedingly difficult to circumvent and blocks Law Enforcement efforts to solve the conflict within our society. Amicable cohabitation of different groups is possible through voluntary commitment but will never be accomplished by force; without resentment by the group that feels offended. If you were born in this country, or a naturalized citizen, adopt the American Way: **Be an American**.

> "There is no room in this country for hyphenated Americanism....The one absolutely certain way of bringing this nation to ruin, of preventing all possibility of its continuing to be a nation at all, would be to permit it to become a tangle of squabbling nationalities."

Theodore Roosevelt,
Speech before the Knights of Columbus,
New York, [October 12, 1915}

G.M. Stratton in his "Social Psychology of International Conduct (1929), states: **"A feature of human nature to be prejudiced in this particular way. Notwithstanding its universality, racial prejudice is seldom or never innate."** Perhaps Oscar Hammerstein's lyrics in the movie South Pacific sum it up best – **"You've got to be taught to hate..."** Perhaps Voltaire (1694-1774),

INTRODUCTION

The distinct character of "Police Humor" may in essence be the duality of emotions and expressions. It is a universal norm to laugh out loud at times listening to a funny joke or watching a crazy act being performed; your reaction is your choice. What is the anticipated norm for a tormented police officer handling a gruesome accident or is confronted by tremendous carnage and death? Despite the revolting horror a police officer is expected to remain at the scene and complete the assignment; cope with it. They are aware of the fact that they will have to face many more grotesque tasks in the future and realize that they must find a way to mask the inner pain. Developing their own somber mood allows them to cope with those agonizing situations; as long as he/she wears a badge. That is why it is called **"Police Humor"**; hard to fully understand for those who never had to hide their tears from the public.

The reader is reminded once again that the following stories span an over a half century timeline and depict occasions when people spoke bluntly and unabashed; without fear of being labeled a "Political Correctness" heretic. Some of the anecdotes reflect moments of the past when respect not only for police, school, elders and our society in general were much more prevalent. It was a time when children were encouraged to stay in school and learn, not to fight and school teachers didn't have to worry about their own safety in the classroom. Youngsters were not allowed to play until homework was completed and checked; they were expected to be home by dark. A simple: **"Do you want me to tell your mom or dad...?"** often solved the problem. It was a time when millions of Americans enjoyed watching the double entendre humor and were able to relate to shows like "Burns and Allen", "The Honeymooners", "All in the Family", "The Jefferson" etc. Back then people used common sense and didn't take offense, nor felt insulted or degraded by the use of certain words or particular phrases that today's insane demands forbid; it was "**comedy**". People didn't lose sight of reality and understood Don Rickles' satirical humor and often laughed until they cried; it was only a **"joke"**. No one cared about a person's sexual proclivity; that was their business. Do your thing, just leave me alone. Unfortunately too many of perhaps well intended changes for the betterment of society, in the form of Political Correctness, have created a plethora of unwanted or negative results.

Technology has made enormous strides to assist Law Enforcement and enhance investigators' ability to fight crime. The unusual responses resorted to and actions taken in these stories by members of Law Enforcement were not committed with malice but for the purpose of inserting their special type of humor applicable to cope with the situation at that moment. Many of the changes made in our laws in an effort to appease opposing views in the quest for a hoped for desired solutions are dismal failures. They in fact contributed to it further. The advent of modern forensic technology and tremendous advances in our ability to communicate, Policing has changed considerably and will continue to do so. Unfortunately these changes have also contributed to the publics' attitude and misperception towards Law Enforcement; which seem to be steadily and dangerously increasing. Despite this negativity threatening the security and stability of our society, members of Law Enforcement are determined to continue their valiant effort to protect society; including their undeclared enemy. However, one thing has remained the same; fighting criminals. Those who have deliberately committed a wrong, have nefarious intensions or refuse to apply common sense remain the primary target and concern of the Police.

> "No man is above the law and no man is below it; nor do we ask any man's permission when we require of him to obey it. Obedience to the law is demanded as a right; not asked as a favor."
>
> *Theodore Roosevelt,*
> *Third Annual Message on December 7, 1903*

Humor In Blue

New on the job and testing his METTLE.

The brand new State trooper has no idea what to expect as he enters through the back door of the troop; certainly not when he reports for duty to the Desk Sergeant. **"Sir, recruit trooper ……. reporting for duty."** With a stern look on his face the D/ Sgt looks at him and asks: **"What did you say your name was?"** Hoping that he is able to hide his apprehension, the recruit repeats his last name. Suddenly the D/Sgt yells: **"Jesus 'effen' Christ we already have enough dumb f*cking Pollacks in this troop and certainly don't need another one."** Shocked by the unbelievable reception the recruit trooper cautiously responds: **"I'm not Polish, that's my adopted name."** Frowning, the D/Sgt growls: **"What are you then?"** Although feeling extremely uncomfortable and hesitating to go on, the Rookie realizes that he has to endure the hazing in order to be accepted and very nervously replies: **"I'm German."** From a back office, a loud male voice is heard: **"Damn, I thought that we killed all of you Nazi bastards."** The young Rookie has enough and boldly responds: **"Well, you thought wrong." "I tried to join the party but I was told that I was too damn young." "Besides that, I had not learned how to read or write yet." "So now you know the reason why I'm still here."** The hearty laughter of the troopers apparently breaks the ice and verifies that he has passed the initiation. All of them stand up and shake his hand and welcome him. In a much friendlier tone the D/Sgt says to the Rookie: **"You will be riding trooper T…, your FTO** (Field Training Officer)." How can the Rookie possibly know that he has just been through only the first phase of the initiation? There is more to come? (Cont'd.)

Where is the turd?

The rookie trooper feels relieved that the initiation is over and he passed. That is until the back door to the troop flies open and in walks trooper T.... Although quite young and obviously does not have that many years under his belt, he acts like an "Old Salt". When he spots the young rookie he snarls: **"Are you the new turd?"** The very moment he stepped through the door, the Rookie already gave him a mental once over and thought: ***"My God if we get into a real fight, this guy couldn't beat his way out of a wet paper bag, yet alone out of a real fight."*** Looking at his FTO, the Rookie simply nods his head while thinking: ***"Oh my God, is this going to be another initiation ritual?"*** Trooper T...'s next verbalization confirms his suspicions when he snaps: **"Are you ready to go turd?"** Without waiting for a response he lifts his foot and shoves his briefcase towards the rookie. Before he has a chance to grab the case, the acting "Old Salt" yells: **"Think fast." "Here, you can carry this too"** and throws his shotgun at him. Well, you do what you have to do. The Rookie numbly sticks his own shotgun under one armpit and "Old Salt's" under the other; then bends over and grabs a briefcase in each hand and obediently follows his master. Since he is the new guy, it is only logical for the Rookie to assume that he should be the one to drive; but fails to take the pretend old-timer's wishes into consideration. Phase III is next.

(Cont'd.)

You have to be a Trooper to drive!

As the Rookie stands next to the driver's side door and waits for the FTO to hand him the car keys, the FTO walks up behind him and yells: **"What in the Hell do you think you are doing?"** Shocked, the Rookie looks at him and as a matter of fact stammers: **"Since I'm the new trooper I thought that it was expected of me to drive."** Glaring at his charge, the FTO growls: **"Did I hear you say that you were a trooper?" "You have not proven yourself to be called a trooper." "So let me tell you something, 'turd'!" "Do you know why you are a 'turd'...?"** The Rookie remains mum and just shakes his head. **"It means that you are**

lower than whale shit, and that's on the bottom of the ocean." Although he finds it very tempting to tell this loudmouth that whale shit floats, he immediately discounts it since technically speaking; he is lower than whale shit in the FTO's eyes.

As soon as he sits comfortably behind the steering wheel he starts his demeaning act again. Pointing to the half chevron sewn just above the cuff on the left shirtsleeve T…says: **"Do you see this hash mark?" "Do you know what that means?"** Having just come off active duty the new trooper has an idea what it signifies. Without waiting for a reply, the "Old Salt" continues: **"That means that this is the closest to God you'll ever come." "You don't talk to me unless I speak to you first!" "Furthermore, you are not going to drive a cruiser until you can prove that you are a real trooper!" "Do you understand that?" "Turd?"** The rookie trooper remains silent and simply nods and wonders: ***"Just how much more vile bullshit is going to spill out of this guy's orifice?"*** They have barely entered the main roadway behind one of the cars in the traffic lane when both of them immediately notice the erratic driving of the car directly in front of them. Glancing over at his passenger trooper T… says: **"Now you will see how a DUI (Driving under the Influence) arrest is made."** The FTO quickly activates the cruiser's lights and siren and motions to the driver to pull over. Two blocks later the car in question suddenly stops in the middle of an intersection and trooper T… immediately jumps out of the patrol car and rushes to the driver's side of the vehicle while the Rookie hurries to the passenger side. In a flash the FTO has the driver pushed against the car. When the passenger sees what is happening to his buddy jumps out and screams at the Rookie: **"Hey, what the Hell do you guys think you are doing to my buddy?" "You can't do that!" "I'm 'gonna' do that to you, asshole."** The irate passenger then commits a major faux pas and pokes the Rookie in the chest and then tries to push him. Remembering what had been impregnated into his brain in the academy –***"If somebody pokes his finger at you or pushes you, you have a right to protect yourself. That person is yours!"*** It is the Rookie's good fortune that his reaction to the assault is second nature. The young "wanna be" trooper instinctively balls his right fist, slightly lowers his right shoulder and comes up with one hell of a "haymaker". He doesn't dare to keep his eyes off his adversary to look at his hurting fist and is prepared to counter an expected response. When it doesn't materialize, he realizes that the passenger, flung halfway over the right front fender of his buddy's car, is half unconscious. A sudden grin from ear to ear appears on trooper T…'s face. When he sees the passenger involuntarily resting on the car's fender he extends his hand across the hood of the vehicle. In a genuine and comrade-like manner shakes the Rookie's hand and says: **"You've made the grade to be a real trooper." "Now you are allowed to drive the cruiser; Trooper!"**

Where are the rest of them?

The D/Sgt (Desk Sergeant.) has been informed that the new State trooper, recently assigned to his shift, has sufficiently proved that he has acquired enough experience and is qualified to handle assignments on his own. It seems that this D/Sgt also feels the need to test the newcomer and decides to send him to execute a warrant on a well known trouble maker; who habitually fights every time troopers attempt to execute an arrest warrant for him. As soon as he has left the troop the D/Sgt grins and turns to the corporal and says: **"Let's see if he is ready for Frank." "If he can handle Frank, he can handle anything."** Before exiting his patrol vehicle he double-checks the address listed on the warrant and walks up to the house. He has barely finished knocking when the door abruptly swings open and a very large and physically fit man appears in the doorframe. It is immediately apparent to him that diplomacy is extremely critical. Pretending to glance at the warrant he asks the big man: **"Are you Frank…?"** The man just glares at him and replies: **"Yeah, what if I am?" "What about it?"** As a precautionary measure, he has already slipped his blackjack into the right shirt sleeve; just in case. Without missing a beat, he once again asks the man his name. Slightly changing his posture and with an annoyed tone in his voice he answers: **"Yeah I am." "What's this all about?"** The trooper replies with a stern voice that he is able to muster: **"Well sir, I have a warrant for your arrest and I need to take you in."**

Apparently slightly amused by the trooper's matter of fact attitude, Frank pretends to be looking over the trooper's shoulder and tauntingly asks: **"Where are the rest of them?" "Cause you ain't taking me in by yourself!"** Hearing those threatening words, an alarm goes off in the trooper's head: ***"Oh my God, the first time on my own and I'm going to get my ass kicked." "At least I am going to try to make it as tough as I can for him and let him know that he has been in a real fight with a state trooper."*** He and his blackjack are prepared for Frank. Concerned about his personal safety, the trooper tactfully replies: **"Sir, I'm here just doing my job." "The warrant only says to bring you in; it doesn't say how." "Therefore, it's up to you in which manner you are going." "I also want to advise you that you are going with me." "If I'm not enough, there is a whole troop full of us."** For a few seconds time seems to stand still. Prepared for the fight of his life, the trooper is absolutely dumbfounded and can't believe Frank's totally unexpected reaction. Frank just stands there and then slowly turns around and says: **"Go ahead troop and 'puddem' on."** Two quick, metallic sounding clicks pierce the silence, with speed that could have been a contender for "Ripley's". That was the fastest he will ever again need to put handcuffs on anyone.

(Cont'd.)

What are you doing here?

With his prisoner secured in his patrol vehicle, the State trooper returns to the troop. The D/Sgt (Desk Sergeant) is flabbergasted when he spots Frank being ushered into the troop by the new trooper and practically yells: **"Frank, what the Hell are you doing here?" "You're going to tell me that you let that rookie trooper take you in by himself?" "Man, you could have eaten him for breakfast and have hardly anything left over for lunch." "How come that every damn time when there are two of us to arrest you, you always fight us?"** With a sneer on his face Frank replies: **"I fight you guys because that is what you expect me to do." "Ya'll think that you can beat my ass." "You know damned well that none of you are bad enough to do that alone." "That's why I have to prove it to you each time you come and get me."** Slightly turning to the new trooper Frank continues: **"He is the first**

and only trooper that just did his job, without looking for a fight." "He is the only one of you bastards that I respect and all you others can kiss my ass."

What telephone pole?

A County officer invites his close friend, a State trooper, to ride with him on patrol; both are in uniform. While on routine patrol they come upon a car partially on the shoulder with the engine running and with the brake-lights on. Upon closer inspection they find the driver passed out behind the wheel and his foot barely resting on the brake pedal. Afraid that the obviously drunk driver could hurt himself, if his foot slips off the pedal, the trooper decides to take immediate preventive action. Hoping that the driver doesn't wake up, the trooper holds his breath and very carefully reaches for the ignition key. All of a sudden the drunk lurches up and his car catapults forwards and crashes into the telephone pole ahead of it; witnessed by a state police unit that just arrived. Happy to grant the newly arrived trooper his request to make an easy DUI (Driving under the Influence) arrest, the two friends in uniform turn the dumbfounded drunk over to him. Glad to be able to dump their potential burden, they jump back into the county car and are out of there.

A "Frisky" matter.

A two-man unit, working the midnight shift, responds to a burglary in progress at an Esso station. As the State troopers approach the scene they spot a dark colored sedan, without its headlights on, speeding away from the gas station. They notify Central and request to have another unit check the gas station and advise Dispatch that they are in pursuit of said vehicle. It is immediately apparent that the subjects in the dark colored vehicle are trying to elude them. Approximately 5 or 6 miles later they finally manage to stop the vehicle and very cautiously approach it. One of them positions himself on the driver's side and orders the driver to exit the car while the other runs to the opposite side and commands the passenger to get out. When the passenger, very arrogantly, claims to have trouble exiting the vehicle the trooper warns him: **"If you make a wrong move, it may be your last one."** In the process of preparing the passenger to be frisked, the trooper forces him to lean against the car and orders him to spread his legs. Once again the passenger moves very slowly. Annoyed with the suspect's antics, the trooper raises his voice and orders him to spread his legs wider and quicker. The passenger yells back: **"F*ck you!" "I'm moving as fast as I f*cking can!"** Keeping his own and his partner's safety in mind, the trooper gives the loudmouth a sharp kick to the inside of his right ankle. Instead of the expected outcry to the painful kick the suspect yells: **"I told you, you f*cking asshole, I'm moving as fast as I can."** Fed up with the suspect's nonsense and verbal abuse, he yells back: **"I'll show you just how fast you can move"**; and gives the creep an even harder kick to the ankle. Again the suspect does not seem to be affected by the sharp kick and screams: **"I keep telling you asshole, I can't move any f*cking faster." "I have a f*cking wooden leg." "Here, I'll show you, jerk-off."** The suspect then bends over and very slowly raises the right pant leg and exposes his wooden leg. Totally caught by surprise when he sees the wooden stump, the trooper is momentarily left speechless until he looks at his partner who is on the verge of losing it with laughter. Fortunately his partner has the driver handcuffed; who would otherwise have had ample time to get away at that moment.

Just another day on patrol. #1

While walking his prisoner down the hallway at the Medical Center a guy lying on a gurney sees the officer and turns the speaker of his cell phone on. As the officer walks past, the guy on the gurney plays the "Imperial March" from Star Wars.

Then this gem of a conversation can be heard from the next room:

Nurse: **"I'm going to have to insert a catheter into your penis."**
Patient: **"You what?"**

Nurse: **"I'm going to have to insert a catheter into your penis."**
Patient: **"Huh?"**

Nurse: **"I'm going to put a tube in your Johnson!"**
Patient: **"Oh, Ok."**

TAXI anyone?

While viewing the northbound traffic on the Interstate, a State trooper spots a vehicle that seems to be in a big hurry. His usual personal policy allows up to 10 miles over the speed limit. That is as long as the operator doesn't do the proverbial zigzagging, practiced by some idiots. The driver isn't cutting in and out of traffic, but is definitely going much faster than 10 mph over the posted speed limit. Despite a fully marked unit directly following behind, the operator fails to slow down. When the trooper stops the car and approaches the driver, the lady driver rolls down her car window and demands to know why she has been stopped. Despite the driver's obnoxious attitude, he politely informs her that he clocked her for a distance of over a mile and that she has been speeding. Totally unexpected, the lady protests in an aggravated tone: **"I don't know what you are talking about." "I wasn't speeding." "The other cars were just going too damned slow." "Besides that, I wasn't even looking at my speedometer."** Fighting not to give a desirable response the trooper maintains his composure and informs her that he is going to charge her for going 17 miles over the posted speed limit and politely asks her for her driver's license and vehicle registration. After a brief moment of undeterminable muttering under her breath the female operator admits that she doesn't have a driver's license. A further check by him also reveals that the vehicle registration is expired.

Complying with state law, the trooper has no choice but to have her vehicle towed. When she realizes that her vehicle is going to be towed, she becomes verbally confrontational and yells: **"You have no damn authority to have my car towed." "That's my car and I'm not a criminal." "If you do, I demand that you take me home since you are going to arrest me."** Without bothering to reply, he thinks: ***"Keep*** *digging your hole deeper"*. When the tow truck driver is finished loading her vehicle onto his truck, he offers to take her with him to the yard where she then can obtain a ride home. Highly annoyed, she screams hysterically at both of them and again demands that the trooper must be the one to take her home; since **he** is the cause of it all. Realizing that any reality check with this woman is futile he decides to apply another technique. Stepping closer to her he points at his cruiser and in a very professional but firm manner says: **"I want you to take a really good look at my car and tell me what is written on the side."** With a questionable look on her face she glances at the cruiser and in an annoyed voice says: **"State Police." "So?"** The trooper just smiles because his moment has come and replies: **"I'll tell you what "Ma'am", when those words written there turn into the word 'TAXI', I will take you home."** Then flicking his thumb over his shoulder says: **"Oh, by the way, I already called one for you." "Your Taxi with the moving parking lot is waiting for you." "Have a nice day."** He is too busy suppressing a laugh as he watches her climb into cab of the tow truck; still cursing him.

A Patriotic Expression

As usual, the State Police Cpl (Corporal) climbs into his personal vehicle and places his 'Smokey the Bear' hat next to him on the front seat and drives to work. When the light at the intersection changes to red he stops behind the two cars in front of him. While he waits for the light to change and glances into the rear mirror he notices a motorcycle approaching from his left and then sees the rider give him a dirty look as he rides past. When the biker peaks back and sees the trooper looking at him, he gives him the middle finger and stops for the light; straddling the bike. Suddenly he stands up and glances back over his right shoulder; as if to make sure that the trooper is able to see him. He then performs a highly exaggerated stretch to expose the American flag sewn to the seat of his pants. In the trooper's opinion, such a gross and disrespectful display of the "Stars and Stripes" needs to be firmly addressed. At the first opportune moment he motions to the cyclist to pull over.

Maintaining a totally professional posture, he politely asks the biker for his license and registration. Standing next to his bike the biker arrogantly demands to know why he should show them. In a slightly demeaning tone the trooper replies: **"Since you apparently didn't hear me the first time when I asked** (with a strong and deliberate emphasis) **for them; now I'm telling you." "I want to see them!"** He then waits for the biker to assume the desired position and continuous. **"By the way, what's on the seat of your pants?"** Defiantly the bike rider snarls back: **"The f*cking American flag." "What's it to you?"** It felt like a wound has been torn open in him. For a split second faces of his friends who didn't make it back from Nam flash before him; and the many caskets that he had guarded in the hangers. It takes every bit of his willpower to hold his temper in check when he asks the dirt bag: **"Do you even realize how many people fought or gave their lives for that flag?" "Is that how you appreciate what those brave souls did to make this country what it is?" "Don't you have any respect for them and what that flag signifies?"** Mocking a sneering laugh the "scrote" (scrota - an endearing term for scrotum in police jargon) replies: **"F*ck the flag and f*ck you!"** Unable to hold his anger in check, he rips the flag patch off the scum's pants. Then with all of the strength that he can muster gives the dreg of society a powerful kick where the flag patch has been. A well placed back-hander to the creep's cheek sends the unpatriotic puke on his way. The corporal could almost swear that his kick had elevated the dreg a half of an inch off the ground. **"Every job is a self-portrait of the person who did it. Autograph your work with excellence."** – *Chinese proverb.*

(Cont'd.)

Later on that day

The corporal has just started his tour of duty and enters the main highway when he gets a call to return to the troop immediately. As he walks through front door of the troop the D/Sgt (Desk Sergeant) just shakes his head and nods over his shoulder in the direction of the captain's office and asks: **"What the Hell did you do?" "He** (captain) **is really pissed and wants to see you right now."** Of course the Cpl's suspicions are confirmed as he enters the captain's office and spots the dirt bag. When he is finished reporting as ordered to the captain (A Marine Corps combat vet who saw action on Iwo Jima) instructs him to sit on the chair next to his desk; directly opposite the biker. The captain has not even finished his sentence when the creep spurts out: **"Yeah, that's the guy who kicked and slapped me."** Without missing a beat the captain turns to the Cpl and asks him: **"Can you explain your side of the incident?"** Well known for his blunt honesty, he doesn't hesitate to express his true feelings and gives a detailed account of the action he took and why. When the complainant is warned for a second time for interrupting the inquiry, the captain gives him stern looks that leave no doubt… and says: **"If I have to warn you again I am going to throw you through that door** (pointing) **without bothering to open it first." "Have I made myself clear?"** Apparently the biker received the message loud and clear and remains mute until the trooper is finished with his testimony. At the conclusion of the proceedings the captain advises the complainant that the trooper's conduct will be appropriately dealt with and punishment will be properly administered for any inappropriate action and will be reflected in his Personnel record. An attempt by the complainant to rebut is cut short and preempted by the captain: **"This concludes the investigation." "Furthermore, this trooper will be adequately punished in accordance with Departmental Rules and Regulations." "You may inquire about the findings in a week or two." "Thank you for coming and have a good day." "Corporal, remain seated!"**

(Cont'd.)

The penalty phase.

As soon as the dirtball closes the door behind him, the captain begins.

> "I realize that you are extremely patriotic and love this country, but you cannot expect others to feel the same way that you do. You know damn well that you were wrong and that you cannot enforce your personal feelings on others. As a result for your infraction I have reached a

> decision and will submit the following recommendation for punishment; which will be reviewed and acted upon by HQ (Head Quarters). I propose that you should be suspended from the Division for one day, without pay and work an additional punishment day. Do you have any questions?"

Keeping a noncommittal facial expression the corporal replies: **"No, sir"**; respectfully salutes and reaches for the door handle. Before he exits, the captain calls him back into the office and demands to know: **"Have you learned your lesson?"** Again he politely answers: **"Yes, sir"**. As he reaches for the door a second time he hears the captain call him by his first name and asks: **"Hey R…., would you pull a stunt like that again?"** Hoping that a fake smile and a phony laughter would disguise his deep honest and inner feelings replies: **"Yes sir, if it happens to be another 'scum ball' like him."** Flabbergasted and annoyed, the captain raises his voice several octaves and sputters: **"That'll be one more day!"** Still smiling, the trooper asks: **"Will that be a punishment day or a one day suspension?"** In a still louder voice the captain hollers: **"I haven't made up my mind yet, now get the Hell out of here."**

As the Cpl walks past the D/Sgt the phone rings and sees him pick up the receiver and almost immediately motions to him to wait. With a concerned expression on his face the D/Sgt tells the Cpl that he has just been commanded to send him back to the captain. Feeling a certain amount of trepidation the Cpl returns to the captain's office; salutes and reports as ordered. In a very stern, yet fatherly way the captain says: **"I know that you are a hard head, but a damn good trooper and I'm totally confident that you can handle any situation." "That is precisely the main reason why I personally asked to have you transferred to my troop." "I also feel that your remarks were made out of anger and frustration, but you must also know that you were wrong." "Therefore, I have rescinded that additional day."** Because he knows that the captain is a fair man, the Cpl is unable to resist a humorous parting remark. **"Permission to speak, Sir?"** The captain nods his head. **"Sir, I would like to know why you had to rescind the extra punishment day." "Is it because you couldn't figure out which**

specific one to give me?" When the Cpl hears, **"Get the f*ck out of my office"**; he quickly closes the door behind him and hurries back to his cruiser.

It's after dark.

It is a nice Fall Friday evening on patrol. A part of the police officer's patrol is to check the county parklands; in and out of his district and pulls into the larger one in his district. They are closed dusk to dawn, but oftentimes kids hang out in them at night as well an occasional dump of stolen cars. He pulls into the rear parking area and douses the lights of his patrol vehicle so he can do a "Poop & Snoop" (police terminology); allowing him to sneak up on any offenders.

As he slides into the parking area he observes a BMW not occupied. A registration check shows that the vehicle is not stolen. Then he spots a second BMW which likewise appears to be vacant. Instinctively he starts thinking: ***"Maybe stolen and not reported yet?"*** He cautiously approaches the BMW; with his "Maglight" off. When he reaches the car he is able to see the rear side of a female; her legs out of the car and her dress hiked up. He immediately also sees a 20 something year old young man on his knees, performing oral sex on the female and clicks on his Maglight. The female's head whips and when she sees the uniform says: **"We were just talking officer!"** Shaking his head he thinks: ***"Yeah, right." "And he can't talk with a mouth full."***

Just then he recognizes the face of the female…his daughter's pediatrician! Well, it wasn't her husband; cougar time he guesses. For some unexplainable reason he feels dirty. He shines the flashlight in their eyes so they can't recognize him. Changes his voice to a deep bass and exclaims: **"You can't be in county parkland after dark!"** He then hurries back to his patrol vehicle and gets the Hell out of there.

He forgot that he could not swim.

A hardened criminal, considered extremely dangerous to the public escaped from police custody in Wuppertal, Germany. During his flight he forced himself onto the "Schwebebahn", a public transportation monorail spanning the length of the river Wupper. When cornered by police, he threatens the officers and disobeys their command to surrender.

As the officers watch the criminal force the door open and ready themselves at the door, they realize that they have to act fast. They are aware of the fact that if the suspect manages to jump into the shallow water below the gondola, he could make a successful escape and continue to be a danger. Faced with a very precarious and dangerous situation, one of the police marksmen takes deliberate aim and shoots the fleeing public enemy in the leg at the precise moment he leaps from his perch. The suspect, screaming from pain, crashes into the water and momentarily disappears; much to the surprise of the police officers.

It becomes immediately apparent that the suspect landed in a deep hole; extremely rare in the shallow river and shortly thereafter resurfaces screaming hysterically. Pretending not to be able to decipher the mixture of pain and words that he is yelling, officers standing on the bridge taunt and laugh at him yelling: **"Oh, we don't want to miss this." "It's not every day that you can watch somebody drown."** When they hear the wet rat's desperate pleas: **"Help me, help me I can't swim"**, a couple police officers quickly sneak into the water behind him. Suddenly four strong arms grab the drowning wannabe' escape and hoist him to the steep river bank. Regrettably, the suspect didn't bother thanking the officers for saving his life and the other officers pretend to be upset for doing so and say: **"Man why did you have to save that piece of shit?" "We wanted to see a real life drowning show." "Now we have to buy some more toilet paper."**

Best defense at arraignment ever. **-"Judge it's not my fault! She has PMS!!!"**

The special of the day.

The light has just turned from green to yellow when the trooper notices that the vehicle ahead of him starts to slow down and stop on yellow. Since the driver had plenty of time to go through the intersection before it would have turned red and thinks that is a little odd. He pulls up behind the vehicle and waits for the light to cycle back to green. But when it does, the vehicle ahead of him does not go on green. As he watches the light make another complete cycle and back to green, the vehicle ahead of him still does not move. Concerned about the driver's wellbeing, he walks up to the driver's side of the vehicle to check on the operator; an elderly lady. Her looks are still fixed on the traffic light as he approaches. Taking her advanced age into account, he wants to make sure that he does not unnecessarily startle her and cause her to suddenly bolt through the light; which once again has changed to red. In a very soft tone and polite manner he asks: **"Are you all right 'Ma'am'?"** With a puzzled look on her face she answers: **"Why of course!" "Can't you see that I am?" "Why do you ask?"** Although surprised by her abrupt attitude, he maintains his composure and says: **"I just wanted to make sure that everything is alright with you."** Visibly annoyed by his uninvited presence and questioning she momentarily glares at him.

Satisfied that the elderly female driver with an ambivalent attitude towards law enforcement is alright, he just smiles and waits for the light to turn green. When it does and once again she still doesn't respond, he bends down and whispers: **"By the way, we have a special on traffic lights today." "You are allowed to go on green."** As he turns to go back to his car he hears her say: **"You little smart ass sonnama' bitch."** Laughing to himself he thinks: ***"At six-two and two hundred and twenty pounds, she calls me little?" "How damn big are they where she is from to call me little?"*** Fearing that she can see him laughing, he isn't able to reply. A subsequent check with DMV does show that the spunky little 81 year old lady still possesses a valid driver's license and has a clean driving record.

The Party is over.

He has just been dispatched to the "Hoodle", a favorite teen-hangout, reference a large group of mostly teenagers drinking and causing a major disturbance. As soon as the rowdy bunch sees the State Police cruiser pull in, many of the group immediately high-tail it out of there. Of course, there are always those who defy police authority and feel safe in their number and decide to stay. The trooper quickly sizes up the situation and recognizes one person in particular. Realizing that he is way outnumbered he holds his 36" long ebony nightstick at the ready; just in case. Before he begins to speak to the undesirable assembly of underage drinkers and revelers, he first makes direct eye contact with a couple of the usual hardnosed trouble makers and then at the rest of their buddies.

Satisfied that he has everyone's attention, he begins:

> "It is very important that all of you listen to me very closely, because I want to make sure that **all of you** understand what is about to happen here. **All of you** know that I likewise know why you have decided to congregate here and I am, therefore, going to give you a chance to stay out of trouble. If you look around, you will see some large drum barrels that have been strategically placed here to serve as trash containers. Here is what I strongly urge you to do. Remember these words of wisdom that I am going to impart on you and thus give you a chance to stay out of trouble! So don't screw it up and piss me off! I want you to empty every bottle and can of beer and liquor in your possession and throw the empty containers into the drum barrels. I do not want to have to make arrests for possession of alcoholic beverages, should I find any of you with booze in your possession. Have I made myself clear up to this point?"

Affirmation is indicated by a multitude of up and down bobbing heads. He then continues: **"Listen up!" "I am going to leave now and I will be back in about five minutes." "When I come back, I do not want to catch any of you with booze." "If I do, you will be arrested."** An advantage to defuse potential discord may be gained with cunning by addressing a crowd on your level of comfort, rather than stooping down to theirs. He then turns around, climbs into his cruiser and drives off.

When he returns more than five minutes have passed and is surprised to find that quite a number of teens decided to stay. Increasing the grip on his nightstick he assumes his previous "ready" posture and addresses the crowd again:

> "As promised, I'm back. Since I don't want to gather dark clouds overhead and hide the sunshine and allow it to rain on you, I am going to ask all of you one more time. Did you pour out **your entire** illegal libation? I tell you right now if I do find some, your ass is mine! For some odd reason I am going to give those of you who did not fully understand me or had trouble hearing me the first time, another chance. So if you still have some stuff left – **pour it the Hell out**, **now!**"

The clinging and thumps of bottles and cans hitting the trash drums indicates that many of the group decided to heed his second and final warning. While he is watching the group, he notices one of the usual troublemakers in particular walk up and glare at him. Displaying a definite sign of hatred, the punk keeps punching his right fist against his left palm and snarls, **"Yo' man, are you that Trooper ……?"** Twisting his name tag and pretending to be looking at his name replies: **"Yup, that's what it says there." "Since I don't know of another trooper with the same name, it must be me."** Still punching the palm of his left hand, the scumbag sneers: **"I wonder if you really are as bad as they say you are."** Hoping to avoid being treacherously lured into a physical confrontation, he assumes an advantages defense/ offense stance and somewhat tauntingly replies: **"No, I'm not bad, I'm just damn good in what I do."** The frustrated look on the dirtball's face and his sudden heavy breathing reveal that the trooper has gotten the upper hand. Barely able to speak because he failed in his attempt to have the trooper throw the first punch, the punk continues hitting the palm of his hand and mutters something under his breath. Only a portion of the debate with himself is decipherable: **"Man, I don't believe he is all that f*cking bad that they say he is."**

When a crowd, obviously anticipating the inevitable, is close at hand begins to gather around them; the trooper decides to turn the table on his antagonist. Feigning a pretext of concern and a desire to help his opponent with the decision making process, he shrugs his shoulders and says: **"Hey, do you know what?" "I'm not going to leave until this place is cleared up." "So if you feel 'froggy', why don't you just leap?" "Rribbit, rribbit!"** No textbook on "Rules of Engagement" exists to adequately describe what to do in this unusual potentially violent encounter; the trooper keeps a tight grip on his nightstick. Suddenly "Froggie" screams a loud **"Yeaaah",** spins around and kicks the driver's side door of his newly restored 55 Chevrolet; resulting in a pandemonium of laughter from the onlookers. Totally embarrassed and with a killer look in his eyes, the self-proclaimed leader climbs into his car, slams the car door and peels off. When the amusement has died down the trooper tells the merrymakers, **"OK!" "The party is over, so get the Hell out of here."** As he is leaving the "Hoodle", he has a sudden uneasy feeling and senses that this is only the first page of an ominous chapter to come.

(Cont'd.)

Time is of the essence.

Several weeks have passed since the precarious incident at the "Hoodle" when the trooper receives a very disturbing message from one of his informants, reference the guy that he almost had a fight with. It wasn't until the very end of the conversation that he realizes the possibility of an extremely dangerous outcome. The informant tells the trooper that because he embarrassed this particular individual at the "Hoodle" and destroyed his reputation, he is planning to kill him and his family. As soon as he arrives at the troop he reports the issue to his Criminal Lieutenant. When he is finished listened to the trooper, the Lt. calmly says: **"Do you realize how many of us**

have had threats made against them?" "I think that you are way over-reacting." "Besides, I don't have that kind of manpower to give you around the clock protection on some hearsay evidence." He has to admit that if the table was turned he would probably have the same response as the Lieutenant. Left with no other choice, he decides to take the necessary course of action to protect his family. Recalling the incident at the "Hoodle", he recognizes the importance of his informant's warning and that time is of the essence.

(Cont'd.)

I don't ever want to see you…

A few days later the trooper and his informant pay "Froggie" a surprise visit and find him leaning under the hood of his 55 Chevy. It takes every ounce of his will power to resist the temptation to lower the car hood on the dirt bag's head. 'Froggie' obviously knows who is standing behind him but pretends not to have noticed. Since it is absolutely critical for the trooper to maintain his cool, he very calmly taps 'Froggie' on the shoulder. You can cut the hateful glare on Froggie's face with a butter knife when he asks: **"What the f*ck are you doing here?" "An' what the f*ck do you want?"** Never keeping his eyes off the wrench clenched in Froggie's right fist, the trooper steps closer to him and in almost a whisper says: **"I am going to tell you this just one time!" "If I ever catch you in my neighborhood, I'm going to pound your ass so far into the ground that you will never be able to extract it."** He then notices the grip of Froggie's hand tightening around the wrench. Not willing to take a chance with Frog's intentions, his fist strikes Froggie's jaw like a bolt of lightning; causing the scumbag's knees to buckle under him and drop him like a sack of garbage in front of his car. After the dirtball has somewhat recovered he yells at the informant: **"Did you see that trooper hit me?"** The informant simply smirks and says: **"I didn't see a f**king thing"** and walks away. A few days later when the trooper is preparing to stop him, 'Froggie' jumps out of his vehicle and frantically waves some papers in his right hand and yells: **"Here is my license and**

registration." The trooper just waives at him and drives off. There is no need for anything else.

All wheels in the air.

Working the midnight shift a senior State trooper, an excellent road trooper, pulls up behind the troop to pick up his partner; a brand-new trooper. While he is waiting for him, he watches the Rookie performing last minute checks of his appearance. A smirk caresses the senior trooper's face when he notices the Rookie paying particular attention to his Stetson; making certain that it is properly centered. Apparently satisfied with his personal appearance, the new trooper climbs into the passenger seat of the purring 440 Plymouth Fury.

Although single strap seatbelts are installed in a majority of cars, their car is still without seatbelts. Departmental "Rules and Regulations" require troopers to wear their head-cover at all times when in uniform; even inside their patrol vehicle. As a matter of fact, communication devices attached to a uniform are still only a dream at best; if even thought of. Thus once a trooper steps out of his cruiser electronic contact ends at the end of the spiral telephone or mike cord. From that point on he is on his own and in God's hands.

Driving further and further away from highly populated or traffic congested places, the senior trooper turns to his partner and says:**"Since things appear to be relatively quiet tonight we ought to take the opportunity and give you a chance to get familiar with the troop area."** The Rookie already noticed the increased frequency of open spaces along the highway; even the road itself doesn't seem to be as wide occasionally. Glancing at the Rookie, the senior trooper advises him to make sure that his hat is on tight and slouches down in the driver's seat. Then grabbing the bottom of the steering wheel with a tight underhand grip he steps on the gas.

Perplexed by the senior trooper's sudden action, the Rookie stares through the windshield and sees the cruiser suddenly and rapidly accelerate towards the leading edge of the slightly elevated roadway of a precariously narrow bridge in the distance. As they approach a little closer, the Rookie is alarmed when he notices that the roadbed of the bridge is six to eight inches higher than both sides of the bridge. As the cruiser reaches the bridge at 60 mph plus and crosses the suddenly higher roadway, the vehicle instantly and forcefully jumps upward; all four wheels off the road.

Unprepared for the unsuspected rapid vertical launch, the recruit trooper's head slams into the headliner of the car and drives his newly-issued Stetson down over his ears; coming to rest on his brow ridges. The senior trooper roars with laughter. Apparently another successful initiation.

Just another day on patrol. #2

"I was told officer that ignorance must have been a requirement when you took the police exam!" The officer just smiles and replies: **"Why yes, yes it was!"**

When a prisoner tells you: **"With all due respect officer, I've been locked up quite a few times." "I think I know the law better than you!"** ***How can you argue with that logic? LOL***

Whoever said: **"There's no such thing as a stupid question"**, never worked the desk at police HQ!!!!

"Ok, ma'am, please explain to me exactly how you pay my salary?" "You don't work and you're on Section 8!!!!" "Although you do keep me busy." "What, with being sent to your residence 20 times in one year?" ***Some people need tickets on the clue bus!***

What do you say to the homeowner when you walk in for a complaint and they have framed portraits of Mussolini and Al Capone hanging on the living room wall? ***They just set back American Italians 70 years!***

"Look lady, I'm a cop not a Magician." "I can't wave my Maglight and suddenly unf*ck your life for you!"

"Please tell the folks in your neighborhood (high falootn' in their minds) **that when you are doing the nasty, don't knock the phone off the hook so it does a 911 hang-up." "And please have your curtains closed when we arrive to check on you!" "I don't need to see old naked hippies ever again!!!!!!"** ***Woodstock be damned!***

I don't care what people think, when you go to talk to a mental patient and they are wearing a T-shirt that says: **"I do what the voices in my head tell me to."** ***Now that's FUNNY!***

Was it simply morbid with a twist of humor?

One of the unique specialties of this particular State trooper is working in Forensics. The facial reconstruction of skeletal or otherwise severely damaged remains of human skulls often requires him to work in mortuaries. On one of these occasions the FBI and a neighboring State Police agency, working on a joined drug investigation, request his assistance to reconstruct the face on a human skull. This rather gruesome case involves a drug dealer who had been knocked unconscious and then locked in the trunk of his car. In an apparent attempt to destroy the victim's identity he had been doused with a highly volatile liquid and set on fire; only charred remains are left. It is now his job to put the pieces of the skull together, hoping to be able to draw a composite sketch of what he envisions the victim may have looked like when alive. Whether the FBI agent senses something is going to happen or not suddenly excuses himself and says: **"I'm going outside for a few and have a smoke."** For some reason the trooper from the other agency keeps hovering over the left shoulder of the trooper working on reconstructing the skull; making it somewhat awkward for him to work. Seemingly undisturbed, he continues with his forensics and nonchalantly turns to the other trooper and asks: **"By the way, how do you like the meat of your steak?"** With a slightly puzzled look on his face he replies: **"I usually like it pretty well done." "Why?"** Pretending to use his index finger the trooper, working on the skull, swiftly rubs his little finger on the burned bones and then sticks the index finger in his mouth. Then with a straight face and without missing a beat says: **"No I don't think**

it's well done enough for you." Without cracking a smile he holds the skull in front of the other trooper and asks: **"Do you want to try it though?"** The out-of-state trooper suddenly covers his mouth with his right hand and runs out of the room, leaving a spotted trail of what he had eaten for lunch earlier in the day. The facial reconstruction is an uncanny likeness of the victim when it is compared to known photographs of him.

Mouth to mouth restitution.

The police officer arrives at the scene of a stabbing and is approached by a person in the crowd. Since the officer figures that this is as good a point as any to start his investigation, asks the young man to tell him what he has to say; and the man begins.

> "Yo', officer, this might be impotent' for your investigation. I just wants to let yo' know there is nothing nobody couldn't do to save him. Even if I had some of dat 'mouth to mouth restitution' like yo' all got, an' dem' medical people that run after yo' all when yo' all go to one of dem' crime happenings. Dat' wouldn't have done nothin' good. Man she done stuck dat' knife in dat' poor boy like she was Dark Vader herself an' done killed his ass dead. When I looked at him an' he already forgot to breathe an' all dat, I knowed' right away that in his head he already done flown away with the birds. Yo' know what I'm saying? I jus' wanned' to let you know that even if I had that stuff yo' all come with, I couldn't have saved him no more. Cause he dead dead, dead. For real. You know what I'm saying? Maybe what I done told you will help you to narrow the time-line. Yo' know what I'm saying?"

Struggling to hold back the desire to laugh, the officer politely thanks the man and begins his investigation in earnest.

A lesson in fingerprinting.

A State Police corporal has been assigned to be the new recruit's FTO (Field training officer). The pair just received a call of a possible fatal accident involving a garbage truck that flipped over on its side; crushing one of the men who had been standing on the running board of the truck. After the scene has been cleared the FTO and his charge drive to the State Medical Examiner's facilities for further investigation to establish the required positive identification of the victim. The new recruit, a former Green Beret and Vietnam veteran, is eager to serve in his new profession. At the ME's office they are informed that the victim's body has been placed in the bottom right hand box of the large cooler housing the cadavers. When the FTO removes the cover from the victim he sees that the fingers of one arm are too mutilated to obtain fingerprints. Noticing the recruit's occasional hard swallow, the FTO decides that he is going to add some fuel to the fire as he holds up the other arm barely still attached by a little sinew. In a matter of fact tone the FTO turns to the Medical examiner and asks: **"Hey Doc, can I borrow a scalpel?"** A voice from somewhere in the back of the room is heard asking: **"What do you need that for?"** Continuing in his casual tone the FTO replies: **"Well, this guy that we are trying to fingerprint has only three fingers left that we might be able to get fingerprints from." "Since his arm is just about off anyway, I was wondering if I could just cut his arm off." "It would make it a lot easier for us." "Besides, he is already dead and won't know or feel a thing."** Somewhat annoyed, the ME (Medical Examiner) responds with a firm and peremptory: **"No way!"** Of course the FTO already anticipated the doctor's position. However, with a fish on the hook, the FTO decides to continue angling and says to the Rookie: **"Why don't you just hold the arm under your arm pit and do it that way?" "You better take one of those paper towels first though and wrap it around the arm." "You don't want to get any of that mess on your pretty uniform." "Sometimes it's difficult to get that stuff out."** The recruit is almost there.

(Cont'd.)

It's lunch time and I'm hungry.

It is lunchtime and they have not eaten yet. **"Hey Rookie, are you hungry?" "It's already passed lunchtime and I am starved." "What about you?"** In a very meager voice the Rookie manages to say: **"No thank you, I'm really not hungry"**. It is no coincidence that the manager of the nearby hamburger joint is also a friend of the FTO and prepares the cheeseburgers to order. On his return the FTO chooses to sit behind a small metal table that still has some residue left on it; the remains of a recently cut open cranium. With very deliberate actions the FTO spreads a couple of paper towels over the bone and hair fragments and grabs the lunch bag. Satisfied with the placement of the paper towels, he begins to dramatically unpack two cheeseburgers heaped to excess with extra cheese, onions, mustard and of course, extra, extra ketchup. He then nonchalantly offers the new trooper one of the cheeseburgers and asks him to sit down and eat. With a suppressed smirk on his face, the FTO tells the Rookie that it isn't polite to refuse the meal since he has bought it and had it especially prepared for him. The FTO then deliberately takes a big bite out of his cheeseburger, making sure that the condiments ooze out just the right way and dribble onto the paper towels. He has hardly swallowed the first bite when his trainee utters a muffled: **"Oh my God"**. In a desperate effort to prevent the escape of whatever was squeezing out between his fingers, the poor Rookie runs out of the back door to get some fresh air. After checking on the wellbeing of his charge and finds him shaking but alive, the FTO returns to his small, makeshift metal lunch room table and finishes his meal.

It took a lickin'.

The patrol unit is in route to a double fatality accident. When the State troopers arrive at the scene and begin their investigation they notice that one of the mangled bodies is missing the left arm. It is absolutely essential for POs (Police Officers) to keep a stoic appearance in the presence of gawking bystanders. Sometimes an officer hopes to find a way that could possibly enable him, at least in his mind, to cope with the cheer brutality of the carnage that he is faced with. In this case that is precisely what one of them feels he has to do. When after several minutes of searching for the missing arm and finds it he calls out to his patrol partner: **"Hey look what I have found."** Dangling from his right hand is the missing arm. When he gets closer, his partner notices the wristwatch and says: **"Man it took a licking and it's still ticking." "Let me see." "Guess what?" "It's not even a Timex." "Do you think we ought to inform Timex that they are not the only company?"** It is a good thing that the trooper holding the arm waits until he gets a little closer to his partner before reporting his final assessment of the watch.

Why don't you meet me at.....

The D/Sgt (Desk Sergeant) tells him that there is a call for him on line 2 and the trooper picks up the phone. The voice on the other end asks: **"Are you that ...... trooper?"** When the trooper answers in the affirmative, the caller continues. **"Since you think you are so big and bad, why don't you meet at the gas station at Atlantic and Maryland Avenue?" "That's of course if you are man enough because I'm going to kick your f.....g ass!"** Without a moment's hesitation he picks up the cast down gauntlet and with a raised voice replies: **"You better wait for me until I get there!"** and runs to the board with the patrol car keys. A very perplexed D/Sgt demands to know what the Hell is going on when he sees the highly exited trooper reach for a set of car keys. The trooper hurriedly replies: **"That call was from some SOB who threatened me and told me that he was going to kick my ass,"** and runs out of the troop to find the cruiser. In his excited frame of mind he almost didn't see the trooper standing outside by the back door; practically doubled over from laughing. Before climbing into the cruiser he is curious about the other trooper's odd behavior and asks: **"What the Hell is wrong with you?" "You look like you're ready to piss on yourself."** Barely able to speak and trying to recover his composure the other trooper blurts: **"You're damn right; I almost did piss on myself when you ran past me."** Catching his breath, the other trooper continues: **"I made the call." "Man did I get you good." "Can you imagine if that dirtball had been there just by chance and you ran up to him and tagged his ass?"** The trooper (Challenged) has to admit that the prank was indeed funny; but swears that he will get even. He eventually does, but not before the other trooper pulls yet another prank on him.

In the courtroom. # 1

#1.

Defendant: **"Your Honor, I'd like to get unsecured bond. I've been having a bad week." "My father died and my mother in trying to make me feel better told me the truth that my uncle is my real father. "Um.......ok.....I'm thinking.. thanks mom?"**

#2.

Judge: **"What is the nature of the relationship between you and the alleged victim?"**

Defendant: **"We were screwing your Honor but we were never formally introduced."**

#3.

Defendant: **"Your Honor, how you gonna' gimme' secured bond?" "Obviously you don't realize I'm dealing with a crazy bitch that's making false accurizations against me!!!!"**

Only in .... could you hear a gem like this. "Look officer, just because I hate one race of people, doesn't make me a racist."

Defendant: **"Your Honor, I can't go to jail." "I just got engaged!"**

Judge: **"Guess your boyfriend should have paid your fines instead of buying you a ring."**

Judge: **"How did the victim get bruised?"**

Defendant: **"It was Witchcraft!"**

Judge: **"How many times have you been to prison?"**

Defendant: **"A few times your honor."**

Judge: **"Young man, any time I see a man who enjoys being handcuffed as much as you do, I'm thinking, he is either very stupid or very kinky!"**

Judge: **"Do you have anything to say before I set bail"**
Defendant: **"Well your Honor if my good decisions were food, I'd have starved to death long ago!"**

Well it took a lot of years, but the officer finally heard it said during an arraignment.

Judge: **"Do you have anything to say before I set bail?"**
Defendant: **"Well your honor, I don't see where incarcerating me would help me or the public at large."**

Judge: **"Shenanigans!!!!!"**

The officer tries extremely hard not to laugh.

You're the cop, take charge.

Just three weeks into the job the Rookie cop in Field Training is riding with his FTO (Field Training Officer) around One Zone, north of the city on midnight shift. It is cold and dead and since he is the new guy he is driving and looking around for self-initiated activity. As they drive into a park land area he observes a lone Cadillac sitting in the darkness and pulls up to the Cadillac. In one fluid motion the Rookie presses the foot switch for the high beams and pulls the mushroom switch activating the 360 red and blue roof lights that turn the darkened park into a 70's Disco. Of course he is just a trainee and no Sherlock Holmes at this point but it doesn't take a genius to figure out what was transpiring in a Cadillac with steamed up windows. The FTO says: **"Go to the vehicle, ascertain if the girl is here of her own will and get both of their ID's and we will go from there"** and remains in the squad car. The young officer exits the cruiser, screws on his cover (police hat) and grabs his four D-cell Maglight in his left hand and approached the vehicle with his right hand hovering over the grip of his trusty Smith & Wesson...just in case. As he reaches the car, he observes that both the male and female were in the rear seat; still as naked as Adam and Eve. Apparently, the police light show hasn't dampened their spirit. There they are friends and neighbors still at work like two rabbits in springtime. Seeing the vigor that they are putting into their "work" he has no doubt that had this been an Olympic event they would have take home the Gold based on concentration alone! There he stands, thinking: ***"Am I going to get into trouble for seeing naked people?" "What do I do?"*** He takes his Maglight and raps several times on the car window. To his amazement, they keep on going! The male half, however, turns his head over his shoulder, looks at the officer and holds up his hand extending his index finger indicating, "One Minute" and goes back to the task at hand. A bit stunned, the Rookie walks back to the squad car...empty handed. The FTO holding his clip board in his lap extends his hand for the ID's, which of course hasn't been obtained. When the FTO doesn't get a response he asks: **"Where are the ID's?"** The Rookie answers sheepishly: **"They weren't done yet Corporal."** The FTO frowns and then begins to explain to the Rookie in language that would make a Master Chief Petty Officer blush and reminds the Rookie that he was the cop and go take charge.

And that folks is how you learn on FTO...LOL

See those pretty boots?

Several weeks have passed when the second prank is carried out; also well executed. When the trooper enters the squad room he notices a young prisoner in his late teens sitting on a metal folding chair. It is alleged by many that this particular trooper has the shiniest boots in the entire Division; he spends at least one hour a day spit-shining them. As the trooper walks past the young man, he hears the arresting trooper say to the prisoner: **"Didn't you tell me that you would kick the next trooper's ass when he walks in here?" "Well, here is your chance." "Look at his shiny boots!" "Why don't you go ahead and kick them."** Anticipating that the young man is gullible enough to attempt to kick his boots he walks past him at a distance where it will be very difficult to make serious contact. However, the young man is more agile than he anticipated and almost succeeds. Without losing his stride, the trooper jumps back and at the same time his fist connects a power punch to the prisoner's chin; collapsing the metal chair with the prisoner flopped on top of it. When he notices that the prisoner's hands are still behind his back, the other trooper busts out laughing and stammers: **"He still has cuffs on".** The trooper swears to himself that this is the final coupe de grace; revenge will indeed be sweet.

Revenge, oh how sweet.

The opportunity, when it presents itself, is totally unexpected and could not have been planned. It is absolutely made to order for the trooper. Many months have passed since the last prank and probably forgotten by everyone; except for this particular trooper. As he walks past the shift commander, the Sgt tells him that his friend (The prankster trooper) needs to see him right away in the Interview room. Before entering, the trooper looks through the glass door and observes a quite attractive female engaged in a conversation with the prankster. When the prankster sees the trooper he motions to him to come in and introduces him to the young lady; whom he is interviewing for a DUI (Driving under the Influence) and who just happens to be German. The prankster then yanks the trooper by the arm and drags him into the hallway and closes the door behind them. Once out of the lady's earshot the prankster, almost begging, blurts: **"Oh man, you've got to help me."** Without looking back says: **"Man, she is German." "Please teach me how to say something very nice to her in German."** In his desire to impress this young lady he is committing a major faux pas by turning to the trooper on whom he has successfully executed pranks on two previous occasions. Since German is one of the three foreign languages the trooper speaks, he agrees to help him; the prankster is thrilled.

The trooper can hardly retain himself and cannot believe what has been dumped into his lap. For him it was an absolute, "Case of non résistance". What was his friend, the prankster, thinking? Has he forgotten the stuff he pulled on him a while back? Has he completely lost his mind, all because of a pretty young damsel? Careful not to reveal his inner exuberance he formulates a sentence with enticing words of endearments; double entendre of course. With extreme difficulty to keep a straight face, he tells the prankster to repeat the sentence after him several times: **"Doo hustn' shunen hoomma"**. Satisfied that his friend is able to correctly utter the sentence he sends the proud prankster back to the waiting female. From his hiding place he is able to observe the prankster open the glass door and enter the interview room and begin speaking to the lady. As he watches in strained anticipation, he sees her suddenly leap from her chair and give him a smarting slap in his face. He just about loses it when the prankster rubs his obviously sore face. When the prankster hears the loud laughter and spots the trooper jumping up and down, he realizes that he has been bested and chases after him.

After the DUI suspect has been fully processed and things have calmed down, the prankster is naturally extremely curious and wants to know what he really said to her. Again, it takes the trooper a moment to compose himself from his new outburst of laughter before he is able to tell him the truth. **"Ok, you simply gave her a very wonderful complement"**. Seeing the extreme anxiety on his friend's face, he wants to relish the moment a while longer and decides to prolong messing with him. Still laughing, he finally acquiesces to the prankster's continual pleas to tell him what he had said to her. Between catching his breath and laughing he tells the prankster that he told the pretty lady that she had a beautiful vagina; but in guttural slang. The prankster screams: **"You no good son of a bitch!" "I must admit, that was hilarious and a fantastic payback"** and busts out laughing.

A midnight Folly.

The midnight shift commander has just finished reading the list of partner assignments for the two-man units. A particular TFC (Trooper First Class) is not pleased to be assigned to the Cpl (Corporal) with whom he had several prior issues during a midnight shift; always falling asleep. Rather than make it an issue tonight the TFC prefers to let bygones be bygones and in all fairness just re-address the issue with the Cpl and stress their safety. Unfortunately the talk did not completely penetrate the Cpl's skull. Less than an hour later his head is resting against the passenger side window;

accompanied by a very faint but audible snore. Thoroughly disgusted with the Cpl's disregard for their safety and the risk of embarrassment for the department, should a civilian see him, the TFC must do something; quickly. Careful not to wake up "Sleepyhead" he drives to the extreme far end of the shopping center's large and empty parking lot; an opportune place to remedy the situation. He positions the cruiser in such way that both headlights reflect in the large plate glass windows of a store; Sleepyhead is still in dreamland. Satisfied and smiling from ear to ear, the TFC clicks on the high beams, activates the red lights and guns the motor. With sirens blaring he screams: **"Oh, nooo"** and heads straight for the store windows and then slams on the brakes; leaving behind a long streak of burned rubber. Horror-struck Sleepyhead recoils out of his seat as if a rocket had been stuck up his ass and expletives coming out of his mouth that would even make a prostitute blush. Neither of them ever mentions the incident to anyone else nor are they ever partners again

It's sleepy time

A trooper, stationed at another troop, had a similar problem with his 'Sleepy'; who likewise did not listen to the admonishments of a junior trooper and would habitually fall asleep. The night finally comes when the junior trooper has enough and decides to take drastic action; he doesn't have to wait too long. About two hours into the shift, Sleepy has assumed his normal and routine position. Assured that his partner is sound- asleep, the junior trooper drives the patrol vehicle back to the troop and parks it in front of a sign marked, "Troop Personnel Only". Hoping that Sleepy is not going to wake up, he carefully removes the key out of the ignition and very delicately closes the car door. Seeing no movement in the passenger side, he briskly walks into the troop. After a brief report to the SGT, he obtains the key to another vehicle and continues with his patrol. His tour of duty isn't quite over yet when he hears a voice on his car radio instructing him to return to the troop. When he arrives he is met by a very annoyed looking troop commander who sternly orders him to meet him in his office. The Commanding Officer listens intently to the whole story and assesses possible negative ramifications if nothing had been done. Strictly out of his concern about the trooper's safety he verbally admonished him for having taken the risk to go out on patrol by himself and dismisses him. On his way out of the office he is somewhat perplexed thinking: ***"By myself?" "How is it different with Sleepy in the car?" "Maybe the Captain just wants to make it look good".*** The two also never ride together again.

Not On My Shift

Sitting in his office, a shift supervisor suddenly hears a lot of commotion coming from the front door area of the troop. Curious to find the cause of the laughter, he decides to investigate and follow the sounds of the amusement. As he approaches the radio room he noticed that several troopers have gathered around the glass enclosed prisoner holding facility laughing at the detainee; a very light skinned black female prostitute. It is immediately obvious that she is not being threatened in any manner and appears to be more embarrassed and certainly not afraid of the troopers who are encouraging her to remove her clothing; **"Come on let us see!"** The supervisor warns them and says: **"Not on my watch!" "Get a female trooper to conduct a body search"**. He barely makes it back to his office and prepares to sit down in his chair when loud laughter erupts again. Puzzled, he rushes out of his office and is shocked when he looks into the holding cell. There, grinning sheepishly from ear to ear stands the totally nude female proudly caressing her shapely and well endowed breasts; obvious implants. When the supervisor, ready to explode, looks a little closer he discovers an appendage dangling between the prostitute's legs. Shaking his head and in total disbelieve the supervisor demands an explanation. Enjoying her moment of notoriety, the prostitute smiles and slowly redresses herself. One of the troopers steps forward and says: **"Sir, please allow me to introduce you to George A….." "I believe that he can explain it to you much better than I ever could." "Hi, George?"** was the only thing that the supervisor is able to say before he is cut off by the high pitched voice of the now fully dressed attractive female looking individual.

Caressing his breasts and imitating a pirouette like turn he smiles broadly at the supervisor and says: **"My name is no longer George". "Do I still look like a George to you?" "I prefer to be called Georgette".** The supervisor wisely decides not to reply or engage the individual any further and simply says: **"Until you legally change your name, you'll be George"** and shuts the door to the holding cell. On his way back to his office he turns to one of the troopers and, with a sneer on his face says: **"Get it out of here".** That will not be the first time for them to meet; the next time it will be the supervisor's choice.

It's in the eyes of the beholder.

Still a rookie, the officer gets dispatched to a report of a drunk and disorderly male. The address as well as the name of the suspect sounds familiar to him. When he arrives on scene, the officer realizes that he has been at the same residence when he was still on field training a few years ago.

There stood "Clarence", drunk off of his ass and harassing family members. Then right in front of the young officer he punches his teenage son in the face. Reacting quickly the officer subdues him, slaps the bracelets on him and throws him in the squad car; off to HQ.

On their ride to HQ the suspect constantly runs his mouth and threatens to kick the Rookie's ass. At 22 and in top shape, the Rookie just smiles and says to himself: ***"Have at it pops."***

When they arrive at HQ and walk into the Turnkey (Holding Facilities), the House Sergeant gives the young officer the ok and says: **"You can take the handcuffs off "Clarence".** The minute the cuffs come off, "Clarence" takes a swing at the Rookie which he managed to dodge causing "Clarence" to be over-extended and off balance. Academy training immediately sets in.

The officer grabs "Clarence" by one of his arms and his shirt and performs a foot sweep; taking his legs out from under him. Unfortunately for "Clarence" the officer's loose grip on him causes him to fall face first onto the tile floor. "Clarence's" body striking the floor sounds like a sack of potatoes while his head actually bounces. As the officer stands there in awe he is horrified when he suddenly sees one of "Clarence's" eyes pop out of his head; skitters across the floor and comes to rest looking at the officer from beneath the prisoner bench. Seeing the total disbelief on the House Sergeant's face, the Rookie yells: **"Holy Shit!"**

To their relief they soon realize that thank God, that it is a glass eye which "Clarence" had acquired since their last meeting.

Psychic police officer? (In his own words.)

Youths often wonder how cops know that they are up to something. Well, some of it is from training in the academy, some of it is experience gained from working the street but a lot of it is based on the fact that many lawmen weren't angels themselves growing up. Before I was the "Long Arm of the Law", I was the "Short Brain of Stupidity". It was a Fall Saturday night long ago, when I was a teenager. My friend Mike called me and wanted to go cruising down Main St. He had a white Ford Maverick with a V-8 shoehorned into it and all souped up with fat rear tires etc. He had just finished tuning it up. Since my circle of friends were all motorheads, off we went. Now Mike was a damn good mechanic and I'm pretty sure that given the right tools he could make a turd run a 12 second quarter mile. As we cruised around Main St. the usual shit talking occurred car to car and it eventually led to challenges among some of our acquaintances to contests of vehicular superiority. Now we went along to be as they say in Police/Military parlance a JAFO or (Just another F***ing Observer) **LOL**. There we sat on the side of the road watching the drag racing...the air thick with the scent of burning rubber and the rumble of dual exhausts. Suddenly, red and blue lights appeared. Uh Oh! The local police were upon us and two patrolmen walked up to our car. It was their usual routine to obtain the ID's and phone numbers of all the non-adults and afterwards call their parents; even just observers like us. As one officer approached Mike's side of the Maverick he leaned in and the conversation went something like this -

Cop 1: **"You boys have your ID's?"**
Us: **"Yes sir." (Hand him our ID's**

Cop 1: Looks at our ID's and studies mine a little closer and then leans in window and inquires: **"Is your dad ....?" (*He knows that my dad doesn't put up with any shit.*)**
Me: ***("Fearing death; I know my life is over.")* "Yes sir, that's my father."**

Cop 1: **"Does he know where you are?"**
Me: **"No sir!"**

Cop 1: Looks at 2nd cop and yells: **"Cut these two loose."**
Cop 2: **"Why Sarge?"**

Cop 1: **"Because I don't want to have to investigate a Homicide tonight!"**
Me: ***"Yeah, he definitely knows my dad!"***

Us: Start the Maverick and drive off into the night! THANK GOD!
Me: Wait to tell my father years later, when I am a cop.

Yes kiddies, we've all been there!!!!! And Mike and I both ended up in the Criminal Justice field.

A little detour.

A City police patrol unit in Germany gets a call reference a major disturbance caused by an unruly drunk. When the two officers arrive they recognize the individual and remember that he frequently will not go peacefully. He routinely and deliberately causes problems hoping that the police officers arrest him and throw him in jail where he can spend the night for free; thus no punishment for him. Tonight, however, he is going to take a little detour.

When the drunk starts his shenanigans, the officers put their plan into motion. Being careful not to antagonize the drunk and deliberately keep his mind occupied, they invite him to partake in their conversation. Too involved, the drunk fails to notice that the officers are not driving to the station but quite a distance out of the city and stop at the edge of the woods. Suddenly the passenger door flies open and the confused drunk is told to get out. Pretending to administer a sobriety test, the offers tell him to turn on his axis several times and look into the bright beam of a flashlight; followed by a swift kick in his rear. It is pitch-dark and the perplexed drunk is totally disoriented and has no idea where he is. Before he has a chance to somewhat recover, the officers climb back into their patrol unit; and without turning the headlights on sneak away.

Screaming at the top of his lungs, he ends up in a small neighboring village about an hour later and really cuts lose; waking up the villagers. Not being used to such commotion, they call the local police station. Apparently coherent enough, the drunk is able to explain what happened to him and that it was the city police who abandoned him in the woods.

Central dispatch advises the city unit that the town police has the subject that the city unit lost and would appreciate it if they came back and retrieve him so that the community could get some sleep. With heavy heart the two officers return to the woods and pick up their quay and on the way the officers once again invite him to join the conversation. This time, however, he declines and the rest of the night is very quiet. Well, sometimes things happen that way.

Just a quickie?

A State trooper has been assigned to a State Police D/Sgt (Detective Sergeant) from a neighboring state to be trained in Forensic Science and Composite Sketching. While under the D/Sgt's tutelage, the trooper is required to accompany him during investigations and job performance. It is on this particular afternoon when driving back to the troop the D/Sgt recognizes the familiar face of the prostitute walking along the shoulder. The D/Sgt is unable to resist the urge to have some fun with his younger and somewhat naïve student. Looking over at his passenger the D/Sgt nonchalantly asks him: **"Are**

you in the mood to have a little fun?" Receiving an affirmative, the D/Sgt pulls the unmarked police car onto the shoulder and calls the hooker to come to the car. At first she hesitates to approach the car until the D/Sgt assures her that he is not going to arrest her and just wants to talk to her. He then turns to his passenger and asks him: **"Are you in the mood for a little action?"** Not quite sure how to answer that question he softly replies: **"I'm not sure"**. Sounding almost like a father talking to his son the D/Sgt assures him that everything will be all right and that he is going to set it up and says: **"Look, I know her and she is cool and probably won't even charge you as a favor to me." "Here is your chance to get a BJ."** Pointing to the back seat he remarks:"**Right back there."** Noticing the hesitation and a doubtful look in the trooper's eyes, he continues: **"Let me talk to her"**.

"Hey George, I mean Georgette, my partner here wants to know if he can get a little action." The D/Sgt had to remember that it was now "Georgette"; legally. Carrying a big smile on her face, Georgette sashays around the car towards the passenger side and sticks her head through the open window. The D/Sgt is ready to explode and it takes every ounce of his willpower that he is able to muster to keep his desire to laugh in check; as he watched Georgette begin her act.

With well synchronized and provocative gyrations she approaches closer and in an almost whispering and especially accentuated voice leans into the passenger side window and says: **"Honey, I can give you anything you want, you jus' gots to tell me what that is." "Is there anything special that you desire?" "You married an' yo wife don' give ya what-cha want?"** Noticing his head nodding in the affirmative, she smiles and continues. **"I'm sure I can turn yo' on wit' things yo' neva' dreamed of an' fulfill all your dreams for you." "Here, let me get into back seat wit' yo' an' show ya'."** At this point the trooper is left almost speechless and stammers: **"No, that's all right." "No thank you." "I'd rather not."**

The threatening looks in his eyes say it all as he glares at the D/Sgt; his supposed mentor. Miraculously still capable of keeping his composure the D/Sgt expresses a sham apology to the streetwalker and drives off; but doesn't get too far. As soon he has the car safely pulled off the road again, the D/Sgt loses it and laughs so hard that tears run down his cheeks and is unable to talk at the moment. Trying very hard to make some sense out of what just happened, the out-of-state trooper is only able to repetitively verbalize one sentence: **"You son of a bitch, Sir!" "You.....** When he has calmed down enough and is able to talk, the D/Sgt assures his trainee that he had confidence in him and that he would not have allowed it to progress beyond a certain point in the first place. Furthermore, had he detected any signs of weakening in the young trooper's character he would have called the whole thing off immediately and would have told him to look at the whole thing as a learning experience. The D/Sgt is pleased how things turned out and knows that he has a very competent trooper with him; but he needs to know one more thing and asks: **"At what point did you suspect that it was a set-up?" Now also laughing, the trooper replies, "When I noticed the 5-o'clock shadow on his face." "But you are still one crazy SOB". "Sir."**

Keep your hands to yourself.

A State Police D/Sgt (Detective Sergeant) is asked to assist in a homicide investigation by a local police department and create a composite sketch of a suspect; if possibly. Upon arrival, a Lieutenant of the local department ushers him into a small room to afford maximum available privacy. A small military issue field table, with a metal folding chair, has been pushed close against a wall to provide space for the D/Sgt to work on the composite sketches. Three additional metal folding chairs have been placed around the table. Another metal folding chair, facing the table, is placed against the opposite wall. Before leaving the room, the Lt asks the D/Sgt if he would have a problem with a couple of gay guys giving him a description of the possible murder suspect. Frowning, the D/Sgt replies: **"What difference does it make who gives me the description?" "As long as they behave themselves, it won't bother me."** The Lt returns a short time later and guides two obviously gay men to the small table.

After a brief introduction the two men are asked to take a seat at the small table; one opposite the D/Sgt and the other to his immediate right. The Lt sits down on the metal chair on the opposite wall to be available to assist the trooper if needed. He isn't able to explain why, but for some odd reason the D/Sgt has an odd feeling about the "Swish" seated to his right, and the way he kept looking at him during their introduction. Work on the composite sketch seems to be progressing very well. Despite the apparent pleasant rapport between the D/Sgt and the person seated very close to his right, he is beginning to have some concern. He has immense pride in his ability to very quickly assess people when initially meeting them; quite often dead on. This is the very first time he thinks that he may be totally wrong. Or is he? The D/Sgt feels a little edgy when he senses the individual's knee, seated to his right, touching his right leg. Since he doesn't wish to cause any difficulty with the local department he attributes the contact to the cramped quarters around the table and shoves the table tight against the wall and slides his chair as far to his left as he can.

Although it is somewhat awkward for the D/Sgt; at least it affords the person a little more room. Suddenly "Swish's" knee again wanders into the D/Sgt's space and plants itself a little too close for comfort; that definitely was not a mistake. Since there is no space left for the D/Sgt to readjust, he hopes that a stern look at "Gay-blade" will suffice; wrong. His drawing pencil is ready to break as his grip tightens, turning his knuckles white. The detective is having none of that; that was the finale. With lightning swiftness the D/Sgt bolts from his chair and with both hands grabs the "Swish" by his coat collar, practically lifting him off the floor, and threatens to beat the Hell out of him. Alarmed by the unexpected chaos, the Lt catapults from his chair and screams: **"Oh my God, don't do it!"** Still holding onto his prey and glaring back at the Lt the D/Sgt yells: **"Well, then tell this faggot son of a bitch to keep his hands to himself."** Still in shock, the D/Sgt's victim lisps: **"But I was only testing you."** Not sure whether to laugh or remain angry, the D/Sgt releases his grip and in a more relaxed tone that he is able to muster says: **"Well, your test results are in." "You flunked big time." "So sit the Hell down and**

keep your damned body parts away from mine." "Also, make sure that you make a firm mental note of the test results". After the D/Sgt is again composed and things have returned (to normal?), the composite sketch achieved positive results. A few days later the murderer is apprehended; with the aid of the composite sketch.

(Cont'd.)

He should have suspected it.

He is not even finished packing his drawing material when the D/Sgt finds out that his encounter with "Swish" has spread like wildfire throughout the police precinct. The Lt reenters the room and under a faux pretext apology says: **"I know what you have just been through and I want to apologize on behalf of my department and make amends, if possible."** The D/Sgt smiles and accepts the apology and the Lt continues: **"Would I be allowed to ask for another favor?"** Since he has some extra time the D/Sgt agrees and says: **"I'll do it, but there is one condition." "Not with any more gays; at least not today."** The D/Sgt could almost swear that he detected a faint smirk on the Lt's face but attributes it to the comment he just made. Then the Lt begins: **"Look I know that you just had a very traumatic experience, but here is the deal." "This time, would you be o.k. to work with two females, because it is possible that they may be able to help with creating another composite sketch?" "However, if they are satisfied with the one that you already did, then their input will not be necessary."** The voice on the station intercom informs the D/Sgt that two ladies have arrived for their appointment and are waiting for him in the lobby.

Glad to hear that they are females, the D/Sgt opens the door to greet them. He is pleasantly surprised to see two tall, strikingly good looking females with long blond hair smiling at him. However, the brief moment of euphoria is instantly destroyed when he hears a deep male voice asking him: **"Hi, are you D/Sgt....**The sudden burst of laughter tells him that he has been set up. How could he be angry, when he himself thinks that it is hilarious and should have suspected something like that? Even the two Drag Queens enjoyed the scene; especially when the D/Sgt admits that they do look damn good. When they are shown the composite sketch, they are surprised by the likeness and are not able to add anything else. But those were different times and different perspectives. Each lived in a world of their own and crossed borders without forcing personal issues on each other. It took a few more decades for the closet doors to swing wide open.

I'll Jump!

A State trooper responding to a possible jumper (person threatening to commit suicide by jumping off the bridge) arrives on the bridge. As soon as the alleged jumper sees the trooper approaching he straddles the bridge railing and yells: **"If you come any closer I'll jump!"** Maintaining his cool, the trooper tries to keep the jumper's attention and very slowly inches towards him. When he realizes that he cannot risk approaching the man any closer he stops. Not known for any special negotiation skills, he decides to employ his own version of psychological diplomacy and says:

> "Look, I really don't care if you jump or not; that's entirely up to you. So why don't you do yourself and me a favor and give me your driver's license first; before you jump. Because who knows how long it will be before your dead body is washed ashore some place. At least I will know ahead of time what or who we are looking for so I can tell your family that your stupid ass jumped off the bridge."

The man slowly slides off the railing and back onto the bridge. Noticeably shocked he just stands there momentarily speechless; glaring at the trooper. He suddenly bursts into a fit of anger and lashes out at the trooper; literally screaming at him.

> "I can't believe you. You are supposed to show compassion to me. You know that I was going to jump and you just don't give a shit whether or not I did. I can't believe that you can be that inhumane. You are supposed to be a public servant."

During the entire tirade, the trooper manages to get close enough to the subject to quickly subdue and handcuff him. With the subject secured in his cruiser, the trooper heads for the state hospital and a 72 hour commitment. Pleased with himself that he saved a life; even if it was unorthodox what he did.

The following week the trooper is summoned to appear at State Police headquarters; pending an investigation reference a complaint lodged him. After all, didn't he manage to prevent the guy from jumping off the bridge? Yeah, but he practiced without a professional license. Doesn't the end justify the means? A three day suspension.

Just another day on patrol. #2

Subject: **"Officer, you don't know who you are dealing with? I've been going to the gym!"** *(A slight click is heard as the officer puts the shiny bracelets on him.)*

Subject: **"When will the bridge be open?"**

Officer: **"I don't know sir."**

Subject: **"Why?"**

Officer: **"Because I'm a cop not a F*ing Engineer!"**

Subject: **"Can you drive across?"**

Officer: **"Sure, if your car is AMPHIBIOUS!"** *(It just continues......)*

Officer: **"How can you tell if I'm a real cop Ma'am?"**
" Well 'A' – you called the Police!"
"Then 'B' - I'm standing here in the pouring rain in full uniform."
"And - 'C', there's fully marked police car sitting there, that I drove here."

Officer: **"Yes that's right." "When you see me on a car stop, you should run out between my car and the one I stopped and exclaim: "'Officer, will you be long?"**

Officer: **"Ok lady, that's a bar light on my roof, not a Disco ball!!!!!!"** ***(Idiots..)***

Subject: **"Sorry officer, I know I'm revoked and I don't have any insurance but that's why I went out in the rain to get some cigarettes.**

Subject: **"Officer, that girl is crazy! She's suffering from Maniac Depression!"** ***(LOLOL)***

I know what I saw.

A two-man State Police unit responds to the location of a white female reportedly lying in the middle of the highway that, according to the caller, had been thrown out of a moving vehicle. After a thorough search of the alleged scene the troopers are unable to locate her body. Puzzled by the disappearance of the supposed body, they contact the person at the nearby gas station who reported the incident. When listening to the troopers' claim that they were unable to find any signs of the female, the proprietor of the station becomes somewhat irritated and jumps off his chair. Glancing at them with a look that questions their intelligence, he huffs and says: **"Come on, I guess I have to show you boys how to investigate"**. When the trio reaches the edge of the roadway, the gas station owner points to the center of the highway and mockingly says: **"She's right there!"** Flabbergasted when he doesn't see her either, he has to first compose himself before he continues: **"Well, that's where I done seen her." "I saw her gettin' thrown outta' the car and was jus' lying there and didn't move or nothin'." "Hell if I'd know what done happen' to her." "That's your alls' job to find out." "All I know is what I seen." "An' right there is where I seen her."** Satisfied with the garage owner's story they decide to investigate further and climb back into their cruiser and drive in the direction the suspect vehicle was last seen traveling.

About a half of a mile further down the road they spot a white female hobbling along the right shoulder of the highway and stop their unit behind her. When they get closer they notice that the heel of her right high-heeled shoe is missing and that she is extremely inebriated; and ugly. In the process of arresting her, the homely specimen of a female wants to know where the troopers are taking her. She demands that they leave her alone; because she had a little too much to drink and is just out for a walk. Remaining surprisingly professional the troopers explain to her that she is under arrest for "Drunk on the Highway" and that they will take her to a more comfortable place. Adhering to departmental policy (All arrested persons must be handcuffed prior to being placed in the police car) she is handcuffed; for everyone's safety. Because the handcuffs restrict any combative notions that she may contemplate, she makes up for with continual barrages of extreme profanity. To preempt a claim of any alleged improprieties lodged against them by this poor excuse of a human being, the passenger trooper informs the radio dispatcher of the type of suspect under arrest, the cruiser's odometer reading, point of contact and destination; the troop.

While processing her at the troop and under better lighted condition they notice that she is beyond ugly; if that is possible. Every so often they frown at each other and give each other a certain look. The nylon stockings covering her hairy legs are riddled with holes and runners with hair penetrating them like a porcupine and hideous clown looking makeup coating her face. One of them finally has enough with the ridiculous side show, jumps up and grabs her by her throat and says: **"What kind of it are you?" "You've got to be one of the ugliest living things that I have ever seen".** A barely audible reply is heard, **"I...I'm a guy".** When hearing that, the Desk Sergeant runs into the room and says: **"Strip bitch, strip".** The D/Sgt and the troopers watch in total disbelieve as the "Trans" performs a strip tease. Under his tattered and soiled white blouse he exposes a red bra with tassels, amply stuffed with scarves to give it some form. His male member is tightly pushed against his crotch by a G-string type devise and hidden under his red panties. When the strip show is over, the Sgt mutters: **"Get that, whatever it is out of here."** The story does not quite end here.

Besides "Drunk on the Highway" the drunk is also arrested for "Impersonating a Female". Boy times have certainly changed in the last five decades.

(Cont'd.)

Get a load of this.

Shortly after the two troopers are back on patrol they receive a radio call from another unit requesting them to meet at a specific location. When they meet the trooper who called them, he doesn't even give them a chance to get out of their vehicle and starts in immediately:

> "You will not believe this. Remember the arrest dressed like a female? Well, I am handling an attempted suicide of a lesbian. This Dike, in my case, admitted that she kicked her boyfriend out of a moving car because she was so pissed off with him. Yes, your guy. So when she had sobered up somewhat, she remembered that she and her boyfriend had a real down and drag-out fight in the car because he had made some advances on her 'Girl Friend'; quote unquote. I know this is some wild ass shit and it's hard to believe but apparently both of them are gay but are also boyfriend and girlfriend. It gets even better. Then they each have a friend besides that; he has a boyfriend and she has a girlfriend. They also have an agreement between the two of them. Neither of them is allowed to mess with each other's friends; they are off limits. So, believing that she killed him, she became so distraught that she tried to commit suicide. Maybe you guys can figure this shit out, it's too dense for me."

Laughing hysterically, the three say good bye to each other and climb back into their respective cruisers. What is the world coming to?

Was it a yellow sub?

An extremely unruly drunk in the State Police Troop holding cell is vehemently complaining about the lack of windows and has finally reached the end of the troopers' tolerance. In an effort to shut his trashy mouth they devise a very unusual plan. First they make sure that the bullhorn functions properly and the bucket filled with water is stored outside the holding cell where the drunk can't see it doesn't leak.

Under the pretext of being concerned about the lack of windows they ask the drunk: **"Man, what are you hollering and complaining about?" "Windows?" "Don't you know that there aren't any windows in a submarine?" "Are you really that stupid?"** Totally dumbfounded the drunk blurts out: **"What the Hell are you talking about?" "Who said anything about a sub?" "What sub?"** Straining to hold back their laughter they reply: **"We couldn't find a place fast enough so we had to put you on the sub."**

Before the drunk has a chance to reply one of the troopers keys the button on the megaphone and..."**Dive, dive, dive."** Then out of the drunk's view one of the other troopers grabs the bucket and pours water onto the cell floor. Suddenly, an alarming voice on the megaphone: **"Sir, we are taking on water!" "I repeat, we are taking on water!"** Panic struck the drunk holds onto the steel bunk for dear life and screams: **"Nooo!" "We're going to drown!"** Just then a much calmer voice is heard: **"All clear, all clear!" "We stopped the leak!"** Refusing to release his grip, the drunk meagerly asks: **"Does that mean we are safe?"** Miraculously holding back his laughter one of the troopers replies: **"Well, not quite yet."** Once again a voice, drenched in fear, quietly asks: **"But they said - all clear, all clear."** Still managing to control his composure the trooper replies: **"Well, yeah." "But only if we remain very quiet." "The least bit of noise could rupture the bladder."** Somewhat lessening his death grip, the drunk asks: **"Oh, did I cause the problem?"** Only the trooper able to keep a straight face responds: **"I'm sorry, but that is quite possible."** With fear still imprinted on his face the drunk slumps on the bunk and whispers: **"Well, you don't have to worry about me!" "I'll be totally quiet." "Ok?"**

The submarine is miraculously transformed into a library for the remainder of the night.

Pay back. **(*A motorist's explanation of his contribution to the trooper's paycheck.)**

An aggravated motorist stopped by a State trooper says: **"You ought to be careful about charging a motorist." "Do you even realize that I pay part of your salary?"**

Amused by the remark, he reaches into his pocket and pulls out two cents and hands them to the motorist; hoping that he swallows the bait. Dumbfounded by the trooper's action the motorist asks: **"What is that for?"** The angler smiles back at him and replies: **"I'm just paying you back your contribution to my salary." "Oh by the way, how about a little raise?" "Please press hard, you're making a copy for yourself."**

Where is the target?

It was the first day on the range for the new recruits; for several of them it was the first time that they ever fired live ammo. After many hours of classroom instructions, learning the nomenclature of their duty weapon and target acquisitioning; now they have a chance to put into practice what they have learned. When the senior range officer is finished explaining the range procedures and with special emphasis placed on range conduct and safety, the Rookies walk to their assigned positions. The range personnel have plenty of experience with new State trooper "Wanna Bees" and are prepared to handle pertaining issues and are prepared to make on the spot corrections. Everything seems to progress fairly smoothly; except for one female cadet who constantly slows down the pace. Despite the fact that he observes that she has good target acquisition and steady hands, her assigned block officer becomes irritated by her inability to hit her target. After a few more repetitive corrective efforts have been made by him, he calls for a "cease fire" and begins personal, deliberate on the spot instructions. To be able to scrutinize her more closely, he shifts his position and stands to her right. Suddenly he yells: **"Are you for real or just acting stupid?" "What in the Hell are**

you doing?" "How in the Hell do you expect to hit the target with your damned eyes closed?" In a very soft whisper the scared recruit replies: **"I'm afraid something might hit my face".** After hearing that, the block officer looses it and screams: **"The only thing that you should be afraid of hitting you is my boot up your ass." "How can you get hurt when you are holding your own gun out here and you are the one who is pulling the damn trigger?" "Now get your dumb ass up here and do exactly what you have been doing, but keep your friggin' eyes open." "Do you understand what I just told you?"** When he receives an affirmative nod, he continues; but in a much more fatherly tone. **"All right now." "You know that you can do it." "Now show the rest of them that you also want to be a trooper".** Apparently, it is quite possible that a good ass chewing can achieve the desired results. Or was it the tone of his voice? Well, either way, she hits the target and eventually qualifies.

Out of toilet paper.

When told that he has an urgent phone call on line one, the Troop Commander lets go of the bathroom door, marked for "Troop Personnel Only" and returns to his office. Standing close by, the trooper cannot believe his luck to finally have the opportunity to execute what he has planned for such a long time. Smirking to himself, he reaches into his pocket and pulls out a small plastic container with his concoction of peanut butter and chocolate mix and without being noticed by anyone disappears. Before leaving the bathroom, he quickly hides the toilet paper. Luck still seems to be with him as he reemerges out of the bathroom without being noticed by the other troopers and melts back into the group. Just in the nick of time as the captain rushes past them to visit the facilities.

Loud screams, laced with an abundance of profanity, emanating out of the bathroom's interior disturb the tranquility at the troop. Suddenly the door of the bathroom flings open with such force that it could have ripped off its hinges. His face swollen like a bullfrog and holding his partially dropped pants by the belt, the red faced captain momentarily stands there looking like a perfectly framed picture. The captain's stammering and muttering seem to have quickly recovered and turn into a rant. Still tucking at his pants he bellows: **"What no good sonnama' bitch ran out of toilet paper and smeared his shit on the wall?" "Who was the last person to use the toilet?" "I can't believe that someone just stuck a finger up his ass and used the wall for toilet paper." "It looks like it might be pretty fresh, since no one else has seen it before." "When I find out who did it, that bastard is going to pay for it!"**

Making sure that his plastic dose is still securely secreted in his pocket and surprisingly maintaining a concerned look, he asks the irate captain: **"Sir, do you mind if I take a look at it?"** The captain turns abruptly and says: **"What's there to look at?" "Shit is shit." "What's the matter?" "Haven't you ever seen shit smeared on a wall?" "Well, go on Defective', see what you can come up with."** The trooper merely nods his head and walks into the bathroom; leaving the door wide open behind him.

When he is sure that the group is watching him he walks up to the tiled wall and takes his right index finger and wipes some of the brown stuff off the wall and then rubs it between his finger and thumb. Those watching him are in utter disbelieve and are horrified when they see him smell his finger and then reach into his pocket and take out a napkin and nonchalantly wipe his finger. He could swear that he heard a gag or two when he took his finger and wiped the rest of the brown residue off the tile and transfer it likewise to the napkin. Apparently numbed by his display and staring at him the trooper simply smiles at them and says to the captain: **"Well sir, you are right." "It is rather fresh but surprisingly doesn't smell bad at all." "One good thing though." "Whoever did it was careful enough not to get his deposits into the grout." "It's all cleaned up." "The only thing we need now is just some toilet paper." "Oh, by the way; does that qualify me to become a detective?"**

Whether by choice or an inability to find the proper response to the trooper's comments the captain shakes his head gives him a stern look and finally says: **"You know something?" "You either have an occasional screw loose or some unknown or weird fetish." "Shouldn't you be back out on patrol?"** It is not known if the trooper ever revealed his prank.

Total absence of logic – go figure.

"Yes sir, you are absolutely right....this is a speed trap." "I trapped you into doing 58MPH in a 25MPH by sitting in broad daylight on the side of the road in a neighborhood.........."

I think I just threw up in my mouth.

Officer: **"Sir, you really need to call it quits with your girlfriend. This is like the fourth time I've dealt with you over her!"**

Subject: **"I tried!" "I just can't!" "The sex is so good with her!"**

Officer: **"Yeah but she's sleeping with all those other guys too." "It can't be that good or worth it."**

Subject: **"Sergeant, you don't understand!!! She's my Fifty Shades of Grey!"**

Uhmmmm yeah..........Fifty Shades of Grey in a trailer....Fifty Shades of Filth is more like it! LOL

Lucky Charm.

A City police department in Germany has been issued new BMW motorcycles. The administration claims that the new machines are of a better quality than the older models. As a cost-saving measure it has been decided to limit each rider to 30 miles per shift. Whether the actual fuel consumption truly interested anyone in leadership position is questioned. To many it appears that the main emphasis is strictly on the mileage driven by the operators. There are also those who claim that the new wheels do not nearly have the pep as the old ones.

As usual, there always seems to be an individual who needs to be personally convinced. Careful not to be seen the officer makes some final adjustments to his BMW, climbs on and drives to the Autobahn on the outskirts of the city. At the top of a high elevation he floors it and kicks the lame mule in the ass. When he reaches a speed in excess of 130+ km the rear tire of his motor cycle suddenly explodes. It is impossible for him to regain control and the bike tilts on its right side, sliding several hundred meters across the asphalt; with his right leg pinned underneath it. Although most of the true circumstances will very likely remain clouded in mystery; some unknown individual comes to his aid. Whoever he is takes the officer, miraculously only slightly injured, to a telephone booth. Cell phones have not been heard of yet. The officer's lucky charm still appears to be functioning perfectly.

He manages to get hold of a private (?) towing service and requests to be picked up. Everything works according to plan. (It should be noted that at the time there was already a stretch of autobahn within the city limits – extremely important because of the 30 mile patrol limit.) It is to this location where the private (?) towing service brings the totaled bike. The tow-truck driver and police officer throw the wreckage off the flatbed and then tie a rope to the motor cycle and climb back into the truck. With what remains of the police motor cycle in tow the truck drags it in snake fashion for several hundred meters, making sure that ample traces are left behind on the asphalt; proving that of the accident happened here. As further proof, the cycle cop reattaches the tachometer and radios central.

When the division head of the motor cycle unit arrives at the scene and surveys the many skid and gauge marks, he is also able to determine that the lucky police officer has only part of his pistol. In fact the pistol may have actually protected him and saved him from serious injuries when he slid across the highway. The steel of the pistol looked like the missing part had been machine routed off.

The question remains – is the new motor cycle slower? Well, now and then we deserve some luck in life.

A clandestine transaction.

Several individuals informed a State trooper, working a special duty job at a hamburger establishment and Teen hangout, to keep a watchful eye on the operator of a particular older green station wagon. According to them, the station wagon is usually parked on the elevated section of the shopping center's parking lot allegedly conducting clandestine business; selling alcoholic beverages to minors. Later that evening he observes the vehicle in question backing into the previously mentioned location. Pretending not to pay particular attention to the operator's conduct, he climbs into his POV (Privately Owned Vehicle) and adjusts the mirrors. He doesn't have to wait too long when he notices a number of youngsters gathering around the station wagon. After a few handshakes with the operator, the station wagon drives off. Not expecting any further action involving the station wagon, the trooper is surprised to spot it again about an hour later. He decides to preempt further activity to be conducted and nonchalantly meandered in the direction of the station wagon. In the meantime he discovers why there has been no transactions taking place until now. During the young teens' initial contact with the operator they only placed their orders and paid him. Startled when he recognizes "Jimmy"; a low level criminal whom he arrested some time ago for burglary verbally engages him. **"Surprised to see you." "What are you doing here tonight?" "How come you are sitting alone all the way up here and so far away from the hamburger joint?" "Are you practicing to be anti-social since you are not eating?"** Jimmy's annoyed look portrays his great displeasure with the trooper's presence.

(Cont'd.)

Start pouring.

Delighted to see Jimmy beginning to get fidgety, the trooper starts his spiel. **"What's that hump back there under the blanket?" "Isn't it kind of warm this evening for that?" "I'm sort of curious." "So may I take a look what you have there?"** Unable to respond clearly, Jimmy just mutters: **"Do I have to?" "Don't you need a warrant or sometn'"?** Having difficulty to suppress his laugh, he continues: **"Well, I don't have a warrant but I have already told you that I have the something; curiosity." "Besides that, I believe that a crime is about to be committed." "Now pop the lid and let me have a look".** Another mutter is heard: **"Do I have to?"** Unwillingly, Jimmy climbs out of his wagon and walks to the rear of it. Any further questions by him are cut short by the trooper's nod of his head. The tail gate has barely been opened and the trooper reaches inside and pulls the blanked off the hump and confirms his suspicion; a treasure trove of booze. With a big smile on his face and a fatherly tone the trooper asks Jimmy:

> "Oh my, look at what I have discovered. Are those a couple cases of cold beer in bottles? What did you do Jimmy, have three birthdays at once? But wait a minute Jimmy, I realize that you look to be in your early twenties, but didn't you just turn eighteen when I arrested you the last time? Of course you know that with all of that alcohol that you have here, you could end up in big trouble; another big arrest and all. So what are you planning to do with all of this?"

Not bothering to wait for a reply the trooper says: **"Here, let me help you."** Holding the first case high above his head, he mockingly exclaims that the case is much heavier than he expected it to be and can't hold it any longer. Pretending to struggle with the weight and very much assisted by him, the case of beer crashes to the ground. The explosion of broken glass bottles is followed by volumes of foam oozing out of the cardboard case. Shock fails to describe the horror on Jimmy's face as the trooper reaches for the second case; which because of the excessive weight suffers the same unfortunate accident. In a very polite tone, laced with fake sadness, the trooper asks if that is all of it. With tears in his eyes Jimmy mumbled: **"Yah, that's it".** The trooper then slowly reached behind the back seat and pulls out the bottles of liquor that he had noticed earlier. Putting on a show of total surprise holds up the bottles and says: **"Look what else I have found." "Boy, aren't you glad that I found them?" "I guess in all of the excitement you must have completely forgotten all about them." "They must have accidentally rolled behind the seat, huh?" "Well I tell you what I will do just for you."** After he unscrews and removes the cap of one of the bottles he hands it to Jimmy and says: **"I'm sorry for being so selfish, so let me make it up to you." "After all, these are your bottles, so you may now have the honor and empty the**

bottles yourself." "Start pouring." When the three bottles are empty he smiles at Jimmy and says: **"By the way, you ought to ask your young buddies over there to help you clean up this mess." "I'm sure that they are anxious to hear about your unexpected misfortune."** Looking at the still intact bottles of beer mixed in with the soaked card board and shards' of glass, he cautions Jimmy to be careful not to get cut picking out the unbroken bottles and empty them. While Jimmy is busy collecting the trash the trooper notices the group of young teens approaching and waves goodbye. Since Jimmy's burglary charges are still pending, he decides not to arrest him but instead hopes that what he did tonight has taught the troublesome young man a lesson. Apparently Jimmy failed again; several weeks later he is arrested for DUI.

Request an intercept.

In the process of making a right hand turn, at a major intersection, the State trooper's attention is drawn to the sound of loud screeching tires and noisy throbbing mufflers. Twisting his head in the direction of the sound, he spots a souped-up silver grey pickup truck exiting the corner restaurant at high speed; leaving behind a long trail of burned rubber in the traffic lane. The trooper punches the gas pedal and quickly accelerates to maintain visual contact. It is immediately apparent that the driver of the pickup has no intension to allow the pursuing cruiser to catch him. When reaching speeds of over 100 mph, going north towards the neighboring state, he calls dispatch and requests an intercept by the bordering state's State Police; and keeps a safe distant visual of the truck. As the two of them approached the state line a couple of semi-trailers straddle the shoulder partially blocking traffic; one facing north and the other facing south. The driver of the pick-up truck has no choice and pulls over; with the pursuing trooper right on his tail. Anticipating a possible escape attempt, the trooper jumps out of his vehicle and runs up to the driver's side of the pickup, rips open the door and grabs the shook-up driver by the collar and yanks him out. Startled, the driver demands to know where the trooper came from. In disbelief that this guy has the audacity to ask that question, the trooper replies: **"I came from cloud nine and you're under arrest."** At the approach of two neighboring state's State troopers the subject suddenly develops a defiant posture towards the trooper who chased him and sneers: **"You can't arrest me now, I'm not in your damn state any longer." "I guess you have to go back now where you just came from, ha, ha, ha."** The three troopers can't believe what the civilian, now laughing just said. One of the neighboring troopers walks up real close to him and pretends to whisper into his ear, yet loud enough for his two colleagues to hear him say: **"What did you just tell that State trooper over there?"** Still smug, the pick-up driver repeats what he told him, emphasizing again that he was in another state. The trooper balls his fist, the loud mouth never saw it coming; it was that sudden. Then the trooper says to the trash mouth; somewhat groggy from the punch: **"Now your ass is back where you just came from." "Go get him Troop."** The trooper handcuffs the now speechless arrestee and places him in the backseat of his cruiser. After a hearty laugh he expresses his gratitude for the neighbors' help, climbs back into his car and heads back to his troop.

Flashback

A two-man State Police cruiser is approaching the outskirts of the town when they hear the crackle of the Town cop's radio message. The passenger trooper can't figure out why that voice seems so familiar to him; suddenly he has a flashback. Five years have passed since his run-in with this "Townie".

He and his buddies had been celebrating his seventeenth birthday and spent a whole week frolicking in Ocean City, MD and were driving through the town on their way back home. Although the speed limit sign read 35 mph, he figured that a couple miles over the limit wouldn't cause any problem and kept an eye on the needle. As he happens to glance in his driver's side mirror, he noticed a car quickly approaching on his left and then slows down; then staying even with him. Too engrossed in conversation with his buddies, he didn't pay any further attention to the car next to him; until he heard the other car's engine rev up and the driver beep his horn. It was a little tempting for him not to give it a go since his own car had been somewhat modified and wasn't too bad, but decided against it since he already noticed the Town cop's car in the distance. Under pretext of having accepted the other driver's challenge, he nodded his head and gunned his engine. He recalls how the other car took off a hellin' fishtailing through a cloud of burned rubber smelling smoke and disappear in the distance. A heartless attempt by the police officer to catch the drag racer failed and left him in the dust.

It is quite possible that by the time he reached the cop car and the police officer pulled him over that he was clocked on radar going close to 40 mph. He didn't want to create any unnecessary problems and just held his license and registration in his hand and gave them to the cop. Then in a very annoyed manner the officer demanded to know why he didn't obey the posted speed limit and was speeding through his town. When he politely replied that he was only going a couple of miles over; the officer glared at him and said: **"Well, you'll do."** Shocked by the cop's attitude he decided not to give in without a fight and told the cop: **"The only reason you are burning me is because you are pissed off at the other car that left you in his dust." "You couldn't even catch a cold in the dead of winter, yet alone catch him."** The cop's looks could have killed him. Unfamiliar with the legal practices of the law, he obeyed and followed the cop to the Magistrate or Justice of the Peace court in town. With the help of his buddies his fine was paid and they continued on their way; him holding a grudge.

Who would ever have believed that five years later the moment would come? It isn't until now that the former teenager knows that the law in the state demands that all teens, under the age of eighteen can only have their cases adjudicated in Family Court.

(Cont'd.)

Let me drive.

The same familiar voice out of the past is heard again, telling Dispatch that he has radar set up; the same road where the junior trooper had his encounter with the town officer back then. As far as he is concerned, it would have been a cardinal sin not to punish past unwarranted conduct. When he is finished with his dissertation, emphasizing that he doesn't just want, but needs to drive the unmarked State Police cruiser; the senior trooper relinquishes control and slides over to the passenger side. Because of the early morning hour, he doesn't have to wait for the roadway to be clear of other traffic; turns off the lights and pushes the gas pedal to the floor. The speedometer needle quickly reaches past 100 mph as he blows past the radar; producing an instant reaction from the Townie. Practically incoherent and stuttering the voice on the radio screams: **"Aah, aah, I'm, I'm chasing a fast one in excess of a hundred, going south."** With extreme difficulty to suppress his hysterical laughter the junior trooper picks up the mike and asks the Townie whether he still has the car in sight and is able to describe the make and model. While waiting for the confused reply, he slams on the brakes and quickly backs the cruiser into a side street. Seconds later comes the Townie's reply: **"I, I don't really know what kind of car it is." "It's cream colored and turned onto Maryland Ave."** Sitting in their hiding place and howling with laughter the troopers hear the wail of sirens and then see the Town cop blowing past them. One of them manages to calm his laughter and asks the Townie: **"Do you still have him in sight?"** The Townie responds immediately, claiming that he can still see the car's taillight; followed by: **"I just lost it." "I don't know where the car went."** Still not fully recovered from laughing, the troopers reply: **"Sorry we weren't of any help." "Hopefully you have better luck next time."** The Townie never finds out the truth.

A Semi-truck?

Driving southbound on the Interstate a State trooper notices a set of tail lights, some distance ahead of him; suddenly accelerate for no apparent reason. Attempting to get a clock (speed check) on the vehicle he increases his speed to close the gap between them. He is puzzled that, although he has increased his speed considerably, he is not getting closer and the two red eyes are still walking away from him. It isn't until he reaches 105 mph that he is able to keep pace and has to increase his speed to get a closer look. Realizing that the vehicle he is chasing is quickly approaching the Toll Gates, he calls ahead and requests the Toll taker to retain the next vehicle approaching the toll booths. When he arrives at the Toll booths, there is no car; just the cab of a "Kenworth" 18 wheeler truck. Aggravated that the Toll taker has failed to stop the car he has been chasing, the trooper bolts out of his cruiser and storms over to the booth; ready to jump on the Toll taker's case. When the Toll taker sees the trooper storming towards him he hollers: **"There was no car that came through here, only that "Bob-cat" over there." "So I had him pull over."** Not quite sure what to make of the Toll taker's story, he decides to check out the truck. Before he has a chance to address the individual sitting behind the steering wheel the truck driver says with a slightly raised voice: **"Trooper, before you say or do anything, will you please tell me how fast I was going when you tried to catch up with me?"** He can hardly believe what he hears and replies: **"At least a hundred plus."** With that the driver turns his head and holds out his hand to the person sitting next to him and says: **"You done heard' what that trooper jus' said." "Yup', you owe me two hunnerd' big ones."** Curious about what the driver said to his passenger, he cautiously approaches the cab a little closer. The truck driver laughs and says: **"I just won a two hundred dollar bet." "So let me tell how." "You may not wanna' believe me, but lemme' tell ya' anyhow."**

(Cont'd.)

A $200.00 bet.

Then he begins. **"As we were drivin' down here, me and my buddy here kept arguing jus' how fast this baby could go jus' by itself without a trailer." "I done told him I didn' know exactly but I was positive I could git up to a hunnert' if ya' were to gimmi' nough' stretch a road." "That's when he said that he'd bet me two big ones (**waving the $200.00

in his right hand) **that I couldn' do it." "En' that's when I done kicked it in the ass comin' down here."** Even though the trooper has to admit that it is funny, he cannot let them get off scot-free. He decides to arrest the driver for excessive speed and takes both of them with him to the Justice of the Peace. When the judge is finished listening to both sides, he slams the gavel on the bench and assesses the driver a $200.00 fine. Either way, the only guaranteed loser is the passenger who lost the bet. On their return trip to the truck, the driver boasts that he could probably get his truck up 110 mph; if the stretch of road was straight and long enough. Who knows?

Hey it's Sunday.

A couple of State troopers honor the request of a local minister to visit his church and allow the congregation to see another side of policing. As they walk towards the church and pass a group of young teenagers one of the boys snarls at them in a very sarcastic tone: **"Hey, what ya' think ya'll' gonna' do?" "Arrest someone in church?" "Can't you bad poelice' wait until tomorrow?" "Don't ya'll' know it's Sunday and yo' pose' to take a day off too?"**

One of the trooper's replies: **"Well, since you obviously seem to be concerned about our welfare and asked so politely, I will tell you why we are here." "You see, we received an urgent call from someone at the church, complaining that the choir was singing too loud." "So we are here to check it out for ourselves and see if there is enough to make an arrest for Breach of Peace."**

Stunned by the trooper's unexpected reply, the young boy straddles his bike, grunting some expletives and peddles off; followed by the rest of the group still snickering.

What oil change?

While on patrol on the Interstate, a State trooper spots a disabled vehicle parked on the shoulder and stops his cruiser behind it to investigate. The upset driver, an elderly lady, states that her only three year old car suddenly stopped running. She also claims that she couldn't be out of gas because she gassed up earlier that day and everything was going well up to that point. Not being a mechanic as such, he decides to follow a simple process of elimination and starts with the key in the ignition. Finding no response, not even a familiar click, he opens the hood. A check for a possible problem with the water level in the radiator as well as a cursory inspection of the battery and wiring proves negative. As a last result the trooper decides to examine the oil level. He finds a piece of paper towel and pulls out the dipstick. When after three or four attempts no sign of any oil appears on the dipstick, it is apparent that there is no oil in the motor. Holding the empty dipstick he walks over to the driver and asks her whether she recalls the last time she had her car serviced and had an oil change. Obviously shocked by the question, she responds: **"Oil change?" "Why would I need an oil change?" "I just bought the car three years ago and they told me then that everything was fine with the car and I just had to occasionally put gas in it." "Is it too late for a lawsuit against the car dealership?"** The trooper is left speechless because he has never heard a story like that. In comparison to her understanding of mechanics, he is an absolute genius. He walks up to her and in a very diplomatic way says: **"Ma'am, I'm sorry but I did everything that I could do, unfortunately your engine froze up." "The only thing that I am able to do for you is call a tow service." "Then you may either go with them or I can transport you to the troop; where you can place a call."** A few hours later her sister arrives at the troop and picks her up.

But not in my neighborhood.

The State Police Troop, located just south of the city, receives a call from an individual complaining about marked State Police units driving through the area where he lives. The somewhat aggravated sounding person claims that he is seriously concerned about how the marked State Police units are being utilized. In his opinion, he finds their presence in his well known, upscale area extremely degrading. While listening to the caller lament, the Desk Sergeant detects a definite dislike for police in general when he hears the haughty remark: **"After all, look at the real estate value of our domiciles." "I'm upset that it could give a false impression to the outside public when they see police vehicles coming through our community."** With tongue in cheek, the D/Sgt politely assures the caller that he will implement corrective measures. He slams the phone back on the cradle and mutters: **"That pompous, arrogant bastard." "You bet your ass, I'll take corrective measures."** When the D/Sgt is finished briefing his men about the caller's complaint, no further instructions are needed. Responding with appreciative smiles his men are determined that they are going to take appropriate and adequate action to remedy the highly insulting offensive act perpetrated against the caller. The caller is obviously not aware of the number of recent burglaries and property thefts that demand increased State Police presence.

(Cont'd.)

A highly motivated response.

According to the State troopers, concerned about the noticeable spike in burglaries the preceding weeks, just a few miles away from the area where the previous night's caller lives, the State Police decided to increase their patrol in the area. It is certainly not uncommon to have an occasional motorist stupid enough and drive through the streets of an exclusive area trying to get away from the police. But a couple of them, two nights in a row? The troopers feel it necessary to have their cruiser's emergency equipment, i.e. lights and siren activated when chasing the vehicles trying to elude them. Unfortunately there is a sudden increase in the phenomenon; the previous night and again tonight. For some unexplainable reason, when the vehicles enter the particular highfalutin area in question and the troopers attempt to stop them, the "four-wheeled" entities suddenly disappear. Several days later the reason for marked units is revealed to the public. The detailed plan to have marked State Police units patrol the community, in order to combat crime, had already been drawn up and implemented several weeks prior. Community leaders agreed to pay for extra off-duty troopers to be specially assigned to patrol the area in marked units. To insure success and coordinate things, a retired State trooper was hired as chief of their fledgling one-man police department. Although the program was relatively successful for several years, budgetary restraints eventually forced the project's closure. Complaints about marked State Police units and phantom cars seized to be an issue.

Porn emergency.

A young County officer with barely a year on the job, thinking that he is going to save the world is working a Friday midnight shift. It is very cold; 15 degrees not including the wind chill and the wind howling. At around 0030 hrs a call of what sounds like a woman screaming comes in to central and he is dispatched to the address. Not too happy about having to pour his fresh hot coffee out of the window the officer starts rolling Code-3; lights and sirens the whole way taking corners on two wheels. When he approaches the neighborhood he goes by the book; turns the lights, siren and headlights off and parks his squad car within five houses of the location.

In case he needs to move quickly the officer doesn't bother putting on his overcoat; big mistake. By the time he reaches the front door of the house he is frozen. With his sidearm in hand he is met by a little girl standing in the doorway. Like in a movie; flannel nightgown and cuddling a stuffed animal. Tears rolling down her cheeks she tells him: **"Someone is hurting mommy!"** Suddenly feeling in a hero mode he tells the scared child: **"Go down to the basement and don't come up until I tell you!"** As he begins to investigate he hears a woman's voice yelling: **"No! Don't! Stop!"** and cautiously follows the direction of the sound. About the same time the officer's partner arrives, two years his senior and like a god. On the plus side, he's big into martial arts. Following the screams, they slide down the hallway and find the door to the master bedroom locked.

The senior officer tells his partner: **"I'm going to kick the door." "You go high and I'll go low!"** With a masterfully executed karate kick the door flies off its hinges and slams to the floor, followed by a duo gangbuster charge; bringing the younger officer's hero mode to a crashing halt.

The officers and uninvited guests momentarily freeze in their tracks by the porn show they are witnessing. Kneeling on the bed is a nude midget holding a dildo; grasping it like a soldier would load a round into an artillery piece. Lying on the bed is his also his nude wife. Angered by the officers' intrusion the midget jumps off the bed yelling: **"What the f*ck!"** and shoves the senior officer. Reacting instantly the officer grabs him and cuffs him. It is readily apparent that the midget is hung like a horse; proof that God has a sense of humor. When the wife jumps out of bed the officers are surprised to see that the wife is almost as tall as the younger officer who is 6'02". Even more disturbing is her huge bush which looks like "Buckwheat" in a leg lock. Apparently not concerned about her nudity in the presence of two strange men she still has not bothered to get dressed. She then grabs the dildo and waving it close to the younger officer's face and in a twang southern accent says: **"I don't mind him wanting to have sex with me, but I don't want him sticking this ole thing inside of me!"** The officer doesn't dare verbalizing what he thinks: ***"Lady, it ain't much bigger than what he is packing."*** She then tops it off and shoves the dildo even closer in the officer's face and says: **"Officer, do you need this for evidence?"** The officer backs off slightly and thinks: ***"Yeah, I'm a real hero and a possible short-lived career."***

(Well, the officers will keep their job, despite the fact that they crashed a porn sideshow. Lucky for them?)

A day in court. ***#2***

Defendant: "**You are judging me as a criminal, based on my dreadlocks!"**

Judge: **"Me?" "No, I'm judging you as a criminal based on your 30 page history of felonies."**
"Of course your knee socks embroidered with Marijuana leaves are not helping my opinion of you either."

Judge: **"Do you have anything to say in reference to your bail?"**
Defendant: **"I ain't got sh*t to say to you man!"**
(The defendant found out $16,000.00 **Cash - only bail** later...........)

Defendant; **"Your Honor, I know my rights." "I got a license not to incriminate myself!"**
(Wonder if he got it at the DMV?)

Word to the wise:

When a Judge asks you if you have anything to say, it is **NOT** the time to throw your feet up on the table and tie your shoelaces. So now someone at the local Correctional center is getting a new roomie'.

Defendant Quote of the night:

Defendant: **"Officer, what was my total bail again on my three capiases?"**
Officer: **"$2,000.00 secured ma'am."**
Defendant: **"But the judge said $500.00, $500.00 and a $1,000.00 secured?"**

(AND this Def. is a teacher in one of the local schools!!!!)

Under suspicion.

Daylight has just broken the horizon when a State trooper takes a closer look at the car ahead of him and recognizes the operator; a known burglar. An affirmative reply from radio dispatch confirms his suspicions. Without PC (Probable Cause) the trooper is, nevertheless, determined to deprive the suspect of any profit for his illegally procured gains. Considering the character of the individual (burglar) and early hours of the morning, he feels it wise to call for backup. When he sees the other the trooper approaching, he flashes his lights and signals for the suspect driver to pull over. After the other trooper has positioned his vehicle in the front of the suspect's vehicle both troopers cautiously approach the suspected burglar; the initial trooper approaches on the driver's side and the other on the passenger side. The suspect has an immediate dejected look on his face when he recognizes the trooper who stopped him. It should be noted that it is this particular trooper's custom to verbally mess with scumbags. While conducting a customary cursory, visionary search of the car interior, the trooper immediately spots the partially hidden burglar tools on the floorboard behind driver's side seat; his intuition has proved him right again. When noticing the dirtball's "oh, shit" expression, he knows that he has struck gold. Thankfully dirty looks don't kill as the scumbag says: **"I donno' why you're stoppin' me cause' I ain't done nothin'." "I'm jus' comin' from a friend's house".**

Holding back the desire to laugh, the trooper keeps a stern face and continues:

> "Oh, yeah? What's your friend's name? Isn't it kind of early for you to be out here roaming the highway? So, don't tell me that you are going to work. Remember, I know that you don't have a job. Oh, wait a minute! I'm sorry, let me rephrase that. I meant to say, 'Legal'. Because I know, of course we both know what illicit profession you practice. I thought for sure that with all of your training behind you, you would be slightly better at it. Well, that may depend upon in the way that you look at clams. Aren't they supposed to be dumb also? I tried to tell you the last time to knock it off because your professional skills suck. By the way, do you still have to take your shoes off whenever you have to count past ten? What are you going to do when it's cold and nasty outside? Well, in your job you have to primarily count on not getting caught. Right? Did the cat get your tongue? You still haven't answered me why you are out here so early. I'm patiently waiting for your answer. Well?'
>
> (Of course the trooper's remarks are frequently interrupted by grunts and short expletives.)

After a brief moment of silence the suspect drops an obviously bogus name. **"Where does your buddy live?"** Only too familiar with the usual rhetoric of lies routinely spouted out by guys like him the trooper had enough. Not willing to listen any longer to the liar, the trooper orders him to get out of the car and bends over to reach into the suspect's car.

(Cont'd.)

Oh, look what I just found.

All of a sudden the trooper stands back up, holding the burglar tools which he spotted earlier. Feinting surprise, he turns to the suspect and says: **"Look at what I just found." "What are they doing in your car?" "Tools of your clandestine profession?" "Did you just forget to put them back into your toolbox?" "Why don't we just put them back into the toolbox in the trunk of your car?"** Displaying a mixed look of hatred and anxiety, the burglar grunts: **"F*ck you."** Smirking at him he coolly replies: **"Really?" "I didn't know that you went both ways." "Well, anyway; I'm straight." "So just open the damn trunk because I have very reasonable suspicion a crime has been committed."** When seeing the suspect hesitate, the trooper waives the tools at him and says: **"To start, I'll just lock your ass up for possession of burglar tools." "That will definitely help your presently pending case."** Mumbling something undecipherable, the suspect walks over to the trunk of his car and opens it. It is immediately apparent to the troopers that the items in the trunk have not been purchased. Looking at the loot, one of them remarks: **"Well, well, well!" "What do we have here?" "Boy, you are doing your Midnight Christmas shopping really early this year." "Aren't you?" Holding up one of the boxes, the trooper asks, "What's this?"** When the suspect doesn't answer, the trooper wants to know where he purchased it and asks for the receipt. After a litany of the usual investigative line of questioning, laced with mocking remarks, he orders the burglar to remove all of the articles out of the trunk and put them into the trunk of the cruiser. The trooper then advises the suspect that he has five days to come to the troop and pick up any of the items that he is able to produce a receipt for and sends the "dirtball" on his way. Of course none of the merchandize is ever reclaimed by him. Hampered by the lack of recorded serial numbers or detailed descriptions provided by possible victims, he is able to return only a small portion of the stolen items to the rightful owners. When the search to locate other original owners has been exhausted and reached a dead end, the remaining, unclaimed, goods are auctioned off at the State Auction.

Baseball pitch?

Confronted by an unusual situation, officers of a Municipal department are unable to figure out what to do. A couple of State troopers who some would say look like the odd couple respond to the emergency call. The taller of the two, resembling a pro football player, would be considered big by any standard. In addition to the ogre looking trooper's apparent strength is the fact that he is also very well trained in martial arts. When they arrive at the scene, they are immediately confronted by the individual who threatens to commit suicide. For some odd reason the Municipal officers are nowhere to be seen. As the troopers approach him, he dowses himself with gasoline and holding a lighter in one hand screams: **"Don't come any closer, or I'll do it!"** Suddenly out of nowhere a large solid oak table flies through the air and strikes the suspect on the forehead, knocking him unconscious. Momentarily dumbfounded by what just happened the smaller trooper says: **"Man, all I saw was a table fly through the air like a Frisbee and nail that guy square on the forehead." "That was a perfect strike-out pitch."** Smiling back at him, his partner replies: **"Strike-out pitch?" "What the Hell are you talking about?" "That was no damn baseball pitch." "That was a perfect touch-down "Hail Mary" pass."**

The suspect is arrested and taken to the hospital for observation. A few weeks later the ogre is honored with a "Lifesaving" award.

<u>Prisoner quote of the day:</u>

> **"Your Honor, how they going to charge me with DUI? I wasn't driving drunk." "I was idling drunk!" "The car wasn't even moving!"**

There is this prisoner.

A rather "flamboyant" prisoner filled out her court pedigree with the following details - EYES="**dazzling**", HAIR="**beautiful**".... ***(Well, at least her beehive hairdo was......different....)***

Two things seem to be apparent. (After listening to defendants address a Judge.)

Prisoners arraigned on a new warrant with a possible commitment claim that they have just started a job or are about to start a fantastic job.

Prisoners getting arraigned on a capias (failure to appear in court) claim to have been out of work or on death's door. Even if they have over $1,200.00 occasionally in the property locker (Secured personal items when processed in jail or holding cell.) and NO job.......

(So, the lesson here is if you want a job...get charged.. LOL)

A close call.

An off duty State trooper with his family, driving his privately owned vehicle, stops for a red light. When the light turns green, he glances at his left side mirror and spots a vehicle approaching from the rear; straddling both lanes of traffic. In the last split second the vehicle swerves to the left and barely misses striking the trooper's vehicle in the left rear and then continues on to the next intersection. As both vehicles approach the next intersection, the trooper watches as the lights start cycling from red to green and slows down. He then notices the other vehicle, which by then is a couple of car-lengths ahead of him proceeding through the intersection before the light completes cycling to green for him. It appears that several traffic lights later the operator, of the same vehicle, wants to take the chance and beat the red light, but is forced to come to an abrupt stop when the vehicle ahead of him stops.

(Cont'd.)

See you in court.

The trooper uses the opportunity to confront the driver and bolts out of his car and runs over to the vehicle in question. Since he is dressed in civilian clothes, he makes a deliberate effort to properly identify himself. When the trooper has the driver's attention, he holds his I.D. folder and badge for the operator to see, and makes sure that both the operator and his female passenger understand that he is a State trooper. The trooper first asks the driver if he was alright and whether he realized that he almost struck his vehicle and why he had taken the chance and go through the red light. The operator arrogantly replies that it is none of the trooper's damned business since he is not in uniform and, therefore, didn't have to tell him a damn thing. At that moment the trooper wishes that the circumstances could be different and that he was on duty and could administer a sobriety test. Maintaining a professional attitude, he looks at the man and in a very stern tone tells the operator to meet him at the Magistrate Court the next day at 10:00 a.m. Satisfied that the man understood the instructions, the trooper says: **"Don't forget, 10 o'clock tomorrow morning." "Have a pleasant evening."**

(Cont'd.)

I know my rights.

The following morning, now dressed in his uniform, the trooper reports for duty and shortly thereafter drives to court to sign a couple of warrants; then waits. When it is almost 11 o'clock and obvious that the suspect is not going to show up, the trooper grabs the warrants and decides to contact the suspect at his home. The butler greeting him at the front door wants to know who it is who wishes to speak with Mr. So-n-so. Somewhat amused, the trooper looks at his uniform and replies: **"Just tell his highness it's the State Police."** Suddenly the front-door is jerked open wider and a man dressed in a smoking jacket, the trooper's arrogant suspect from the previous evening, demands to know what right the trooper has to disturb him. The trooper smiles at him and politely says: **"These papers here in my hand give me the**

right, and place you under arrest." With a look of disbelief on his face at what he just heard, the man exclaims: **"I know my rights." "I have a right to a telephone call."** A size eleven and a half boot stops the door from slamming shut. A short time later the man reappears and with a smirk on his face tells the trooper that he is not required to go with him. The trooper just looks at him and nonchalantly replies: **"These warrants in my hand say that you do." "However, the way you go with me is entirely up to you." "But I assure you that you are going, with me." "I will extend you the courtesy though and allow you to drive your own vehicle and follow me to court."** About five minutes later an Alfa Romeo follows a marked State Police unit to court.

(Cont'd.)

Wife or Girlfriend?

When finished reading the charges to the defendant the judge asks him how he wants to plea. The defendant haughtily replies: **"Since the trooper was not in uniform at the time, I plead not guilty."** The trooper looks at the judge and politely requests a short recess to allow him enough time to get a hold of the defendant's wife. He also quickly emphasizes that he is not calling her as a witness to the incident but only to have her verify that he properly and sufficiently identified himself. It is a good thing that looks can't kill as the defendant glares at the trooper as he turns to face the judge and says: **"Your honor, I would like to change my plea to 'guilty' on both charges."** Obviously surprised, the judge responds: **"Do you fully understand what that means?" "Because when you plead guilty, that's it." "The case is over and done with and no appeal."** In a slightly muttered response the defendant says: **"Just give me the papers that I have to sign and how damn much I owe you and I'm out of here."** After the defendant has left, the judge asks the trooper: **"Is there something else that I should know or be made aware of?"** Keeping a straight face, he glances at him and replies: **"Well, he seemed to have a question about my identity last night, that's why I had a question about the identity of his female passenger." "Oh, I mean girlfriend, to verify my position."** Shaking his head, the judge looks down from the bench and says: **"I'm glad**

this case is over with." "Only God knows where it could have ended up." "See you next time trooper."

Send me a Tow Truck.

A State trooper's repeated warnings for the owner to remove his unregistered and derelict car out of his drive-way fall on deaf ears. Judging by the man's flippant replies, the trooper suspects that the owner is aware that, according to the State Motor Vehicle Code, it is not against the law to park his car in that condition in his private driveway. But unaware of the County code. After many months of exposure to the will of the elements, the backseat of the badly rusted vehicle has become a permanent home for rats and the debris underneath the vehicle shows traces of hiding places for other creatures. Concrete blocks that replaced the two missing front tires are now supporting the front part of the frame. The deteriorating piece of metal is truly a health-hazard and waiting to be pushed the wrong way and fall on an unsuspecting child. Since the State Code only applied to the public domain and not private property, he needs to look somewhere else and finds the applicable charge in the County Ordinance code. Armed with the authority of the County Code he returns to the owner's residence and issues him a written order to have his vehicle removed within five days. When he returns, five days later, and finds the vehicle still in its original place he immediately calls for tow service. Just as the tow-truck driver has finished hooking up the piece of junk, the owner suddenly drives up, almost crashing his car into the mailbox as he jumps out. Flailing his arms in the air and shrieking like a wild animal the highly irate owner runs up to the trooper and hollers: **"What the Hell do you think you're doing?" "You can't do that, you're on private property!" "That is my own personal driveway!"** Puzzled by the commotion, the tow-truck driver stops momentarily what he is doing and waits for further instructions. When the trooper gives him the go-ahead, the owner goes berserk and starts screaming at the top his lungs: **"You son-of-a-bitch." "I just told you, you can't do that." "According to your MV code I'm not in violation."** The trooper smiles and looks at him and points at the tow-truck and calmly says: **"Now watch closely, there it goes."**

"Wave bye-bye." "You can probably visit it though at the junkyard." "By the way, I do know who my father is?" "I also recommend looking in the County Code."

Quotes of three defendants vying for first place:

(3rd place)
Judge: **"What is the victim's relation to you?"**
Defendant #3: **"Well your Honor, he's a great baby's daddy to our kid but he beats the shit outta' me!"**

(2nd Place)
Judge: **"Do you have anything to say before I set bail?"**
Defendant #2: **"Yo', your Honor, fo' real though. This is some crazy shit!"**

(1st place)
Judge: **"To defendant #1 "Your bail is set at $2,100.00 cash."**
Defendant #1: **"$2,100.00!" "Your honor, you crazy or what?"**

Give me your hand.

Responding to a call of a suspicious person in the neighborhood the officer carefully exits his squad car and quietly walks around and observes the suspect walking in the darkness. Instead of getting close like he should have, the officer yells: **"Halt Police!"** Just like in a 1930s film. Suddenly the suspect takes off running with the officer in hot pursuit. After chasing the suspect for about a block the officer starts catching up while running parallel to a hedgerow. Remembering some of his football days, the officer executes a flying tackle and both go down into the shrubs in a heap of arms and legs

When the officer has the suspect pinned to the ground he slaps a cuff on his left wrist and then grabs his right wrist and slaps a cuff onto it; only to have it slide off! Pumped up on Adrenaline, the officer did not immediately notice that the suspect is missing his right hand!

It's just a bullet.

It's a Friday night and one of the newer County officers made plans to meet a female friend after work got lucky and pulls the 3x11 shift. It is a relatively slow night; what a shocker. When 10:30 rolls around he is chomping at the bit and thinks: ***"If anything comes along now I'm screwed." "Since I'm the young guy; I'm getting it." "But this close to the end of my shift, what can possibly happen?"*** Then with only 20 minutes to go fate strikes and seems to say: **"Here hold my beer!"** The radio blares out his call sign; he is instructed to respond to a specific address reference the discovery of a bullet at the residence. Did someone whisper "Murphy's Law"? Annoyed and frustrated he drives to the location muttering to himself: ***"What the f*ck!!!" "It's just a damn bullet!"***

When he arrives at the residence, he rolls up the driveway to the rear of an old Victorian era house and knocks on the door. He is greeted by the caller, a nervous looking female residence who says: **"Oh, thank God you're here!" "It's in the basement." "The basement has a dirt floor." "I was cleaning out a corner and this bullet rolled out on me."** Attempting to ease the woman's obvious anxiety replies: **"Ok, go ahead and grab it for me and I'll dispose of it"**; thinking: ***"Trash can at HQ."*** Looking at him with a very concerned look on her face she asks: **"Are you sure it won't explode?"** The officer calmly replies: **"No ma'am." "You're safe as long as it is not in a gun."**

Reassured about her safety she turns and walks down to the basement. After anxiously waiting for about two or three minutes she finally reappears carrying something wrapped in a blanket. As she enters the kitchen the officer's mouth falls open when he sees what she is holding in her arms. He sees "her bullet", except it's not bullet…it's a WWI British artillery shell with the primer still intact, with the date 1916 on the rim. With his speech quickly returning, the officer yells: **"Ma'am! Slowly put that down on the floor!" "It can explode!"** Horror struck, she screams back: **"You said it wouldn't explode!"** Fearful of a mishap and in a scene resembling a Vaudeville act, he yells back: **"You told me that it was a bullet!!!"**

With the artillery piece secured in the patrol car, his newly converted EOD vehicle, he feels that this call is the closest he has ever come to needing Adult Depends. If it taught him anything, it is to ask for more details in the future.

Very reliable sources claim that it will take at least another 100 years to clear the former battle grounds in France of deadly, unexploded ordinance still buried since 1914-1918. Occasionally a farmer is killed while plowing his fields.

A rather arrogant, local politician stopped by the police.

Motorist: **"Do you really know who you stopped officer?"** (With obvious distain for the officer.)

Officer: **"Is this your license?" "Well then you are ...."**

Motorist: **"That's right." "And what does that name say to you?"**

Officer: (Pretending to be listening to something.) **"If it's talking to me, I can't hear a thing."**

Motorist: **"Is that so?" "Well you will."**

Officer: **"Pump up the volume."** (Mimicking a poor quality rapper.)

Motorist: (If looks could kill.)

Just call this trooper!

A State trooper spots a vehicle parked on the shoulder of the opposing traffic lane and makes a U-turn to investigate. When he gets close enough he notices that the vehicle is still running with the windows open and a very large man sitting behind the steering wheel. Relieved to find that the man is still breathing and judging from the strong odor of an alcoholic beverage emanating from the interior of the car; it is likely that the man is passed out.

Sizing up the situation, he immediately realizes that he will be no match for an irate, lumberjack-type drunk in a physical altercation. Before taking further action, he notifies the troop and appraises dispatch of the situation and requests assistance. When a couple of other troopers arrive he advises them of his plan of action and sneaks up to the driver's side of the drunk's vehicle. He hopes that he will be able to engage the drunk in a friendly conversation should he come to while he attempts to turn off the car and remove the keys. The troopers are extremely fortunate that the initial trooper's golden tongue keeps the drunk calm when he awakes. Tremendously disturbed the drunk fumbles through his pockets and then hands them a card and demands that they contact the trooper named on the card first before they arrest him. When he notices them looking at the name says: **"You'll see." "He will help me get out of this mess."**

They giggle when they read the name of the initial trooper on the card and chime in unison: **"Hey, you better call him right now." "Remember?" "That's a good friend of his."** In the most sincere manner he is able to fake, the initial trooper tells the drunk that he happens to know the trooper personally very well and will try to contact him. He also notices that the other troopers suddenly cover their face and quickly turn around. After failing the field sobriety test, the drunk is transported to the troop.

When the metal bars of the holding cell clank shut, the drunk's initial request steadily escalates into violent verbal demands. Holding back their laughter, the troopers respond: **"We are trying everything to get a hold of him." "We have no idea what's taking him so long." "All right, we'll keep on trying."** etc. As the evening drags on it becomes very apparent that the only thing preventing a serious physical confrontation are the metal bars encasing the angry drunk.

Lesson learned.

Possessing an understanding of human nature, the State Police training academy considers the need for repetitive reminders an important part of the training. Great emphasis is frequently stressed on such issues as paying attention to detail, securing and the continuity of evidence as well as the responsibility when carrying a weapon and all other issued items. Unfortunately the semi-permeable membrane is not always penetrated the first time and some recruits require a quick jolt during their osmosis. This happens to be the case at this troop when the young Rookie trooper rushes in, stammering: **"I gudda' go!"** With an urgent need to visit the facilities he casually throws his Stetson hat on the counter next to the D/Sgt's (Desk Sergeant) desk and runs into the locker room.

When glancing at the Rookie's hat, the trooper manning the desk suddenly has a flashback and knows exactly what he should do. After all, the Rookie failed to secure a piece of issue equipment by simply discarding it. Without even the slightest thought of harboring malice, the trooper genuinely just wants to see a replay of the act that he had been a victim of some years ago. He jumps up and hurries to tell his supervisor; a Cpl (Corporal) well known for his antics. The Cpl was just waiting for a moment like this and opens a filing cabinet door and pulls out a slightly crumpled up issue Stetson.

With the trooper keeping watch for the Rookie, the Cpl lifts one end of the D/Sgt's desk and with his foot shoves the hat under it; crushing the crown of the hat and flattening it. He barely has time to grab the Rookie's hat and sneak back into his office to hide it when he hears the rookie coming up the staircase. When the Rookie reenters the dispatch room everything appears to have returned to normal. The trooper is still sitting behind the desk and the Cpl has come out of his office and is leafing through the logbook; both fake a stern and businesslike appearance.

Only with extreme difficulty are the two culprits able to keep a straight face when the Rookie walks to the counter where his hat had been. As they watch the Rookie in his frantic search they almost loose it when he suddenly mutters: **"Excuse me, but has anyone seen my hat?"** To their amazement both of them respond in unison with the same puzzled look and ask:

> "Do what? What are you looking for? Where did you put it or see it last? Isn't that your hat? How did you lose it? You do realize of course that you are held fully responsible for it. Don't you remember what they taught you in the academy? So what are you going to do now?"

The Rookie suddenly stops and stares at the floor and swallows a big gulp of air and hesitantly bends down for a closer inspection. His face turns ashen and then instantly turns into a look of horror when he spots the crushed Stetson under the D/Sgt's desk. Barely just able to mumble, he asks the culprits to help him lift the corner of the desk so that he can retrieve his hat.

It isn't until the Rookie is in the process of attempting to reshape the Stetson that he notices the State Police hat pin missing and gives the two pranksters a look that is understood without words. The two are unable to hold back their laughter and tell him what they did and why. The Cpl momentarily leaves and comes back and returns the Rookie's Stetson. Relieved to have his hat returned unscathed, he thanks the two and acknowledges that he has been taught a valuable lesson.

How many Tow-trucks are available?

Very familiar with the neighborhood the State trooper can't recall how often he has been sent here by Dispatch reference a Domestic Violence, Drug Deal or other crimes; but today he requested to have it included as a part of his patrol area. All of his previous warnings to remove all the unregistered and non-operable vehicles off the street by a specific time have so far been ignored; that's why he is there to send an impressionable message. His records confirm that twelve of the cars, whose owners have previously been warned on numerous occasions, are still in their original places. Well, the date when the vehicles had to be removed by the owners has expired, so the trooper is going to be kind enough and help them and do it for them. A call to Dispatch requests every available tow-truck to be sent to his location. About an hour later twelve vehicles that unlawfully occupied spaces on a public street are hanging from the rear of tow trucks; despite the violent and threatening verbal objections by their owners. Although law suits are threatened, only one vehicle is ever reclaimed. This time the upstanding citizenry must have gotten the message, at least during the time that he is stationed at that particular troop. Even the number of complaints seemed to have dropped noticeable; and he is happy with the people's terminology of endearment for him. "**He's one crazy and hard-nosed son-of-a-bitch who can't wait to bust your ass if you step oudda' line.**"

Just couldn't resist the temptation.

A couple of State troopers picked up a box of illegal fireworks that were left behind by a group of teenagers who ran away when the marked State Police unit approached. On their way back to the troop, the temptation and a desire to have some fun seemed to be too enticing to resist, as the trooper sitting in the passenger seat holds the match against the fuse of the cherry-bomb he is holding. Alarmed by the rapidly moving spark he quickly flicks the firecracker out of the car window; almost instantly followed by a loud boom. Shocked, he looks at his partner and with a nervous laugh says: **"Man that was a close call." "Did you see how fast that thing went off?"** The driver suddenly slams on the brakes and screams: **"You dumb son-of-a-bitch." "Look at what you just did." "I can't believe that anyone can be that stupid".** He then jumps out of the cruiser and runs to the passenger side and is horror-struck by what he finds. Flipping a still partially attached piece of the blown-up side mirror the driver screams: **"How in the Hell are we going to explain this?" "They are probably going to fire both of us."** The troopers are extremely fortunate that their Sergeant has connections and is willing to help his "Stupid dumb-asses". By the end of the shift the mirror has been replaced, at the troopers' expense. In gratitude, both volunteer to perform needed odd jobs at the troop on their next two days off, and work for free.

Do you want me to drive?

A couple of State troopers working midnight shift pull out of the troop parking lot; the driver a Corporal and his passenger a two-year veteran junior trooper. About an hour into the shift the junior trooper notices that the Corporal appears to be a little sluggish and asks whether he would like to switch drivers. The Cpl replies that he is going to be all right and continues driving. Satisfied, the young trooper continues with his cursory visual checks of the businesses as they drive past them. As the cruiser approaches a left-hand curve, suddenly a telephone-pole pops up; seemingly out of nowhere. Panic-struck, the passenger trooper is only able to blurt out: **"Watch out the…"** then a loud bang and the cruiser jolts to an abrupt halt. Both troopers jump out and are shocked to find that it is far worse than they expected it to be. The impact pushed the bottom of the right-front fender against the right-front tire, rendering the vehicle inoperable. It is immediately apparent that the extensive damage will require more time to repair than they have available.

(Cont'd.)

Help was not too far away.

Fortunately the accident occurred within a short walking-distance of a garage with towing service and a very good friend of theirs. The Cpl decides to stay with the unmarked cruiser and asks the junior trooper to walk up to the garage. Luck is with them once again. Although the garage closed for business a few hours earlier, the proprietor decided to stay in his office and attend to some needed business matters. When the owner has recovered from laughing, he immediately goes into action to help his uniformed friends out of their predicament. By 3:00 a.m. the cruiser has been relocated in a nearby body-shop and is feverishly worked on by the shop owner and his son. Time, literally, is of the essence for this clandestine operation to succeed and avoid possible repercussion. It is absolutely critical for the cruiser to be back in the Troop parking lot, no later than 7:45 a.m. In order to ward off any additional attention to the incident the

Cpl remains at the troop and the junior trooper manages to obtain another cruiser and returns to patrol on his own.

(Cont'd.)

Asking for a miracle?

Adding to the troopers' already existing tension the body-shop owner calls and says that he may not be able to get done in time but will move mountains trying. It has to be Devine Intervention that made it possible; when the anxiously awaited call finally comes. The troopers are absolutely beside themselves when they hear the owner report that he and his son have performed a miracle and that the car is finished; but with one serious stipulation. Unfortunately the time restrictions that have been placed on him, it is impossible for him to complete the job in the short allotted time. Since it is not possible for him to keep the car in a drying chamber, he stresses the absolute necessity of following his instructions. He hopes that the troopers will be able to hide the car for the rest of the day and allow Mother Nature complete the drying part. When the tow-truck arrives at the troop, the driver is instructed to put the cruiser behind the garage in one of the parking slots designated for vehicles to be serviced.

(Cont'd.)

Just leave the cruiser sitting here.

The junior trooper has an instant worried look on his face when he hears the Cpl sitting next to him say: **"Oh shit! We've had it." "I might as well kiss my ass goodbye." "Trooper H… just asked for the car keys."** Since the junior trooper has an excellent rapport with that particular trooper eases the corporal's mind and says: **"Look he and I are pretty good friends." "So, first let me see what I can do before you jump off the deep end of the cliff."** The junior trooper rushes over to his friend and quietly explains to him that he needs to address an issue of extreme urgency with him in private. Puzzled by the junior trooper's serious look he follows him outside. As soon as the two of them are outside the junior trooper explains the previous night's mishap and the absolute necessity of keeping it a secret. Finally, he requests that his friend fills out a garage work order for the car and then tell the mechanic to hold the work off until the next day. The junior trooper then tells his friend what the body-shop stressed. Fortunately the plot is not uncovered until several months later when the cruiser is placed on the State Auction block and the Troop commander calls the Cpl and his riding partner to step into his office. Both have a suspicion why they are called in and make a pact not to volunteer any information. When entering the captain's office their anxiety is relieved when they notice a slight smirk on the captain's face and surmise that it can't be all that bad. Looking at them through squinting eyes the captain says: **"Corporal, I believe that Unit #... is your assigned vehicle?" "Well I just came back from the State Auction and I noticed that the right front fender of Unit #... was a little bit lighter than the rest of the car." "Someone also told me that you might be able to tell me something about the difference in color."** Neither of them utters a word and just sit there with a puzzled look and a frown on their face. Sensing that he isn't getting anywhere, the captain stands up and says: **"You little bastards pulled one over on me." "I must admit, not bad." "Now get the Hell out of my office and get back to work."**

A product of the times.

The County officer grew up in the 60s and 70s when gay people weren't open and out like they are now. The only guys he ever saw and knew and obviously gay were the really flamboyant ones. At that time he didn't know that gay men came in all shapes, sizes and colors. Thinking back, it may have been just a product of the times.

Still relative new on the job the County officer is dispatched to an apartment in reference to a "Domestic in Progress". Since he already has been on his own for several months he thinks: ***"OK, I can handle all this; no problem." "Just separate the guy from the girl; problem solved."***

When he does a "Cop knock" a huge, manly dude answers the door. A guy about 6'05" and looking like Rusty Jones (Mascot from the auto repair product) greets him at the door. In a deep booming voice the man says: **"Hello officer, come on in." "I'm having trouble with my better half and I don't know what to do."** As the officer enters the apartment he is left flabbergasted. Suddenly another gentleman, wearing one of those poet blouses depicted on the cover of a Harlequin Romance novel flits by in the hallway. As he runs past and in a very effeminate voice yells out: **"You Bitch!"**

With a sad face, the big man looks at the officer and says: **"You see sir?" "I love this man and this is what I have to come home to every night!"**

The officer just sits there with his mouth open. ***(Who knew?)***

The only reason you done stopped me is...

A State trooper watches as two vehicles traveling in tandem run through a red light and stops them. Before he even finishes explaining to the operator of the first vehicle, the driver hands him his driver's license and car registration. Then in a very apologetic manner says: **"Trooper, you caught me and I deserve the ticket for my stupidity." "As soon as I committed myself I knew that I couldn't make it." "I know that I'm not in a position to ask for a favor, but would it be possible for me to get a couple of day's extension for my court appearance?" "Or can I just send the fine in?"** Impressed with the driver's humble demeanor he replies: **"Let me see what your driving record tells me."**

On his way to his patrol car the trooper glances at the second vehicle that also ran the red light; behind the first one. Due to the glare on the windshield he is only able to see a set of hands drumming the steering wheel impatiently; a total opposite behavior of the first driver. When he hands the first driver his citation he tells him that he may send the payment in. The driver thanks him and drives off. As he approaches the second car he notices that the operator is a black male.

Since the first driver readily acknowledged that he went through the red light, it is a no-brainer that the following car definitely also had gone through the red light. The trooper doesn't even have a chance to get the first syllable out of his mouth when the black man crudely cuts him off and screams: **"The only reason you done stopped me cuz' ah' is a nigga'!"** Finding it immediately necessary to defuse the trash-mouth's extreme belligerence, the totally flabbergasted and highly embarrassed trooper sternly looks at him and replies:

> "I'm sorry that you must suffer from such a debilitating mental disorder. But since it is not a part of my vernacular, I'm not familiar with that verbiage. I stopped you for going through a red light. But for legal reasons I need your real name as it appears on your driver's license. However, since you apparently prefer to be addressed by your adopted name rather than your given name; you are under arrest for going through a red light "Neger" (***naygare***). Let me clarify that for you. I mean that light there *(pointing)* and not a red-light district."

Huffing, the driver retrieves his registration and arrogantly grabs his driver's license out of his wallet and then almost throws them at him. The trooper politely takes the documents and says: **"Thank you sir." "Please wait here." "I'll be back shortly."** A few moments later, as he respectfully hands him the traffic ticket, the subject yells: **"You haven't heard the end of this!" "I'll see yoh' ass in court!"** The trooper tactfully smiles at him and replies: **"Oh, I'm looking forward to it and make sure that my belt is on tight."**

Several months later the trooper is subpoenaed and sits on the witness stand in court. Well known for his over-dramatization and adopting an Oxford English accent, the defense attorney makes an elaborate performance as he gestures towards his client and begins.

Attorney: **"Troopa', do you recognize the person seated next to me?"**

Trooper: **"Yes, I certainly do."**

Attorney: **"Will you please tell the court under what circumstances you two met."**

Trooper:

"While I was on patrol on ....., I observed two vehicles traveling in tandem, that's one behind the other; going through the red light. When the first car went though the red light, your client followed directly behind it. I then pulled in front of both vehicles and stopped them. I specifically remember the difference in attitude towards me between the two drivers. The first was very polite and was immediately apologetic and readily admitted having gone through the light. In total contrast to the first driver's behavior; your client had a noticeably different attitude and was extremely belligerent."

Attorney:

"Objection your Honor!" "Those remarks are strictly the trooper's supposition and I request that they be stricken from the record."

Judge:

"What is your objection, council?"

Attorney:

"That remark is strictly a matter of opinion."

Judge:

"Did you ask for an interpretation?" Didn't you ask the trooper to tell the court where and how he encountered your client?" "Your objection is overruled." "You may continue."

Attorney:

(Gesturing towards his client again.) **"Do you recall what you called my client?"** ***(Overdramatizing even further.)*** **"Isn't it a fact that you referred to my client as a nigga'?"**

Jury: Despite barely audible gulping sounds from the jury, a pin dropping to the floor would have been heard.

Judge:

> *(Looking at the trooper with a very concerned look.)* **"I hope that you are able to explain yourself sufficiently trooper."**

Trooper:

> *(Nodding at him in the affirmative.)* **"I certainly can your Honor. It was NOT exactly like that your Honor. To begin, the defendant didn't even give me a chance to inform him of the reason why I pulled him over. As a matter of fact, as soon as I opened my mouth to speak he shocked and severely embarrassed me. He began screaming at me, claiming that the only reason that I stopped him was because he was, and I quote, a nigga'. I realized that I had to immediately find a way to prevent the situation from escalating and apologized to him for him having to suffer such a debilitating mental deficiency. I also told him that I needed to know which name I should use, since I am required to use the name that appears on his license. He then almost threw his license and registration in my face. Then I said to him: "Since you prefer to be called by your adopted name, you are under arrest "Neger"; pronounced naygare. By the way, the origin of that word 'neger' is spelled n, e, g, e, r. I just pronounced the word correctly. Incidentally, it is still in use today and quite simply means "Negro" in German. Then when I returned and handed him the traffic arrest ticket, he yelled something like: "You haven't heard the end of this." "See your ass in court." "Well, here we are."**

In addition to his attorney's fee, the afflicted individual with his identity problem is assessed a fine for the traffic violation and court cost; and the jury left slightly spellbound.

(Fortunately there is no physical debris to wipe off, despite the accuser's attempt to vocalize through both orifices.)

Honesty paid off.

With his attention suddenly drawn to the noise of roaring car engines and squealing tires the State trooper swings his cruiser around and drives towards the direction of the sound. His suspicions are confirmed when he spots two drivers in the process of parking their vehicles on the shoulder of the highway and pulls up behind them. He is surprised by their polite attitude and candor with which they answer his pertinent questions. They readily admit that they had "punched the pedal to the medal", just for a short distance and suspected that that was the reason why the trooper stopped behind them. Further inquiry reveals that both drivers hold respectable jobs and just happen to have a yen for fast cars; and as excellent hobbyist mechanics have the means to satisfy their desires. Impressed with the guys' honesty, he gives them a verbal warning and cautions them about drag-racing and tells them that this time it is on him and that the next time it will be on them; he climbs back into his cruiser and drives off.

(Cont'd.)

Caught in the act.

Several weeks later the trio meet again under very similar circumstance; only this time the trooper catches them in the act. Unbeknown to the two dragsters the trooper already spotted them earlier at a local eatery and suspected that the two were making plans to do their thing. He drives to the two suspects' favorite road-strip and hides on one of the side-roads and patiently waits. He doesn't have to wait too long when he hears the familiar sounds. As soon as the cars race past him, he activates his lights and siren and punches the gas-pedal. He already knows that neither of the guys will try to elude him and just stays behind them as they slow down and pull over. The trooper has to laugh to himself and is unable to hide the smirk on his face as he approaches the cars. Both drivers exit their vehicles and with an embarrassing smile hand the trooper their driver's license and vehicle registration, and in unison say: **"Yeah we know, this time it's on us." "At least we always wait until the road is completely clear**

of any other cars." Just to make sure that the message has more of an impact; he charges both of them for having loud mufflers instead of going over the speed-limit. Several weeks later the two dragsters finally call the trooper's bluff once too often, and are arrested for "Speed exhibition"; a more serious offense than speeding, points and possible loss of license. It's quite possible the two continued doing their thing, but someplace else.

(Cont'd.)

Get to know Brian.

During the course of the next year or so, the trooper has the opportunity to get to know one of the drivers, Brian, on a personal basis and eventually befriends him; they are still friends today. On occasions he made it a point to stop by Brian's garage and ask him to work on his private vehicle. During one of those initial times, when driving home after completion of his 4–12 shifts, he decides to briefly stop by Brian's garage. He is surprised to find him in his garage still working on his new masterpiece, an old Ford that he just converted into a Bucket-job. Brian is excited to see the trooper and tells him that he can't wait to give his Roaster a try-out and suggests to ride along with him. Since he is still in uniform, he somewhat reluctantly climbs into the roaster's passenger-side.

(Cont'd.)

"Hold on".

When they enter the highway, the trooper breathes a sigh of relief when he sees that they are the only vehicle on the road. The long and straight stretch of pavement is the ideal place for Brian to have the opportunity to show off; much to the trooper's chagrin. With a broad grin on his face, Brian glances at his passenger and says: **"Hold on!"**, and they are off. The quick and unexpected acceleration lifts the front of the roaster off the ground and forces the trooper's back hard against the backrest of his seat. Shocked and totally unprepared for the speed-exhibition, he yells a barrage of expletives at Brian that would have made a whore blush. The loud droning of the motor, however, drowns out most of what he is saying and Brian just laughs hysterically and screams: **"I can get a little more out of it"** and the front of the roaster lifts up once again. When Brian sees the serious look on the trooper's face he immediately slows down and turns around and heads back in the direction of home; but he has one more trick up his sleeve.

(Cont'd.)

How about a hamburger?

Grateful that no one has spotted them, the trooper is relieved and able to relax, until he notices that the roaster is heading towards a busy hamburger joint and a favorite teen hangout. As the roadster turns the last corner before entering the parking lot, he expects the worst. An anxious and worrisome thought races through his mind, where or how to hide in the open cockpit of the bucket-job; it's impossible. At that very moment God must be with him; the parking lot is practically empty. On their way out he politely declines Brian's offer to go through the drive-through and order a hamburger and replies: **"You little bastard, if you don't leave here right now your ass is mine."** He has difficulty suppressing his smile and hopes that Brian has not detected it. By the time they arrive back at Brian's residence both have to wipe tears of laughter from their face. Before the trooper leaves, Brian admits that he realized that the trooper was serious about arresting him if he had continued his game. Today, the episode continues to be point of humor at parties that they attend together.

I want fresh air.

A State trooper is instructed to contact the troop and pulls into a gas station to make the call (Cell phones have not been invented yet). As he exits his cruiser his attention is drawn to a verbal confrontation between an annoyed elderly female and a young gas station attendant and walks over; hoping to defuse the situation. Aided by his uniformed presence, he tactfully asks: **"All right folks, that's enough." "Why**

don't we try to settle your differences without putting the gloves on." "So 'Ma'am', ladies first."

> "Well, when I pulled up to the pump to get some gas I noticed that my right rear tire was kinda' low and needed some air. So I decided that since I'm here I might as well get all of my tires serviced and asked this young man to help me. I then told him about my tire and that I wanted the air let out of all my tires before the foul air had a chance to rot out my tires; I needed them to last. He just looked at me and then I heard him say to his buddy over there (pointing) that I was an 'Old Kook'. That's what got the whole thing started."

Before the young attendant has a chance to voice a sly response and rekindle the situation, the trooper intercedes and says: **"OK, here is what we are going to do."** He then turns to the young man, hoping that he is going to understand his double entendre, gives him a certain look and continues.

> "I see that you service automobiles and that you seem to be quite busy with some major service jobs. Wouldn't it have been a lot easier to just tell this lady that you were too busy at that particular moment. You certainly didn't have to call her a name because she didn't understand your scheduling methods. So here is what I suggest should be done. (Again a look that says you better read the hidden message of what I'm saying.) There seems to be a lull right now so why don't you put her car on the lift and let that foul air escape? Since all the car weight is off the tires there will be no pressure on them. When you remove the valves and the air escapes instantly. Then you pump them back up with all that fresh and good smelling air. Right? Right? Yeah, you already knew that. So for all tires the entire service should take no more than fifteen minutes. Does that make sense?"

The trooper's obvious **"Don't you dare"** look immediately erases the dumbfounded expression on the attendant's face and silences any possible rebuttal. Seeing a satisfied look on the lady's face he enters the station's office and calls the troop. Oh what a pleasant ride on fresh air.

Through the red light.

A State trooper, driving an unmarked cruiser, slows down when he sees the traffic light ahead of him cycling to red and notices the driver in front of him quickly glance left and right and then bolt through the red light. The trooper instantly activates his red lights and siren. Instead of the driver pulling over, as he anticipates, a volley of loose stones pelts against the cruiser's grill and the other vehicle suddenly shoots forward at a rapidly increasing speed. Although the trooper has the license plate number of the vehicle, he wants the driver in case he is not the owner, or the vehicle has been stolen. The trooper informs Dispatch that he is in pursuit of a vehicle (Gives number and state of plate.) which refuses to stop.

Rather than allow the dull-witted suspect to continue his reckless driving in his attempt to escape capture, the trooper slows down and drives out of the heavily populated area. Under the pretext of having called the pursuit off, he turns his siren off and quickly drives back close to the point of entry from the main highway and waits. A short time later he spots the suspect attempting to re-enter the main highway. Determined not to allow the suspect to elude him again, the trooper releases his foot off the brake pedal and rockets forward. Since the suspect just entered the main thoroughfare his speed was still slow enough to allow him to take evasive action and execute a quick u-turn when he sees the trooper rapidly approaching from behind him. Unfortunately, he is going too fast to be able to do the same and is forced to stop first and then turn around. Reacting to the suspect's evasive action, the trooper quickly shifts his vehicle into reverse. That would have worked except that his adrenaline is pumping overtime and fails to wait for his cruiser to come to a complete stop; when he punches the button on his 65 Plymouth into drive. A subsequent loud crunching of metal gears brings the chase to an abrupt end. Embarrassed, he returns to the troop as a passenger in a tow-truck. Two days later the trooper brings the suspect to court.

A day in court. #3

Wrong response.

Judge: **"State your name for the court."**
Defendant: **"Why? You have it right there in front of you on the warrant!"**

Judge: **"What is the nature of the relationship between you and the alleged victim?"**
Defendant: **"Good, right up until I found out our kids weren't mine!"** *(You can't make this stuff up folks.....)*

What **NOT** to say to the judge when asked why you didn't appear for court and/or pay your fines.

Defendant 1: **"Well, your Honor, we seem to be living in a depressed economy and it's trickled down to me."**

Defendant 2: **"Your Honor, I've just been trying to maintain!"**

Judge: **"Do you have anything to say for yourself?"**
Defendant: **"Yeah, ain't this some bullshit?"** ***(Is NEVER the answer.... Just saying.)***

Defendant: **"Your Honor, how they gonna' charge me with Terroristic Threatening?" "I ain't no Terrorist!"** ***(Hello, Darwin Awards, we have a winner.)***

Defendant: **"Your Honor, that baby ain't mines!" "I want my girl to take a"Denny test."**

Judge: **"A what?"**
Defendant: **"A 'Denny test' to see if the kid is mines!"**

Judge: **"You mean a DNA test?"**
Defendant: **"Yeah, that too."**

Apparently, the defendant didn't realize that addressing the judge as ***"Hey Sister"*** was wrong. .....***(who knew??)***

Where is the state line?

A Rookie State trooper and a former City officer riding together respond to a robbery at a liquor store close to the state line. By the time they arrive at the scene the suspect has already fled. While searching for the robber, the trooper is advised that the thief has been caught by police officers in the neighboring state. When the trooper arrives at the scene he is informed by the officers of the neighboring state that the thief is drunk and that he kicked and spat at them and is extremely violent.

Since the trooper is new to the area he asks where the state line is. One of the officers informs him that the white, 4 ft. tall, fence he is standing next to is the state line. While he attempts to arrest the drunk thief kicks at him. Rather than prolonging the culprit the opportunity to resist, the trooper balls his fist and with a heavy punch knocks him through the flimsy fence.

The following day the suspect pleads guilty as charged in JP (Justice of the Peace). The Rookie trooper must have had a flashback. ***(What state lines?)***

Possible burglary in progress.

A Town–police department contacts the nearby State Police troop and requests a trooper to assist a member of their department to investigate a possible burglary in progress. The trooper arrives at the possible burglary in progress location and is met by an excited Town officer who points to a possible point of break-in and immediately wants to force an entry into a slightly ajar door. A closer inspection by the trooper reveals that it is highly unlikely that a burglar would have been able to squeeze through that slight opening and suggests checking the outside of building further. Claiming that he has already checked the premise, the Town-officer attempts to force himself through the small split between the door and the doorframe but stops when the trooper cautions him to wait and says: **"Why don't you just secure this part of the building while I check out the rest of it?"**

When the trooper returns the Town-officer is gone and then sees the splintered doorframe and an open door.

(Cont'd.)

I thought that the burglar was inside.

Annoyed by what he finds, the trooper climbs through the newly created opening and cautiously moves forward. His eyes have barely adjusted to the interior when he hears a gunshot. Concerned about the Town-officer he calls out his name and is relieved when he sees the officer coming towards him holding his gun in his hand. The sheepish look on the Town-officer's face indicates to the trooper that it wasn't a burglar that he has to be concerned about but the Town-officer's stupid stunt and demands to know what happened. The Townie tells him that he had been certain that the burglar was still inside and accidentally broke the door when he tried to squeeze through the small opening. Then he says: **"While I was in the process of checking things, I pulled my gun out just in case I needed it." "I must have done something wrong, because when I pulled my weapon out it went off accidentally and I shot a hole through my holster."** In total disbelieve the trooper shakes his head and replies: **"Well, the main thing is that you are alright and scared the shit out of your ghost burglar." "What I can't understand is why in the world you broke the door to get in." "It should have been obvious to you that no one could have gone through that opening." "I guarantee you that it was the wind that pushed the door open just far enough to set off the alarm." "You dumb ass." "You are aware of the fact that you are going to have to pay for your stupidity, right?"** Still in disbelief about the Townie's stunt, the trooper climbs into cruiser and drives off.

A reflection on the good old days.

As he sits there on a mind numbingly cold day sipping his Dunkin Donuts coffee, his mind goes back many years. Back to the days of Dodge Diplomats…ah yes..a cold 19 degree day paired up with a hard plastic steering wheel and of course, his cup of coffee. Young cops will never know the feeling of, shall we say exhilaration as one's backside and unmentionables strike that cold, hard vinyl seat. Then, to top off the cold you got to look at the "Block-Off" plate where an AM-FM radio should be and those God-awful manually wind up windows....Ah yes, heady days. So as he sits there in the comforts of a modern patrol car, with cloth seats, padded steering wheel, AM-FM-CD player, electric windows AND a laptop he wishes to give a hearty thanks to the visionaries in Detroit. Then he realizes it's 28 years later and he is still in a squad car, on a cold day drinking coffee....the more things change, the more they stay the same..

It's almost Halloween.

It seems to be a typical midnight shift for the County police officers working the cell block at HQ (Head Quarters); drunks etc. The anticipated tranquility is suddenly disrupted by a drunk banging on the cell door and yelling obscenities; in a deliberate effort to annoy the officers. Well it has the desired effect, but lucky for him it is close to Halloween. The officers head for the House Sergeant's office and the stolen and recovered Halloween decorations temporarily stored there.

Rooting through the pile they find what could fit their plan. Excited one of the officers pulls out a life-sized, glow in the dark, human skull with an electronic speaker that gives off a shrieking sound. Still better yet, a black robe about 7 feet long is attached to it. It is apparently made to hang on a house wall or tree and moves by the wind. The officer, about 6'-05" tall, starts laughing; he has a great idea.

Making sure first that the electronic component works the officer pulls the cloak over his body and places the skull on top of his head. Satisfied with the fit and looks for his planned appearance, he turn the lights to the cell block off and walks towards the cell holding the rowdy drunk.

The drunk, nosy to see what is going on, is standing at the door of his cell. He takes one look at the approach of the "Grim Reaper" and lets out a blood-curdling howl. Shaking like a leaf in a storm, he cowers in the corner of his cell screaming: **"NOOO! NOOO! NOOO!"**

Needless to say, not a peep is heard out of him the rest of the night.

I want your badge number!

Police Officer: **"No, it's assigned to me."**

"Having my number doesn't make you a cop."

"What did you do?" "Forget yours?"

"I can't it's a part of my badge."

"You'll be issued your own when you graduate from the Police Academy."

"What are you planning to do with it?"

"Oops, not enough numbers to make a Social Security number."

Just for the bang of it.

The young State trooper, a recent graduate of the State Police academy, is excited that he is assigned to the troop a relatively short commute from his residence. As soon as he finishes reporting for duty the telephone rings and the D/Sgt (Desk Sergeant) picks it up. It is like watching a slow-motion movie when he sees the Sgt's facial expression change to extreme concern and then hears him say: **"All right, I'll get on it right away."** Turning to the trooper who just walked in says:

> "I just received a phone call from someone who claims to have planted a bomb behind the garage that is set to go off in thirty minutes if we don't release .... There is no way that we can do that. Even getting the bomb squad needs more time to get here. At least it's a Saturday and none of the civilians are working. So we just have to evacuate a handful troopers. Well, let me think what I can do."

Still looking extremely concerned he continues.

> "Look, I watched the bomb disposal guys a couple of times when I was in the military. If those guys were able to do it; I think I have a pretty good idea how to disarm it too. So let's find it first, maybe I can figure out what to do."

One of the trooper's listening intent volunteers to help the Sgt and the two walk towards the garage. A few anxious moments later the Sgt reappears from behind the garage holding up some wires and a small clock attached to a pipe. Claiming that he might be able to disarm what appears to be a makeshift bomb tells everyone to clear the immediate area.

Holding the device and pointing to one of the wires he explains to the trooper that he thinks that (pointing) is the wire he needs to cut. He then orders the trooper to stay behind the partition in back of the garage so that he is able hear him when calls out which wire he is going to cut; just in case. A protest by the other troopers falls on deaf ears as the Sgt and his trooper volunteer walk behind the garage.

A total hush falls on the area; only an occasional car in the distance is heard. The silence is momentarily interrupted by the Sgt's voice cautioning his helper that he changed his mind and is going to cut the other wire. Suddenly a loud explosion freezes the new young trooper in place while the eyes of the other troopers are fixated on him.

When the Sgt and his volunteer suddenly reappear and the whole group bursts out in laughter, the young trooper realizes that he has been had. Patting him on his shoulder, the Sgt says:

> "The whole thing was a set up and part of our initiation to test a newcomer's mettle. When the trooper motioned for me to answer the telephone call I knew that he had hidden the fake bomb and went into my spiel. Then when I told him that I changed my mind and was going to cut the other wire, I was giving him the signal to set off a cherry-bomb firecracker. I must warn you though not to broadcast our initiation practice. I hope you understand."

The young trooper smiles and heartily agrees to keep his mouth shut. Having proved that he has what it takes, everyone shakes his hand and welcomes him as a new member to the troop. Unfortunately the fun is eventually halted when another young trooper lodges a complaint because he had been embarrassed by the explosion. He apparently experienced a leaky bladder when the firecracker went off and probably forgot to slip rubber pants over his diaper; leaving a telltale sign running down his pants. Some people just don't know how to have fun.

Just another day on patrol. # 3

They say if you live long enough, you'll see everything. The officer sees a car driving up a major road with a 10 speed bike duct-taped to the trunk lid! As he passes the officer the driver yells: **"I don't have a bike rack!'**....**(The officer doesn't even want to know....)**

Quote of the day: **"You can't arrest me in the hospital!" "You don't have jurisdiction!" "Besides that, you're not the Medical Police!"** *(Ah stupidity, the real opiate of the masses...LOL)*

(Folks, you can't make this stuff up. When you stop a car and the occupants are named Cinderella and Fountain. Well, you just have to laugh. You know what I'm saying?)

Apparently, the defendant didn't realize that: **"Yo, check this shit bud.."** *is NOT the way to address the judge! LOL*

How not to plead your case to the judge: **"Yo your Honor, I'd like unsecured bond." "You don't know my baby's mom." "That b*tch is crazy!"**

Defendant: **"Officer! I have a right to a courtesy call!"** ***(Apparently the officer is unaware of this.)***

Judge: **"Do you have anything further to say about your bond?"**

Defendant: **"Well Your Honor, I know I have these drug and weapons charges but I shouldn't get secured because it's my birthday." "And as for the capiases well, I have a bad memory but if you release me I'll make sure I post it on my refrigerator so I don't forget."**

Judge: **"$81,000.00 secured!"**

A new police station.

It has taken him almost three years of politically prostrating himself before the small-town mayor. In a Machiavellian way, it was worth it. Standing in front of their new police station, a renovated old fire station, the chief and his personnel are assembled for the dedication and await the arrival of the mayor and his entourage. They are elated to finally have a building of their own; with enough space to function as a genuine police station.

The young officer, a recently accepted candidate for the next State Police academy is assigned to escort the mayor. He is also one of the few individuals in the department familiar with what the chief has previously been subjected to. When the limousine arrives, the officer recalls how often his chief had to play the mayor's sycophant. He quickly grabs the small pack of peanut butter and briefly disappears into the police locker room and returns just in time to see the mayor strut his pompous derriere towards the building.

Barely able to hide his disgust, the young officer anxiously waits for the arrogant peacock to stop bragging about his accomplishments; finally he shuts up. Still holding his fake smile, the mayor turns to the young officer and says: **"Well officer, let's see what I have worked so hard for to get for you guys." "Lead the way and let's see my creation."** Struggling to maintain his composure, the officer swallows hard and thinks: ***"Man, where is a barf-bag when you need one?"***

Emphasizing the department's appreciation for having an actual locker room with a private toilet for police personnel, the officer tactfully guides the mayor towards the room. Making certain that the mayor is not going to miss it; the officer deliberately holds the door to the toilet stall wide open. With somewhat exaggerated disgust in his voice, the mayor suddenly points at the toilet bowl and blurts: **"Just what in the Hell is that?"** The officer can't believe that everything is going according to plan and how easy it was to lure the mayor into the trap.

The officer replies: **"I don't know"**. Looking puzzled and concerned, the officer bends down and dips his index finger into the bowl and swipes some of the brown stuff smeared on the inside of the toilet bowl. Holding up his finger and looking at the residue on his finger tip the officer notices that the mayor's eyes appear ready to pop out of his head. Ready to inflict the coup de grâce, the officer looks at the brown stuff again and then sticks his finger in his mouth and calmly says: **"That is shit, sir."** Left speechless by what he just witnessed, the horrified mayor starts to gag and quickly covers his mouth with his hands and runs upstairs.

Was the chief's smirking a sign of gratitude? He undoubtedly realized what the young officer had done and why. He also knew that prior to the mayor's visit the brand new toilet had never been used since it was installed.

Rats and more rats.

The City, plagued by major problems, asks the State Police for assistance. During a meeting one of the City officers says that the abandoned dog food plant on the Eastside has the largest rats he has ever seen. Curious about the claim a trooper asks whether it was possible for him to see for himself. That evening the City officer sitting in the passenger side of the trooper's cruiser advises Central that the State Police needs to conduct a security check on the Eastside.

Prior to entering the plant the City officer instructs the trooper to dowse his lights and very carefully edge forwards and allow his eyes to adjust to the darkness. Squeezing the steering wheel with a death grip, the trooper stops the cruiser and gasps: **"Oh my God." "Oh my God." "They are the biggest rats that I have ever seen." "They**

are almost as big as groundhogs." When he turns the headlights on he has another shock and involuntarily draws his heels back against the front of his car seat. Suddenly there appears a 5 to 6 feet tall, honeycombed, mound of rotting dog food in front of him; covered with rats scurrying back into their holes when the lights came on. The following evening two more State and two more City units join them at the plant. It isn't long before the troopers and officers boast about their marksmanship prowess; what better place to prove it? A week later the group meets again.

It is decided that numbers will be drawn to see who shoots first and that each kill of a rat has to be verified by members of the group, then each member must pay the shooter one dollar. However, if it is not a direct kill the shooter has to pay each member a dollar. Neither the Pellet nor the BB gun is powerful enough so it is decided to shoot live ammo. Since a .38 cal revolver would be too loud they chose the .22 cal rifle a trooper brought with him.

One of the trooper's claims that he did kill the rat sets out to prove it and requests a member of the group to light a couple of flares and follow him up the mound. Since no one is willing to follow him he grabs a flare removes the wire stand, lights the flares and uses the wire to dig out the dead rat; lying at the very edge of the hole. A couple of the participants claim that they would have been willing to pay him regardless, just because he is crazy. The rats must have gotten wise to the group's intention; their numbers dwindled dramatically. So what to do next; outsmart the rats?

The next time, the same crazy trooper takes the wire stand from a couple of flares, straightens the wires and sticks a couple of slimy, spoiled hotdogs he obtained from one of the local street venders on the end of each. He then places a piece of cardboard in front of him, places lighted flare next to him and sticks the improvised rat lure on top of the mound and requests lights out. Several minutes pass and members see shadows attempting to climb up the wire. This puts an entirely new meaning on marksmanship. Realizing that he has only about two seconds to engage the target, the shooter anxiously waits for - **"Lights!"** Then a radio-call from Central: **"Unit#... check on**

the welfare of the community reference numerous shots fired on the Eastside." As quick as rats the group suddenly disappears. The party is busted by a bunch of spoil-sports in the community.

"Roll Call".

A police Lt (Lieutenant) conducting "Roll Call" is addressing a group of new personnel on his shift. While emphasizing the importance of writing supplement reports in order to finish up outstanding initial reports he yells: **"Doing an initial crime report without writing a supplement...why that's like getting off the toilet without wiping your ass!"**

What ya' doin' here?

A State trooper, ordered to disperse rioters from a sensitive area, notices a young black boy glaring at him. Surprised to see such a hateful look in the child's eyes he decides to find out the reason. Maintaining a fatherly posture the trooper asks: **"Just how old are you young man?"** Looking at him through squinting eyes the little boy says: **"Eight." "What's it to ya?" "Ya white motha' f**kin' big hat." "Yo' man what ya' all doing here anyway?" "You don' even belong here."**

Totally taken aback and acting out of instinct, the trooper grabs him by the scruff of his neck. Suddenly a very corpulent black lady appears and waddles towards them hollering: **"Whatya' think ya'll' doing with my son dare?"** Relieved to see the youngster's mother he replies: **"I was just getting ready to scold him for his filthy mouth."** Practically screaming at him the lady says: **"You crazy or somt'n?" "What ya' gonna' do dat' fo'?" "Pour hot water on him?"**

Suppressing a laugh he replies: **"I didn't say that I was going to scald him; I was going to give him a severe lecture."** Waving him off, the heavy set lady asks: **"What he do?"** Somewhat surprised by her careless attitude the trooper replies: **"Excuse me for the language, but I want you to know that I'm only going to repeat the words that your son used." "Well, your son called me a white mother f**king big hat."**

Appearing to be undisturbed by the trooper's remarks she replies: **"I got it from here on an' gone to take of it."** She then snatches her offspring by his shirt collar and mutters: **"Get yo' mutha' f*ckn' ass inna' house."** When he finally realizes that he has been standing there, frozen in place for several seconds, he just shakes his head and slowly walks back to his cruiser. Still in disbelief he asks himself: ***"Was that for real?" "It certainly was different."*** Childcare anyone?

Specialized unit volunteers to be called first.

A State trooper, assigned to a specialized and flexible patrol unit, volunteers to take some slack off the regular patrol units and requests to be the first notified in complaints involving physical confrontations. That particular evening the trooper just dropped his partner off at the troop when he receives an urgent call to respond to a bar-fight in progress. Elated that he happens to be nearby and possibly able to help, he hurries to the scene and finds the fight still in full swing when he arrives a few minutes later. As he storms into the bar he suddenly remembers that in his excitement, he forgot his nightstick. He immediately realizes that he is already committed and can't go back to his cruiser because that would be misinterpreted as a retreat by the rowdy bunch; but he must do something, and fast. He is relieved when he spots a derelict barstool close-by and doesn't waste time to break it apart and create an instant make-shift nightstick out of a chair leg and joins the crowd. As usual one of the big guys intent on proving how big and bad he is, falls like a sack of potatoes from a well-placed nightstick to his left shoulder and a quick trooper's fist to his solar plexus. A sharp strike to the upper leg causes a second brawler to buckle under and drop to the floor: then it is over. Before leaving he asks the unruly bunch if any one of them wants to play some more with him, but receives no response. As he reaches for the door, the trooper turns and says: **"As all of you just saw, since you invited me too late, I was forced to play the games by my rules." "Because you had already started the game and obviously played outside my game-rules, I need to know whether any of you knuckle-heads prefer to press charges against any of the other players." "Since your response is a bunch of blank stares, I interpret**

that as a no response." "Oh by the way, I want to thank you for the invite though." The trooper takes one last cautious look at the motley crew, just in case, and leaves.

(Cont'd.)

You owe me for a barstool.

Several days later the trooper is working an extra duty job at a hamburger joint when a man approaches him and in a somewhat demeaning tone demands to talk to him. When he recognizes the bar owner from the bar-fight the trooper says: **"Just who do you think you are talking to in that manner?"** Glaring at him the man says: **"Well, you owe me for the damned barstool that you broke into pieces when you charged into my bar like a wild-man the other night."** In a very calm voice, that even surprises himself, replies:

> "Listen to me mister, if you didn't invite such riff-raff into your joint, you wouldn't have to bother to call me to bail you out. You know what? Why don't you get a better clientele to visit your place? Then you can choose your own tools to clean up the scum: I just used what was conveniently available. You know damned well that bar stool was a piece of junk and could no longer be used. Since it was on its last leg anyway, I made good use out of it. Now get the Hell out of my face."

Surprised by the curt response, the owner mutters something about reporting him. Well, the trooper didn't have to be concerned too long, the bar changed ownership and a better repellent for unwanted barflies.

Early Halloween trick.

One of the difficulties of being a cop is finding a quiet, yet tactically safe place to type reports. Working the evening shift, a County police officer and his sector partner decide to go to the local cemetery to type their reports. It is a rather cold night and almost

Halloween and they also recognize that there is always some jerk who will mess around with tombstones.

They pull their units next to each other; driver's side to driver's side. While they are busy writing their reports they notice a car pull into the far side of the cemetery; park and dowse the lights. One of them remarks: **"Here we go." "Probably some asshole that's going to mess with the cemetery." "I'm going to check it out, wait here."** He carefully opens his car door and stealthily approaches the parked vehicle; making sure not to step on anything that could make noise.

He manages to reach the passenger side of the parked car undetected; with a young couple making out. When the officer, standing on the outside, looks inside through the rolled down windows he sees a bare set of buns staring back at him. Known for his sense of humor, the officer can't resist the temptation to exploit the opportunity. He leans down and closer to the open window and sarcastically goes: **"Boo!"** Although his intensions were not necessarily to scare anyone; but it worked. The male's body goes instantly and completely rigid in the seat. He then lets out a long, high pitched scream that would match any schoolgirl. Unable to breathe because he is laughing so hard the officer just wave them toward the exit.

Are they real?

A County patrolman sent to investigate a theft complaint arrives at the residence and is invited in by the victim; a lady in her 80's. She ushers him into the living room and asks him to take a seat and also offers him a cup of coffee. With an affirmative reply from him she goes into the kitchen to get some.

As he sits in one of the high-back chairs and gazes at the elegant and tasteful décor, his eyes are suddenly fixed on a pair of knick knacks displayed in the curio cabinet; two shrunken heads. He is slightly shocked by what some may call morbid and mouthing under his breath says: **"Holy shit!" "Are they real?"** He knows that according reliable research most of the heads panned off as human are in fact primates; but considering her age he is curious.

When she returns to the living room the officer asks: **"Pardon me, but are those 'Jivaro' shrunken heads?"** Surprised, she happily replies: **"Oh I see you're familiar with them." "Yes officer, my father brought them back from Ecuador when he was down there working with an oil company in the 30's."**

Certain that the lady has long passed since then, the officer still thinks about her now and then and wonders: ***"Whatever happened to those heads?"*** It's the kind of stuff you only see in a museum.

Great way to start a day.

Officer: **"What in the Hell is that smell?"**
Defendant: **"Oh that's my feet; these are my lucky hunting socks!"**

Officer: **"Don't you ever wash them!?!?"**
Defendant: **"No."**
Officer: **"WTF?"**

Prisoner quote of the day.

Judge: **"Where would you like your charges heard?"**
Defendant: **"They're just some bullshit traffic charges your honor, so wherever you think is best."**

(***Followed by this gem from the same prisoner.***)

Judge: **"How do I know you'll show up?" "You have prior capiases."**
Defendant: **"Your Honor, I got you man!" "We cool!"**

What???

The motorist hands the State trooper the documents he asked for and says: **"Here is my driving license and rederation."** Although tempted to ask the driver what type of test his license had to take and what he had read about the ration, the trooper decides to leave well enough alone.

He then recalls a statement made by someone at the motor vehicle accident scene. As soon as he had stepped out of the cruiser, a man rushed up to him and in a very excited manner said: **"Trooper I want you to know that I minstrated'** (administered) **first aid and stopped some of the bleeding."** It took a lot of willpower then also not to ask the Good Samaritan whose blood he had stopped.

Lost and spotted.

A local police department K-9 unit involved in a high-speed chase requests assistance from the State Police. According to the City Police, the K-9 unit lost the vehicle that it has been chasing when it entered unfamiliar territory outside the city. The troopers responding position their cruiser at a location where the vehicle most likely escaped to in an attempt to hide; then turn the cruiser's lights off and wait. Peering through the darkness, one of the troopers catches a quick blitz of a car's brake lights and carefully edges the cruiser a little closer to the car parked only halfway in the driveway. From their new position the troopers are able to detect the movement of four individuals in the vehicle. Suddenly two small dots of white light shoot out of the driveway and then followed by a flash of brake lights, and the dark silhouette slides down the street in the same direction they are facing. Not wishing to take any unnecessary chances, the troopers decide to follow the suspects from a safe distance and just follow the occasional blink of brake lights. As soon as the suspect vehicle exits the darkness and enters the main highway, the headlights come on and are instantly followed by a loud roar of a car engine and squealing of tires; the chase is on again. This time, however, the hunters know the roads well and are determined to catch their quarry.

(Cont'd.)

The Chase is on.

The city K-9 unit and a regular patrol unit have already prepositioned themselves to block off the southbound escape route. A few minutes later and less than four miles away, troopers successfully place four suspects under arrest. When the K-9 handler positively identifies the vehicle that he had been chasing earlier, they turn the suspects over to the City Police. It is quickly established that the vehicle was stolen earlier that day and the suspect driver doesn't have a driver's license; of course; **"No hablo ingles." "No hablo ingles."** The troopers are shocked when they hear the K-9 handler tell the four suspects that they are free to go and to get out of there. Before they have a chance to intervene, the suspects have already cleared the road and are climbing up a steep embankment. Seeing that the troopers are upset with what he did, the K-9 handler calmly says: **"Yeah, I know that you got them for us and we appreciate it." "I just want to prove to you that these bastards, who act like it's a joke, speak English."** He then opens the back door of his vehicle and releases his dog and it disappears over the embankment. Suddenly the troopers and City officers hear screaming. **"Aaah." "Get deez' mother f...er offa' me."** Having proved his point, the K-9 officer yells to the suspects: **"Well, get your asses back over here"**, and calls his dog. Shortly afterwards, four bedraggled and slightly bitten figures reappear; defeated looks have replaced their previous smiles.

Soft landing.

Momentarily stopped at the intersection, the State trooper quickly finishes jotting down the incidentals of the stolen car broadcast. As he glances across the intersection he is shocked to see the stolen car; driven by a young male. When he is certain that it is indeed the stolen car he immediately informs Dispatch that he will be in pursuit. Hoping not to alarm the suspect or panic other motorists, he doesn't immediately activate his siren or flashing lights, he wants to wait until the suspect car is in less traffic. The pursuit has not quite reached the outskirts of town when he sees the suspect vehicle quickly accelerate; an obvious sign that he has been made. He is relieved to see the suspect head for the open road, probably in an effort to pick up more speed and elude him. Feeling confident that his experience in pursuit driving and his 440 Plymouth give him a definite advantage, he follows the stolen vehicle at a safe distance.

After about fifteen minutes into the chase, with speeds often exceeding 100 mph, the pursuit car suddenly swerves off the road, catapults over a shallow drainage ditch and across the lawn of a farmhouse; then through a wooden fence; rails flying through the air. Lucky to immediately find a shallow approach, the trooper is able to stay close behind the suspect and sees the stolen car jolting to an abrupt stop. The trooper's concern about the driver's wellbeing is immediately diminished when he sees the suspect struggling to get out of the stolen car, partially imbedded in a large mound of sodden hay and animal dung, screaming: **"Get me out of here."**

Undoubtedly alarmed by the noise and a State Police cruiser, the panic-stricken farmer comes running out of the house hollering: **"Oh my God!" "What is going on?"** Attempting to calm the farmer's frayed nerves, he tells him in a very soothing tone that no one is hurt and it's nothing that a couple pieces fencing can't fix. When the trooper sees the extremely dumfounded look on the farmer's face he motions to him to take a closer look at the scene; both of them muse at the suspect's predicament. Making certain that the trapped thief is within earshot, he nonchalantly asks: **"Is that what I think it is?"** Grinning from ear to ear the farmer replies: **"Yup that's what it is." "A whole year's worth of good ole' hay soaked in urine and cow manure."** Then laughing out loud says: **"I sure hope that he didn't contaminate my fertilizer that dem' cows worked so hard fer'."** Laughing now also, the trooper says: **"Maybe he just wanted to show off his new car."** The farmer chimes in and says: **"You know what they say about dem' birds of a feather flocking together." "Well, here you have turds that crash together mash together." "He probably just wanted say good bye to his family before you throw his ass in jail and slipped on some of his family members."**

Since only the suspect's pride is hurt, there is no need for either of them to wade through the squishy landing strip. Rather than soil their attire, they wait patiently for the tow truck.

I'll empty every nook and cranny....

State troopers stationed a relatively short distance from the city are faced with the same problem every weekend; repeat offences by the same criminal derelicts. It eventually has a tremendous negative impact on the efficiency of their policing; something needs to be done. Finally fed up with the criminal nuisance it is decided to send the habitual troublemakers into the nearby city; at least they will be out of the troopers' hair for the weekend. Everything appears to work smoothly for a few weeks. Then one day the troop commander receives a call from the city's police chief. Since the commander is unaware of the derelicts' transfer he is shocked when he hears the obviously highly annoyed Chief complain:

> "Look, I don't know what kind of game you boys think you are playing. But I tell you right now, your going away games better stop right now! If you don't, I will pull every homeless person out of every nook and cranny and tell them that somewhere in your troop area is going to be a big party; free for all. I assure you that I will find a place. An' let me tell you, we have a Hell of a lot more of them than you have of weekend dregs. So don't even doubt me. I hope that I have I made myself clear!"

Left totally flabbergasted and momentarily speechless, the Troop commander finally regains his composure and in a somewhat angered tone demands to know what the Chief is talking about and explain to him what the Hell is going on.

Rather than open a can of worms, the Troop commander orders an immediate halt to the transfers and things gradually return to normal. Much later on both the Chief and the Troop commander find humor in the incident and call it a draw.

Wedding Invitation.

A State Trooper receives a wedding invitation from a very good friend and fellow trooper. Since he and the groom will pull a prank on each other whenever an opportunity presents itself, this time the guest trooper has a doozey planned for the day of the wedding. To enable him to pull it off, he needs to entrust another trooper to help him. Once the groom's car door is unlocked, the troopers pull the latch and open the hood and go into action. To make sure that they will not leave a tell-tale sign on their fingers, they wear surgical gloves and carefully un-wrap a hunk of Limburger cheese and thoroughly spread the cheese over the engine manifold and noiselessly close the hood. They then take the remaining cheese and hide it under the driver's seat and rejoin the celebration.

(Cont'd.)

Several weeks later.

Several weeks later both troopers are invited to a cookout at the newlyweds' residence. On their way to the backyard they notice a brand-new car parked in the driveway. It wasn't necessary to say anything; their looks at each other say it all. If either of them is tempted to ask about the new car, those thoughts are cut short as they enter the backyard and the new husband walks up to greet them. Extending his hand to his friend says: **"You're just the guys I've been waiting for."** The fake puzzled looks on their faces does not seem to convince the newlywed of their innocence as he continues.

> "So let me tell you what happened to us on our Honeymoon trip. About an hour into our trip we smelled this ungodly stench of rotten crabs that kept getting stronger and stronger; so I pulled over to check it out. It was only natural to check for a bag, or something with crabs. Then I discovered the Limburger cheese that someone had hidden under my driver's side seat. I thought that I had found the cause and threw it away; problem solved. Boy was I wrong. Instead of the foul odor going away, it seemed

> to get even stronger. It wasn't until we stopped to get gas and the mechanic opened the hood of my car. All of a sudden I heard him scream: "Oh my God, what the Hell…" I thought that he was going to puke. When I took a closer look under the hood I saw the whole manifold completely caked in melted Limburger cheese. Although the mechanic hosed off what he was able to, he told us that only time could possibly make the smell go away. Since we didn't want to wait that long, we decided to buy a new car. By the way, I heard someone say that you two might know something about this."

The two culprits, no longer able to hold back, look at each other and burst into laughter. When they have recovered enough, they tell their side of the story. **"Look, we had no idea it would turn out like that." "You should have seen him here** (as he points at his co-conspirator)**; he was salivating when I started spreading his favorite cheese all over the manifold." "For a moment I thought that he was going to lick it off." "And then he even asked me if I could save him a little piece."** The story of the prank ends up being the hit of the party.

A day in court. #4

Judge: **"Sir, you've failed to appear at two courts dates." "Why did you not appear?"**

Defendant: **"Well your Honor, I think it's a postal problem." "I haven't received any mail about it at…."**

Judge: **"Sir, they gave you the paperwork the night you were arrested!"**

Defendant: **"Ok your honor, you right, you got me there. I was lying.. ha, ha I just didn't show up."**

Judge: **"Your bail is $5,000.00 cash only." "Do you have anything to say about that?"**

Defendant: **"HOLY F*CK your honor that's a lot of money!!!!!!!!"**

Delightful little exchange in Turnkey (prisoner processing) when searching an arrestee and checking his pants for contraband:

Prisoner: **"Sir, just a little warning." "I was pretty scared when I got arrested because I have outstanding warrants and well, I shit myself pretty bad."**
Officer: **"Well I guess that explains the lump in your pants then...."**

Prisoner: "**Sorry sir, do you think when you get the cuffs off and I can do a courtesy wipe?"**
Officer: **"Sure thing." "Thanks for the warning man!"**

Prisoner: **"I have a right to get a ride home!"**
Officer: **"Actually, you don't!"**

Prisoner: **"Are you sure?"**
Officer: **"Yes, they actually told us that in the police academy."**

Prisoner: **"That's not fair; you drug me down here in the middle of the night!"**
Officer: **"Yes, in handcuffs, because you were under arrest!"**

Prisoner: **"Well what if you needed a ride?"**
Officer: **"I'd drive my police car and I wouldn't be arrested for assault!"**

Prisoner: **"This is what I pay taxes for!?"**
Officer: **"Yes sir, that's why we didn't charge you a fare."**

Do you smell what I smell?

A couple of State troopers working extra duty at a hamburger joint suddenly get a whiff of a peculiar odor lingering in the air and the Sergeant, humming a Christmas tune, says: **"Do you smell what I smell, dum dee de dum?"** The Corporal responds: **"Yeah, I do but it's over at Arby's and that's not part of our area and we're not getting paid for extra duty by them."** The Sgt snaps back: **"Oh, I see." "So let me get this straight." "It's ok to steal, as long as it can be concealed in a person's pants pockets." "Is that what you are telling me?" "Well let me enlighten you." "Since both of us smell marijuana, detected by one of our senses, it's a crime committed in our presence." "That in 'legalese' is P.C., probable cause." "So here is what we are going to do**

Cpl." As he points at a specific corner of Arby's, the Sgt tells him to walk around that corner while he is going to sneak around the opposite corner and converge on whoever is smoking pot and cut off their escape route. As the Cpl comes around the corner he spots a group of three teenage males and sees one of them flick something away. Assured that any inclination by the group to run away has been negated by the Sgt's sudden appearance, the Cpl asks: **"Ok you guys, what are you doing back here?"** In a very arrogant manner, the group's self-appointed spokesperson says: **"Why do you want to know?" "We are allowed to be just standing here and talk."** The Cpl replies: **"What I want to know, who is holding?"** Again answering in the same tone the punk says: **"Man, I already told you, we are clean and just standing here and I don't know what the Hell you are talking about."** Tired of listening to the nonsense, the Sgt pushes the steel-ball end of his nightstick hard against the bigmouth's rear end and whispers: **"Do you feel that?" "You know what?" "I am going to ram this stick so far up your ass that it is going to make your eye balls play ping-pong if you don't change your attitude."** He then tells the Cpl to ask the punk again. The smart-mouth is only able to spout: **"Man I just told you, ugh…"** as the Sgt pushes the nightstick hard between the pothead's butt-cheeks and whispers: **"Where punk?"** Practicing a poor imitation of a pirouette, he stammers: **"It's in my left boot trooper."** The shocked look on the Cpl's face is priceless as the Sgt retrieves a bag of marijuana from the teen's boot and empties it on the ground. When the Sgt is finished scattering the weed he hands the empty bag to the wise-guy and a back-hander to his cheek. Before leaving the Sgt says to the three teens: **"You may consider yourselves lucky that we don't arrest you and you don't have a criminal record." "Now pull your head out of your ass and start using the common sense that I'm sure you are capable of using, before you destroy your future with this crap."**

Just another day on patrol. #4

If you ever want to lose total faith in humanity and truly experience the abject stupidity of mankind - you need not go to war, rather attempt directing traffic. You will be assured within five minutes that you will have more stupid questions and reactions directed at you than in any other circumstance. You probably will also learn to create and flow curse words much like a Renaissance poet! What is it about manually directed traffic that forces everyone from a GED to a PHD to lose all common sense? Who could forget these gems?"

1. **"But I live here!"**
2. **"But I need to go this way!"**
3. **"Is anyone dead?"**
4. **"Is it a bad accident?"** ***(There are good accidents?)***
5. **"But I'll be late."**
6. **"How long will this take?"**
7. **"Why do I have to go back a little ways?" "But I just came from that way."**
8. **Individual first looks at police cars with flashing red and blue lights and flares; then asks: "Is this road blocked?"**
9. **"But that's quite a bit out of my way!"**
10. **"Is that detour really necessary?"**

(UGH! LOL)

Late for the party.

Arriving at the scene of an alleged loud party with reports of drinking and gambling, a State trooper turns on his flashlight and sees a large group of people jump up and run helter-skelter; like roaches suddenly exposed to light. He cautiously checks and finds the area littered with partially full and empty bottles of beer and liquor. Taunting his audience in hiding, yells: **"Yoh', where is everybody?" "Looks like I'm a little late." "Well, at least you left me some of your party-favorites."** Careful not to soil his uniform, he begins pulling off the caps of all the unopened beer bottles and unscrews the lids of the liquor bottles. While searching for more bottles he spots four cases of beer placed together into a square and is curious to find out why. Upon closer inspection he finds playing cards and paper money and coins scattered on the empty beer cases and nearby on the ground; remnants of someone having left in a sudden hurry. He empties a discarded paper bag and collects the forgotten money and hollers: **"Yoh', does this money belong to anyone?" "Well, I guess I'll have to take care of it."** When he doesn't receive a response, he climbs back into his cruiser and drives to a church a couple of miles down the highway and knocks on the door of the church rectory and hands the secretary the fast-food bag with the money and says: **"Here, I found this thrown on the ground." "I was not able to find out where it came from and thought that the church might make good use of it."** Caught totally by surprise, the secretary stammers: **"Thank you trooper." "Do you…?"** The trooper just waves her off and says: **"Glad to have helped." "Have a blessed evening."**

Adhering to the establishment policy.

The fast-food place is the favorite teenage hangout in the area, perhaps even in the whole county. Whatever action you are looking for, you can be certain to find it here. In an effort to promote business, the establishment implemented specific policies. According to the cash-register receipts, the predominance of business comes from adults and families. Preempting teenagers' unnecessary lengthy stay, the establishments put into effect a specific time limit for customers on busy weekends and also pay for two extra duty State troopers in case of trouble. It is the usual busy Saturday evening when they arrive and notice four motorcycles parked side by side belonging to a notorious local motorcycle gang. After the gang members, four males and their women have been there for at least twenty minutes and their presence is obviously intimidating to other customers; the troopers have to do something. The first trooper says to his partner: **"I'll go and talk to them about the time restrictions,"** and walks towards the group. At least ten more minutes have passed when the second trooper says: **"Hey, I thought that you told them that they had only five more minutes to finish and then they had to leave." "You know**

what?" "I think that I still see them there." "Do you want me to talk to them?" The first trooper snarls at him and in a very emphatic tone says: **"No, I know how you will handle it." "I'll go and talk to them again."** Standing close enough to hear what is being said, the second trooper can't believe what he is witnessing when he sees his partner assume a very submissive and highly inappropriate posture dealing with these known criminals. Rubbing his hand together the first trooper begins: **"Now ladies and gentlemen I already extended your stay and now ten minutes later you are still here." "I suggest that you leave now."** One of the gang-members snidely remarks in a somewhat mocking tone: **"Well, we are still not quite ready yet"** and ignoring the trooper simply turns away and talks to his friends.

(Cont'd.)

I guess I have to talk to them.

A short time later the second trooper says: **"Guess what?" "They are still here." "Looks like I have to talk them since I'm multi-lingual and speak their language."** Disgusted with his partner's demeanor, the second trooper walks over to the scruffy-looking bunch and says: **"Your mental acumen is apparently severely challenged by your obvious deficient knowledge of the English language." "So I will make an attempt to bring it down to your level."** Then walking over to the first of the four motorcycles, lined up side by side, puts the sole of his boot against the seat of the bike and says: **"I strongly suggest that all of you leave right now because if you don't, you will see what is called the 'Domino Effect' of bikes."** With that, the owner of the bike sputters: **"Man, are you some crazy 'Mother f*cker'?"** The trooper nonchalantly replies: **"Yup, about as crazy as they come and you are going to find out just how crazy if you don't leave right now."** While keeping a watchful eye on the rest of the creeps, he notices how one of the females busies herself with the heavy chain on the back of her bike. Before she can manage to get the chain into a threatening position, he places his hand on the butt of his gun and says: **"Whatever you have planned to do with that, I want to warn you that I have quite a few more friends on my side." "Not to insult your obvious lack of intelligence, I strongly advise you**

to get your fat ass on your bike and get the Hell out of here." Apparent unwilling to challenge the trooper's mettle, four bikes and eight hoods wheel out of the parking lot. When he returns his partner (the first trooper) mutters: **"I can't believe how you talked to them."** With a look of obvious disgust on his face the other trooper replies: **"Let me ask you, did your ladies and gentlemen listen to you?" "Or did the derelicts I talked to understand my way of talking to them better?" "Are they still here?" "No." "I can't believe how <u>you</u> talked to them." "You pussy."**

A High School lesson.

A State Police sergeant, slated for retirement, decides to take his five months accrued vacation and sick time he was able to accumulate during his twenty year Law Enforcement career and stay on active duty. A position as a substitute teacher has become available at a local high school and hopes to use it as a foundation for future teaching endeavors. Since the Sgt has taught specific subject matters at his local State Police academy as well as guest lectured at police academies and colleges in other states, he wants to continue teaching as a civilian. The school considers having the Sgt as a member of the faculty an added bonus. Two weeks later the school principal asks him to be the hall and school lunchroom monitor and assist in curtailing the occasional disruptive students' behavior. After the Sgt completes his check of the hallways and enters the cafeteria, his attention is immediately drawn to the far end of the cafeteria and a group of burly male students; obviously members of the school's football team. When the Sgt finds an empty seat and sits down at the long table, the commotion ceases. Noticeably disturbed by the trooper's presence, one of the footballers says: **"Yoh' man, what yo' think yo' doing?" "Daz' our table." "Yo' can't jus' sit at our table, jus' like dat."** Mimicking a puzzled look, the trooper puts the bait on the hook and calmly brushes his hands across the table surface pretending to be searching for something. As anticipated, "Big mouth" swallowed the bait and says: **"Man what yo' all looking fow'?"** Without looking at the student and still pretending to be searching the Sgt calmly replies: **"No matter how hard I look for it, even as a trained investigator, I can't find it."** Totally confused, the student asks: **"Do what?" "Man,**

what can't yo' find?" With some difficulty suppressing his laugh, he responds: **"I'm looking for the 'Reserve' sign." "Well, since you have forgotten to display it in a conspicuous place, I thought that I'm allowed to sit here." "Why don't you just sit down and eat your lunch?"**

(Cont'd.)

What yo' gonna do?

Sensing a possible physical confrontation when he notices the angry look on the football player's face, the Sgt stands up and places his back against the wall; just in case. Glaring at him the student snarls: **"Yah, yo may think that yo' some bad-ass State Trooper, but yo' ain't all dat." "So why don't yo' jus' get away from our table and leave us alone?"** Smiling at the student, the Sgt says: **"Well, young** (pause) **stud you obviously have no way of knowing because intelligent people have told me that I am excellent in the performance of my duties."** Bothered by the snickering of some of his playmates, the student is hardly able to restrain himself and sputters: **"Yea, yo' think yo' so big an' bad!" "What yo' gonna' do if I smack yo' along-side yo' ugly heead, cause yo' ain't allowed to touch me or nottin'?"** The trooper instantly realizes that he must be prepared for a possible physical confrontation and calmly replies: **"Let me tell you something young man, and excuse me for misusing that term." "Should you decide to pull such a foolhardy stunt, there will be two hits." "The first one will be when my fist hits you in your trashy mouth and the second one when your nasty ass hits the deck."** Apparently having his attention drawn to the commotion the vice-principal approaches the group and "Big mouth" stammers: **"Did yo hear what that State Trooper done told me?" "He said he go kick ma' ass." "He ain't allowed to do nottin' like dat."** The vice-principal looks at him and asks: **"Did you really say that to this student?"** It is apparent to the Sgt that the vice-principle doesn't seem to be interested in finding out the real cause of the incident or why the trooper made the remark. The Sgt replies: **"Well, not really like that, but I suppose in a way." "Here is what really hap…"** The vice-principle holding up his hand and cutting him off in mid-sentence says: **"You can't just hit the students." "I think you better**

leave trooper." Somewhat caught off guard, the trooper whispers: **"And you wonder why you have problems?" "It's called 'no balls'."** Disgusted with what just happened, the Sgt turns and walks into the office and tells the secretary where she should send the check. Confused by what the Sgt just said, the secretary objects and reminds him that he still has two more classes to teach. He doesn't even bother to fully respond and whispers: **"Past tense"**; politely smiles at her and closes the door behind him.

I can read.......

A State trooper pulls his cruiser behind the car he just stopped for speeding and walks up to the driver's side. Before he has a chance to tell the female operator why he stopped her she unleashes a verbal barrage against him and in a very irate voice says:

"Just because I didn't go to some fancy pouelice' academy like you, doesn't mean I can't read plain and simple signs; which apparently you failed to see." Without losing his composure he smiles and politely asks for her driver's license and vehicle registration. Glaring at him, and almost throwing her license at him she snarls: **"I have you know, I obeyed the speed signs." "I did exactly what the first sign said – 45 mph minimum speed – and sped up like I was supposed to." "Then at the next one where it suggested a 65 mph speed I went beyond that because I was in a hurry." "So since when is going a little faster than the suggested speed breaking the law?"**

Barely holding back what he really wants to say, smiles and replies: **"Ma-am, how much longer you want to bake a loaf of bread beyond the suggested time is entirely your choice." "However, for your information, the recipe for how fast you should go is not just recommended but demanded by law." "Please sign on the bottom, acknowledging that you received the ticket."** Hesitating briefly and visibly annoyed, she snatches the book and signs the ticket. When she hands it back to him, she remarks in a somewhat threatening tone: **"I'll definitely see you in court on this one!" "Believe you me!"** Before she is out of earshot he replies: **"And I can't wait for this one!" "Believe you me!"** ***(Yes, as a matter of fact, she had blond hair.)***

The Defense is badgering the Sergeant.

It is the State Police detective sergeant's second appearance in the same courtroom and before the same judge; whom he previously met at a semi-formal occasion. Similar to the first time, he has once again been subpoenaed to testify on a homicide case investigation that he assisted in. When the State Attorney is finished establishing the D/Sgt's credentials, he turns the proceedings over to the defense council. In the process of soliciting specific details in the case, it is very noticeable that the defense attorney is attempting to confuse the D/Sgt and have him contradict himself. The prosecuting attorney suddenly jumps up and in a very agitated tone raise his voice and says: **"I object to the defense council's line of questioning your honor!" "The defense is trying to badger the Sgt., hoping to confuse him."** Sliding his reading glasses off his nose and slowly pushing them against his forehead the judge glances at the Sgt, then at the defense table and replies to the prosecutor: **"Denied, because I don't believe that there is anyone in this courtroom capable of intimidating Sgt.____."** He then looks at the defense council and says: **"You may continue."**

Now everyone has seen your...

A couple of County officers are sent to a residence reference a juvenile suspected of being under the influence of drugs. When they arrive they are met by a hysterical woman (the juvenile's mother) and then hear yelling in the background. Preempting the officers' question the woman says that it was her husband attempting to subdue their son who had taken some type of hallucinogenic drugs. Both officers immediately run up the stairs.

When they arrive they find "Johnny" stark naked, wild eyed and sweating profusely being held down by his father. They couldn't help but noticing both parents hysterically crying while "Johnny's" sister with her horn rimmed glasses on, arms crossed just standing in the corner looking at the event with total disgust.

As the officers wrestle "Johnny" to the ground his sister exclaims in a rather calm voice: **"Well, that's just great Johnny, now everyone has seen your penis hanging out..."**

(Maybe the officers misjudged the seriousness of the situation. After all, it was hanging out.)

Dragnet.

There is nothing worse on this Earth than a bored cop. A County officer and his sector partner recall working a section of the county that had a few rough neighborhoods with the same type of complaints a routine; last night's victim would be tomorrow's suspect. In an effort to pass their time they start taking actual field notes and call it "Dragnet." As they do so, they remain completely emotionless and deadpan like Sgt. Joe Friday and won't crack a smile. When suspects were questioned, whether or not they understood, the officers would reply with some nonsense such as: **"I'm picking up what you're throwing down Ma'am."** Or **"Yes sir, I'm mopping up what you're spilling."** Not once did any of the suspects realize what the officers were doing.

Make him look presentable.

A rookie of a City police department is ordered to accompany two senior officers assigned to investigate a possible suicide. When they arrive, they find the victim naked and hanging from the ceiling. Since they have to wait for the arrival of the Medical Examiner one of the senior officers tells the Rookie to stay with the body while they go outside to have a smoke. Before they leave one of them tells the Rookie, jokingly: **"Keep an eye to on him and make him look presentable."**

When they return from their smoke break, they are stunned not to find the body of the suicide victim where they had left him. Alarmed by his disappearance they turn to the Rookie, who sheepishly points to the nearby couch with the victim lying on it;

fully dressed. Horrified by what the Rookie had done they ask him to explain himself. Realizing that he perhaps had done wrong, the Rookie explains: **"Well, you told me to make him presentable." "So I cut him down first." "Then I went into the bedroom and picked out some nice clothes and dressed him and placed him on the couch." "An' just like you told me, I made him presentable."** Alarmed and left temporarily totally speechless it takes the senior officers a moment to regroup their thoughts and work out a plan before the arrival of the M.E.

Aware that time is of the essence, the officers decide to quickly undress the victim and then hurry to place the rope around his neck and retie him to the ceiling. Just in the nick of time, without the M.E. ever finding out what they did.

Talk about a close call.

She fell out! ***(In the county patrolman's own words.)***

There I was, a newly minted County Patrolman; a regular "Johnny Whitebread" from the suburbs. I was sent to a "First Aid" call and arrived at the scene. When I ran up the front door I was met by a concerned family member and then saw an older female lying on the living room floor. I turned to the family member and ask him what happened. He responded: **"She fell out!"** Somewhat perplexed I replied: **"Fell out of what?"** The man looked at me incredulous and said: **"No man, she just done fell out."** I still wasn't able to make out what he meant.

Just then a couple of paramedics came through the front door. One took me aside and asked: **"What do we have here?" "A DFO?"** Somewhat dumbfounded I said: **"A what?"** Smiling at me he replied: **"Done fell out."**

(Slowly my brain picked it up…)

Are you hungry?

A State police detective sergeant is still somewhat aggravated by his wife's attitude from the previous day. No matter how hard he tried to stress how important it is for him to have an actual human skull to study for his final exam in physical anthropology, she absolutely refused to have him bring one into the house. As a result he spent the afternoon sitting in his cruiser holding the cranium and studying for the exam. It just so happens that the following day he reports to the Medical Examiner to work on the facial reconstruction of the homicide victim's skull that is quite involved. It is lunchtime and due to time restrictions he decides to eat his lunch at the mortuary; an opportune time for a harmless payback. He calls his wife and asks her to save some dinner for him; since he will be late. Somewhat annoyed that he will be late again, she wants to know where he is. Surprised by her attitude, the D/Sgt replies: **"I'm at the morgue and I'm getting ready to eat my lunch"**, in a matter of fact tone. Following a short moment of silence she asks: **"No!" "Are you going to eat your lunch at the morgue?"** The D/Sgt replies: **"Of course, where else would I eat?" "Oh, wait a minute it's impolite to eat in front of others so let me ask her if she wants a bite."** He can barely hear his wife's voice asking: **"Who are you talking to and ask if she wants something to eat?"** Taking a bite out of his sandwich he says loud enough for his wife to hear: **"The burned corpse that I'm working on." "But since she didn't answer me, I guess she is not hungry."** Her reply on the other end is a loud slam of the receiver.

Were you intimate?

A man charged with assault and battery is brought into the J. P. (Justice of the Peace) court by a local police officer and is asked to testify.

Judge: **"I see here that you have been charged for assault and battery." "What is your relationship?"**

Defendant: **"She ain't no relative an' all that." "She my girlfriend." "Well she was; but she done mean nothing to me no more." "You know what I'm saying?"**

Judge: (Frowning) **"OK." "Now let me ask you." "Were you intimate with her?"**

Defendant: **"Yeah I was." "I was like in my own groove." "Ya' know what I'm saying?" "An' that's what got me in trouble wit' her." "Cuz' when I tried to get her to slide into my groove she mad an' all that." "So I had to use a little force." "You unnastan' that?"**

Judge: (Puzzled look on his face) **"Well sir the court would like to know how you plead." "Are you guilty or not guilty?**

Defendant: **"Well maybe I shouldn' have hit as hard." "But your Highness, I needed her to see where I was in our relationship an' where I want her to be at." "Daz' all." "So I jus' told her what she has to do."**

Judge: **"You still have failed to tell this court how you wish to plead to the charges of A & B** *(Assault & Battery)*.**"**

Defendant: **"I guess I'm guilty." "But I want da' court to know that I'm justified cuz' she done needed to be taught a lesson."**

Judge: **"The court finds you guilty..." "Officer he is yours." "You know where from here." "Get him out of here."**

I have no intention paying for this damn ticket.

A couple of friends in their late teens are riding in their souped-up vehicle and are stopped by a sheriff's deputy; the driver is charged for excessive speed. Holding the ticket in his hands, the driver snorts and turns to his buddy and says: **"Wait here; I'll be right back." "I ain't paying for this damn ticket."** Before his friend, sitting on the passenger side, has a chance to ask him what he intends to do the driver jumps out of the car. Puzzled, the passenger watches his buddy briskly walk over to the sheriff's cruiser. When he returns, the driver doesn't say a thing and simply starts up his car and pulls along-side the sheriff's cruiser. Suddenly both cars take off, peeling rubber drag racing down the highway. The results - the sheriff beats the friends at top-end.

Still attempting to recover from the shock of what he just witnessed, the passenger friend is horrified when he sees his buddy pull along-side the sheriff's cruiser again. When the sheriff deputy rolls down his window the passenger hears his friend scream: **"Pull over!" "I want to make a citizen's arrest, charging you for drag-racing."** Certain that they are going to spend the night in jail, the passenger is relieved when he hears the sheriff deputy yell back: **"Go to Hell"** and drive off. As soon as the teen driver arrives at his home he calls the sheriff department and tells the sheriff that he will prefer charges against the deputy when he is going to court.

Two days later, a sheriff cruiser pulls up in front of the teen driver's house and the sheriff walks up to the front door. After some hem and haw, the sheriff finally makes his point. **"Look, I heard about your incident with one of my deputy's." "Here is what I'm going to do." "I've instructed my deputy to drop the charges and not appear in court." "As far as I'm concerned, this whole thing never happened." "I cannot complement you without calling the other party stupid." "However, you might be better off to apply your skillful tenacity in a more meaningful way." "Like I said this never, I repeat never happened." "Have we reached an agreement?"**

Although not fully unexpected by the teen driver and encouraged by the sheriff's professional demeanor, he gives the sheriff his word of honor that he will not talk about the case from this point on. What case?

Just a lineman's opinion.

A witness, called to testify in a Justice of the Peace court is sworn in and takes the stand and begins:

> "Well yo' Awna' since I ain't no lawinforcin' officer or like one of dem' dare' defectives, yo' know what I'm saying? So I'll splain' it my own way. So when I saw the subject, he done looked like he was all hungry and all dat'. Man, yo' shoulda' seen him; that dude was notn' but thin and bones. I'm telling ya'. I would say he was all emancipated (emaciated?) and all dat' and probably looking for some food. Yo' know what I'm saying? I just want you to know that is my lineman (layman?) opinion since I ain't one of those headmasters (psychoanalyst?). Yo' know what I'm saying? Well dats' what I seen and dats' my inpersonation' (interpretation?) of it."

I know who you are.

Leading a handcuffed man, a State trooper walks into the Justice of the Peace court. As soon as the magistrate's enters the courtroom, the man yells: **"These things are hurtin' me!" "That damn trooper put them on too tight."** Ignoring the trooper's strong recommendation to keep the handcuffs on the subject and just loosen them, the judge orders the trooper to remove them completely. With them off, the subject smirks at the trooper. Then, rubbing his wrists and faking an expression of gratitude turns to the judge and says: **"Thank you so very much your Honor"**; smirking at the trooper again. Maintaining his composure, the trooper replies: **"Keep smiling you** ...(pause)." **"Don't forget that you are under arrest and this is a courtroom; my comfort zone." "We haven't even started with your case yet."** Glaring at him with obvious total contempt, the creep suddenly snarls at the trooper and says: **"I know who you are." "I also know that you have little kids and where you live." "Just don't you forget that!"**

The trooper's primeval animal instinct to protect instantly kicks in. His fist flashes and strikes; followed by the thunderous crash of the subject falling into one of the wooden armchairs in the courtroom. Just as he readies himself to administer the coup de grâce a strong hand, attached to a uniformed arm, suddenly grabs his wrist. He quickly calms down when he hears the familiar voice of another trooper telling him: **"That's enough."**

> *Personal threats made against law enforcement officials are regrettably on the increase and are slowly becoming the norm. Whenever possible or practical, the issue is quickly dealt with by the individual offended. Unfortunately, factors such as the validity, the possibility to carry it out, the officer's interpretation, personal danger represented, etc. could have great influence on how and when to respond to personal threats. However, all bets are off when an unmistakable threat is made against the police officer's family or friends; the primeval animal instinct to protect sets in.

The judge slowly raises his head and peeks over the bench and timidly asks: **"Is everything alright?"** He carefully grabs the chair arm and wriggles his chair into position behind bench. When he sees the judge reemerge from his hiding place under the bench, the prisoner climbs out of the wood splinters and screams: **"Did you see that judge?" "I want to prefer charges against that trooper for hittin' me an' havem' arrested!"** The judge seems to momentarily study the loudmouth and then says:

> "Mister, if I were you I would consider myself lucky." You are indeed fortunate that the other trooper entered the courtroom in the nick of time; before the commencement of an encore. Although you are non-deserving of my generous offer, I will soothe your wounds and dismiss the present charge filed against you. If there is nothing else trooper, get him out of here."

Tell me about yourself.

After a he briefly introduces himself, the police academy instructor sits down and takes roll call of the recruit class. When he is finished he cups his chin with his hands and squints at the class; as if studying the students. Then, unbeknown to the students, he practices his usual routine and says: **"All right, why don't you stand up and tell me something about yourself."** Probably believing that he is following the usual practice, the first recruit stands up and begins. He manages to utter only his name when he is abruptly cut off by the bellowing voice of the instructor: **"Who told you to be the first to**

stand up?" "What makes you the sudden self appointed authority of this class?" "Who in the Hell cares who you are or gives a shit what you have to say?" "I've already seen enough." "So sit the f*ck down!" Shocked and visibly befuddled the recruit slumps back into his seat; he certainly won't dare to reply. A sigh of relief is heard throughout the classroom when the instructor tells them that he does that with every class. He just wanted to test them to see their reaction and cautions them not to simply believe that not everything follows an expected routine or anticipated customs; just like in a real situation.

A very close call. ***(In his own words.)***

My sector partner was investigating a three car accident in a semi rural area of the county. I went to assist him because two of the operators were DUI (Driving under the Influence) and the third had several outstanding felony warrants for his arrest. My sector partner was a big DUI enforcer and told me that he would take both DUIs if I would transport the wanted suspect for him. I throw the suspect in the rear of my cruiser and off I go to our HQ. After driving about two miles, my stomach began to gurgle and I broke out in a cold sweat. It must have been bad what I had eaten and the pain was quickly increasing. My ass started to pucker and I knew it was coming. I was still far from our HQ, but I knew there was a nearby State Police Troop. I threw the lights and siren on and (no joke) I'm doing about 80-90mph! I'm thinking: ***"There is no way I'm shitting myself in uniform."*** Meanwhile the prisoner in the backseat is turning white and yelling: **"Slow down!" "We are going to die."**

I roll into the troop parking lot on two wheels. I'm dragging the prisoner with me with one hand while at the same time trying to get my Sam Browne off with the other. I am now "touching cotton!" I run into the troop, throw my prisoner to the Desk Sergeant and yell: **"Please watch him!'** As I crash through the bathroom door I hear the Desk Sergeant shout from the background: **"Hey man, you don't look so good!"** Thanks "Captain Obvious"....made it with no time to spare.

A very unusual animal.

A gentle wind is blowing and rain just starting to spit. The County officer driving down a dark, unlit road grabs the steering wheel with both hands and pays full attention to the road ahead. Suddenly there is a movement and his trained policeman's peripheral vision spots something small and white scurrying across the dark asphalt backdrop. It's the moment when your police emergency vehicle operator's training kicks in. The adrenaline pulses down through his fingertips as he moves the wheel in an evasive arc. His car performs a maneuver worthy of the master Evel Knievel himself and his heart pumps in his chest; awaiting the "thump" that doesn't come. He is lucky, his training was a success. No damage to his squad car and no innocent animal died tonight. He feels confident until he looks in his rear view mirror and watches the unusual white "animal" finish scurrying across the roadway behind him. Then he realizes that he just saved the life of a rare white "Marsh" (Swamp) shopping bag".

The troopers are here.

A pair of State troopers is responding to a frantic call by a female claiming that her son is going to commit suicide. Due to the unfamiliarity of the backwoods area they finally arrive at the scene and spot the pickup truck described by the caller and approach the vehicle with utmost caution. When they get close they immediately notice the red spider hair pattern on the driver's side window and lower left hand side of the windshield and a bloodied person slumped over the steering wheel. One of them carefully opens the truck door and begins to pull the body out by the shoulders while the other trooper grabs the legs. They are shocked when what they thought was a dead man suddenly starts to gurgle and carefully place him on the ground and begin administering CPR. By the time EMC personnel arrive the suspect has been revived and is transported to the local hospital ER. Due to the troopers' quick action the man survives the self inflicted gunshot to his head, which fortunately for him did not fully penetrate his skull; both troopers receive "Lifesaving" awards.

Several weeks later the mother of the subject (attempted suicide) calls the troop and requests that the two troopers come to her residence so that she can thank them personally for saving her son's life. Since it is only natural to accept such an invitation, they go to the residence. When they arrive, they are reluctant to enter because the entire room is engulfed in cigarette and cigar smoke; and feels like a chimney. Both are ushered into the kitchen and become somewhat suspicious why they were invited when they hear the mother repeatedly calling: **"Billy come here." "The troopers are here."**

Suddenly a small door, apparently a service opening between the kitchen and the dining room, springs open and a hand with a raised middle finger pops out; then Billy's face appears. Instead of thanking the troopers, Billy just glares at them and says: **"F*ck you!"** Judging by Billy's unexpected reaction of their presence, both feel that Billy is genuinely angry with them because in his mind they did not save him. They instead prevented him from escaping Hell and put him right back into it.

Billy is under supervised care and no longer lives with his family; his Hell.

I found these…

It is not uncommon for a police agency to receive calls from citizens who are freaked out by things related to war such as guns, bayonets and even trench art made from inert ammunition and wish to get rid of them. Such was the case with the woman who called and asked the D/Sgt (Desk sergeant): **"Do you boys get rid of war souvenirs?"** The D/Sgt says: **"Sure Ma'am."** Before he has a chance to ask what they are, she hangs up.

About an hour later an old woman comes shuffling into the station and walks up to the counter and places a small brown paper bag (the type often used to bring lunch to school in) on the counter. When the D/Sgt asks: **"Can I help you?"** she replies: **"Sir, I found these in my husband's sock drawer and want to get rid of them."** The

D/Sgt, a Vietnam vet, looks into the bag and pulls out two old WWII MkII Fragmentation grenades.

Two or three officers who stuck around, curious to see what she brought in, suddenly scatter and run for cover when they see the grenades. Remaining calm as he can be, the D/Sgt turns around and says: **"What?" "The pins are still in them!"**

The wheelchair.

A State trooper working a special duty job at a fast-food restaurant notices a young man in a wheelchair and finds his actions somewhat odd. It appears as though the man deliberately chooses to avoid the normal activity around the restaurant's parking lot. Yet after a short time of being there groups of young teenagers congregate around him. The trooper finds it particularly interesting that the youngsters do not linger very long and when they leave, just drive off; very few of them actually stop at the restaurant. It becomes very obvious to him that a clandestine operation of some type is being conducted. Rather than just walk into the unknown, he decides to first gather some information to fortify his suspicion. A short time later a reliable source informs him that the guy is in fact dealing drugs. Working the hamburger place the following week the trooper spots the subject again in his wheelchair sitting in his usual place and decides to take action. Hoping not to alarm the chair-man he meanders towards the general area. The young audience hovering around the wheelchair scatters as soon as they spot the trooper walking in their direction, while the subject in the wheelchair busies himself adjusting the armrest on his chair. It is immediately apparent that the guy feels uneasy by the trooper's close presence. When he introduces himself the guy glares at him and snarls: **"Yeah, I know who you are." "What do you want man?"** Although the trooper initially planned to play his usual mind-game with the subject of questionable character, he no longer considers his adversary worth the time and goes right for the jugular and says: **"You better be careful." "I hear that the word is out on your ass."** The wheelchair bound man sputters: **"Man, I don't**

know what the Hell you are talking about." Then the banter vacillates back and forth.

Trooper – **"You know damn well what I am talking about." "So why don't you just come clean and tell me all about your deal."**

Creep – **"Man, I'm just sitting here. You've got nothing on me." "So just leave me alone."**

Trooper – **"What?" "Do you think that I am as stupid as you are?" "Well let me tell you something." "The word is out on you and some people are planning to get even with your crooked, cheating ass." "And guess what? I may not be around to save your rotten carcass."**

Creep – **"I told you, I don't know what you are talking about."**

Trooper – **"Like I said." "The word is that what you are selling is some cheap and nasty shit."**

The trooper has some difficulty suppressing a laugh when he notices the creep practically trying to leap out of his chair and blurt in anger: **"What the f*ck are you talking about?" "My stuff is some of the best that you can get."** Shocked, when he realizes what he just said, the creep grabs the wheels of his chair and pushes with all the strength that he has to get out of there. The creep may have continued dealing; but the trooper never sees him again.

Roll your window down.

Both State troopers notice the car enter the parking lot of the fast-food restaurant and the way the driver looks at them as he slowly drives past them and then head for the drive-thru. A short time later they spot him again, this time entering the rear of the parking lot and park in the darkest area of the place. One of the troopers recognizes the driver; a known burglar. Believing that there is still an outstanding arrest warrant for him, he asks his partner to contact the nearby troop and verify his suspicion while he keeps an eye on him. When his partner returns and gives him the high-sign, the trooper walks towards the suspect's car and notices the suspect quickly roll up his window and push down the buttons locking the car doors. Positioning himself slightly to the right side of the car door, just in case the suspect decides to open the car door and try to slam it against him, he knocks on the driver's side window and says: **"Roll down your window!"** When each repeated demand to roll down the window is replied with a barrage of foul language, abundantly laced with four-letter expletives; he is left with no other choice but to employ drastic action. The strike on the glass with his blackjack is much harder than he expected and shatters the window. It isn't possible to establish which one of them is shocked more when the window suddenly disappears. Before the suspect has a chance to recompose himself, the trooper quickly grabs him by the shirt-collar and pulls him partially through the window frame and gives him a sharp blow to his back. After he manages to open the driver's side door he pulls the suspect off the door and quickly places the handcuffs on him and tells his partner to call the Troop to pick up his arrest. When the trooper looks up he is surprised to see that the parking lot is practically empty. For the remainder of the evening his partner keeps repeating: **"I can't believe that you did that."** He calmly replies: **"Did I get the job done?" "I simply executed an outstanding warrant and just had to help him a little to get out of his car."**

Hey, I'm working down here!

The Troop secretary, a pleasure to work with and well known for her willingness to participate in pulling pranks or commit one of her own, is about to have the table turned on her. When the trooper reemerges out of the Troop Personnel Ladies' room he quickly sneaks back to where he is working; hoping that his visit will work out as planned and anxiously waits. His blood pressure rises when he sees the secretary open the door to the Ladies' room.

Suddenly a blood-curdling scream coming from inside the Ladies' room penetrates the entire Troop. Then the door is ripped open and miraculously still remains attached to the frame. Alarmed by the sound all available troopers rush towards the Ladies' room and arrive just in time to witness the screaming and cursing secretary waddling out. In her desperate attempt to pull her pants up she finally realizes that the drops of liquid trailing her could present a problem and rushes back into the ladies' room.

When it is apparent that it was just a prank and the laughter dies down sufficiently, one of the female troopers goes in to help the secretary regain her composure and also provide her with an overcoat. Desperately trying to find out what happened, the people in the audience beg the secretary to tell them. With a mixture of embarrassment and suppressed laughter the secretary says:

> "Well, when I entered the stall and sat down on the toilet seat, everything was all right up to that point. Then when my full weight was on the seat, all of a sudden there comes a voice from inside the toilet bowl hollering: **"Hey, I'm working down here!"** That scared the shit out of me so bad that I didn't even realize that I wasn't done peeing when I grabbed a hold of my underwear and yanked them up. When I just looked where the voice came from, I found this box under the back of the toilet seat. When I pushed that little button here, I heard: **"Hey, I'm working down here!"** Believe it or not, for a split second I thought: ***"Oh my God, I just peed on somebody."***

Someone says: **"I guess that is your Trail of Tears." "Huh?" "Now can I please have the box back because it isn't mine?"** Once again laughter erupts. When the secretary has fully recuperated from her ordeal, she admits that the prank was one of best ever. In the end, the laundry saved the day.

Stolen Dirt-bike.

A County police officer responding to a call reference a theft of a red dirt-bike is advised to be on the lookout for young black male suspect riding it. As the officer approaches the area he spots a young black male fitting the description riding a red dirt-bike and recognizes him from previous encounters with him. The boy's first instinct is to run but stops abruptly when the County officer calls him by his first name and hesitantly walks over to the police car. Since the officer knows the little thief's family personally he feels confident that his grandmother will meet out better justice than a court and decides to take him home.

When they arrive at the grandmother's house she is already waiting for her grandson and gives him a very suspicious look, but politely greets the officer. It is apparently obvious to her that her young charge is in trouble and invites the officer inside. As the officer walks up the front stairs of the house, the grandmother distinctly observes her grandson's reluctance to walk into the house and says to him: **"You better get your butt in the house before I beat all the black off your ass out here!"** She then turns to the officer and says: **"I just put some fried chicken on the table and there is enough for you too." "So come on in and have some."** Unable to resist the invite the officer follows her into the house. During the meal the officer gives an account of her grandson's involvement with the theft. The grandmother first looks at her grandson and then turns to the officer and says: **"First of all, I want to thank you for doing this." "I guarantee you that I will handle this."** She then looks at her grandson and says: **"When we are done here, you will return the bike and I will make sure that you do." "That is if you are still able to walk with a sore ass." "Thank you again officer."** The officer wants to laugh when he notices the – "I could kill you" look on the boy's face.

Several years later, while working an extra duty job, a young black male dressed in a security guard uniform walks up to the County officer and introduces himself. **"I don't know if you still remember me, but I'm the kid that stole the dirt-bike and had my grandmother beat my nasty ass." "Thanks for doing that instead of arresting me."**

It's better to err on the side caution. ***(In the officer's own words.)***

I'm not one to revel in the misfortunes of others however, when it is said that the other being is a douche bag I say Cheers; and bask in its sweet taste. While I was on patrol today, I erred on the side of caution; due to inclement weather. I drove in a slow, steady pace below the posted speed limit. When I looked in my rear view I noticed a car fast approaching with nary a sign of care because hey, sports cars are immune to the wrath of Mother Nature; apparently on her period. The car came up fast and then quickly changed lanes. As the car passed me, the operator glared at me as if I somehow, was an idiot for being cautious and then sped off ahead of me at a fast pace. When I saw the car change lanes again; that's when it got glorious. The ass end of the car began to argue with itself debating in which lane it preferred to dance an Argentine Tango. Suddenly, it changed styles and performed three pirouettes, worthy of the finest Swan Lake Ballet before launching itself into a Gran Finale of "Off road", snow and grass. I have no doubt had that been an Olympic event; the operator would have taken the gold. As I slowly drove by, I tooted my horn and waved. Yes....there is a God!

A unique way of decorating.

As soon as the D/Sgt (Detective Sergeant) is gone for the day, the Det. (Detective) jimmies the lock and slips into the D/Sgt's office and quietly closes the door behind him and opens the bag of goodies he has brought with him. He then takes the roll of toilet paper and peels off several long strips and thumb-tacks the strips to the drop-ceiling, along with several torn pieces of woman's underwear that he has knotted to a sewing threat. Careful not to attract the attention of the others, the Det. sneaks through the troop and collects every available chair and small pieces of furniture and carries them into the D/Sgt's office. Satisfied with his esoteric collection he begins stacking the items on the D/Sgt's desk and open floor spaces. To further express his unique decorating skills he tapes pornographic pictures on the walls. Before he closes the door, the Det. places a fake pile of genuine looking dog feces that rivals anything left behind by a live animal and locks the door. To make sure that he doesn't miss anything the Det relieves his predecessor a couple minutes early and takes his seat behind the desk and waits. The D/Sgt greets the Det., walks down the hallway and opens the door to his office. Almost instantly the Det. hears the D/Sgt's bellowing voice: **"You no good son of a bitch!" "I'll get even with you; you bastard." "I'll find out who you are." Just wait and see!" "There will be Hell to pay!"** The torrent of fake anger is quickly overshadowed by a burst of hearty laughter by other troopers who ran up to investigate the reason for the commotion.

(Cont'd.)

Paper Snow

While cleaning out a corner in the troop basement, the D/Sgt (Detective Sergeant) discovers an old hole-puncher with the attached tray still full with the little circular dots of punched out paper. He decides to turn his unexpected find into a payback for his favorite Det. (Detective) and undetected by anyone, lifts the Det's spare car key off the board. Later that afternoon the D/Sgt grabs a bag and fills it with special paper graffiti and waits until the Det. is busy with an interview. Shortly after the Det. closes his office door the D/Sgt quietly sneaks out of the backdoor of the troop. Any possible noise that he might make unlocking the door of the Det's car parked outside in front of the Det's office window is conveniently masked by the office air-conditioning unit. To prevent unwanted detection the D/Sgt maintains a low profile; below the dashboard of the car and carefully dumps the contents of his bag into the window's defroster and AC vents. After double checking that no tell-tale signs are left behind, the D/Sgt silently closes the car door and returns to his office. He strategically positions his chair for an advantages view and waits. Somehow the word of the D/Sgt's impending prank has spread throughout the troop but has fortunately not reached the Det's ears; still busy in his office. Hidden behind see-through curtains, watchful eyes of those on duty and are glued to the windows in anticipation. Following his usual end of the day's routine, the Det. locks the door to his office, opens the back door of the troop and nonchalantly walks to his car. Since it is a hot day, he loses no time to activate his car air conditioner. Sudden jubilation and bursts of laughter echo throughout the troop when the Det. laughing and furiously brushing the paper snowflakes from his head and face. He then walks back into the troop and compliments the D/Sgt for a job well done, but also reminds him that the game is on again and that he will have an appropriate response; then carries the vacuum cleaner to his car.

(Cont'd.)

Just one more time.

Memories of paper snowflakes drift through the D/Sgt's mind when he spots the Det's car parked next to his car and a sudden urge to… He reached over the back seat of his cruiser and grabs a small towel out of his gym bag and waits until a few minutes before the end of duty. When he is certain that the Det. is occupied, he slithers out of the back door of the troop and crouches between the two vehicles. Careful to buffer any noise, he presses the towel against the edge of the screwdriver and pops the hubcap of the Det's left rear wheel. He then inserts a couple of small stones into the rim of the hubcap and remounts it. He just reenters his office when he hears the Det. at the back door of the troop. There is no reason to watch the Det. enter his vehicle since nothing is going to happen until he driven some distance on the open highway.

The following morning, the D/Sgt, along with a group of other troopers sees the Det. rush into the troop. With a demeanor fluctuating between laughter and barrages of curse words the Det. begins to tell his story; to the delight of the group who has been anxiously awaiting his arrival.

> "In the very beginning I didn't give the noise too much thought until I was further down the road; then I got a little concerned. My first thoughts were that there was something wrong with my engine and pulled over onto the shoulder and popped the hood. When I couldn't find the problem I decided to drive to the garage where I have

> my personal vehicle served since the troop garage was already closed for the day. The mechanic at my garage, likewise, couldn't find anything wrong and decided to take a test ride with me to hear the noise himself. We had just entered the highway when he told me to turn around and go back to the garage. As soon as we got back he grabbed a screwdriver and started popping hubcaps, one at a time. After he had removed the one on the left rear wheel, holding a couple of pebbles in his hand, he said that he had found my problem. Of course I knew immediately what the source of my problem was you; you bastard!"

Batman couldn't fly.

City police officers in Germany receive a call from a hysterical woman claiming that her husband had a very bad accident and was seriously hurt when they got ready to make love. Suspecting a possible domestic violence incident, the responding police officers approach the house with caution and are met by a scantily dressed female who directs them to a second story bedroom. When the officers enter the bedroom they follow the sounds of loud moaning and find a male suspect crumpled on the floor at the foot of the bed, dressed in a Batman suit. Although the man shows no external injuries and is not bleeding, it is very obvious to the officers that he is in excruciating pain but sufficiently coherent to respond to the officers' questions. While waiting for an ambulance the officers begin their investigation and have great difficulty maintaining their professional bearing when they hear the story of what had gone awry in the planned night of hot sex. According to the love birds, they wanted something different from the usual and routine action. They allege that it was the husband's idea to dress up in a Batman suit the next time they felt the urge to express their amorous feelings for each other. Then the real story begins.

Dressed in a Batman suit, the husband decided to add to the excitement and climb on top of a tall armoire, a couple of feet away from the foot of the bed. Due to the insufficient space between the top of the armoire and the ceiling, the poor slob was unable to squeeze himself into a proper position. The tantalizing looks of his wife and his desire to express his male prowess had unfortunately blocked any common sense; if he had any to begin with. To answer the call, he decided to dive onto the bed in Batman style and accidentally struck the footboard with the full force of his body. Out of respect for the seriously injured man, the police officers refrain from laughing in his presence; but loose it when driving back to the station. It is only natural that the story spread like wild fire when re-told; accompanied by roars of laughter.

Soap could help.

A motorist in Germany is arrested and transported to the station by a City police patrol unit. When they arrive at the station it is very apparent that the uncooperative prisoner will make every attempt not to have his blood drawn. Apparently still able to realize that a blood test would fortify the police officers' case in court he requests to use the toilette. Honoring his request the officers escort the mouthy individual to the toilette; located in the basement. It is also equipped with a mirror and a sink to wash your hands; for those who practice hygiene. While the drunk is using the facilities the two officers position themselves where the drunk cannot see them but is able to hear them.

Unbeknown to him the officers are able to watch his actions through the split of the partially opened door and begin. **"It looks like we are faced with a potential problem when drawing blood from someone suspected of DUI** (Driving under the Influence) **cases." "What do you mean?" "Well, recent studies apparently have shown that if you eat soap before you have your blood drawn; it throws the test out of whack and drastically reduces the actual alcohol level reading."** Ready to go into hysterics, it takes every bit of their willpower not to make any noise laughing. However, they somehow manage to suppress loud laughter and quietly snicker as they see the drunk take a bite out of the soap and watch his distorted facial expression as he chomps on the piece.

While back upstairs filing the paperwork, their subject suddenly complains that he is not feeling well and needs to go to the toilette again. He makes it just in time when the officers hear him throwing up. One of the officer's remarks: **"So much for the blood test."**

Can I be next?"

The younger sister of a local police officer's wife is in attendance at a function and overhears comments made by a PS "Pistol Sniffer" (Term referring to women who are infatuated with police officers in uniform). As she listens to the woman's claim to having occasional amorous encounters with a certain police officer, she is shocked when realizes that the PS's conquest is her brother in law. Pretending to be intrigued by the woman's story she tactfully joins the conversation; hoping to obtain more information. With the sought after information now in hand she is faced with a very complex issue. What is she going to tell her sister? The following day the sisters meet.

Still in the process of figuring out how to approach the delicate issue, the younger sister's anxiety is relieved by her older sister's response: **"I've already been suspicious of his extra marital trysts."** Delighted by her sister's positive reception, the younger sister continues: **"Well I was able to get not only the bitch's name but also where they meet and the approximate times."** Fortified with the new supply of critical information the older sister (PO wife) says: **"Here is what I plan on doing to get even with that SOB, but I need your help."** Happy with her sister's decision the younger sister responds: **"Whatever you need, count me in."**

After several failed attempts, patience and persistence pay off. Ready to call it a night once again, the sisters suddenly spot the police vehicle (driven by sister's husband) enter a shopping center and slide behind loading area of the complex. Allowing enough time to lapse for the couple to be deeply involved and temporarily oblivious to their surroundings the sisters sneak up behind the patrol vehicle. It's a nice balmy evening and the car windows are rolled down giving the sisters a perfect view of a naked derriere in motion. Negating her initial thought of causing serious harm to the couple, the wife gently pats her husband on his bare buttocks and says: **"Can I be next?"** A sudden loud: **"What the f*ck.....!"** Rather than taking a chance with an unpredictable repercussion, the wife follows her sister already in hasty flight. When the sisters are back home they feel that it would be a shame to already call such beautiful evening to come to a close. They decide that it is an ideal time for major house cleaning á la husband's uniforms; the front lawn. Needless to say, hubby has to find a new laundry maid and another place to flop until the divorce is final.

Sorry, but I tried to hold it.

A County police officer operating a moving-radar has a car register traveling in excess of 70 mph in a 35 mph speed zone. By the time the officer makes a U-turn and activates the emergency equipment, the speeder is rounding a curve. Less than a mile later the vehicle, occupied by a lone male, pulls to a stop in the right-hand travel lane. As the officer approaches the driver's side window to begin the process of a traffic arrest and asks him for his license etc. a strong odor of diarrhea suddenly collides with the officer's olfactory receptors - wafting heavily from the driver's seat. The totally dejected and embarrassed driver obviously defecated in his pants. Despite his desperate high speed attempt to reach a bathroom the operator ruined not only his suit, but also the car seat; A very stern verbal warning is issued and the driver is allowed to continue; now at 25 mph to find a shower and a change of clothing. If the officer's warning was not enough, the aroma and car seat helped.

But it's Halloween.

The Dispatch Center is extremely busy handling all kinds of tricks and criminal mischief calls. A police officer, somewhat still a juvenile at heart, procures a "Jason" Halloween hockey mask. Closely resembling the mask used in the horror movie with the same name, it is painted with dripping columns of red splatters. Walking through the telephone relay room the way goes from a break room into the main call center, a diamond plate landing with two steps leadings into the operations center and multiple radio dispatcher consoles. The delinquent officer, wearing said mask and uniform of the day, bounces through the door and jumps onto the diamond plate stairs so that the "BONG" (sound) announces his arrival. All activity in the center instantly stops. The staff duty officer (a Captain) who has absolutely no sense of humor is standing midway across the room begins an immediate foot pursuit of this clown.

The masked officer immediately makes a hasty exit back through the telephone room then the break room and flees via the locker room into the men's restroom. Taking a very careful stance with his feet on the toilet seat he very quietly closes the stall door. His heartbeat starts to rise dramatically when he hears the familiar "squeak-squeak" of Corfam shoes rushing through the locker room. Holding his breath, the officer freezes like a statue when he sees the captain's shadow as he peers under the stalls. Officer "Jason" breathes a sigh of relief when the captain turns and runs back out of the locker room to search other areas of the police HQ building. Apparently the captain, obviously not detective material, is satisfied that the 'Unsub' (unknown subject) isn't there. Cautiously exiting from his hiding place, the pretend 'Jason' cop slithers out through a side door, climbs into his patrol car and drives away. Whew!

Too bad the captain wasn't able to see the "hee-hee, haa-haa" on the face of the uniformed "Jason" raiding the call center.

Just one more spritz for good measure.

An urban apartment complex is plagued by a Peeping Tom. Despite the fact that he has been spotted numerous times peeping through bedroom windows, he is always able to elude the many foot chases in his pursuit. However, on this particular night it is going to be different when police are once again responding to a Peeping Tom call and receive some help from a very unusual and obviously unexpected source. The 'Perp' (Perpetrator) has found a bedroom window with the curtains pushed aside and is able see a woman getting undressed. Totally entranced by the view, the 'Perp' crouches down and watched the woman as she continues changing her clothes. According to the investigation, the victim (woman being watched) claims that at some point that evening, she sensed his presence. KARMA? When she turned around she spotted him looking through her bedroom window and immediately screamed at the top of her lungs. Unbeknown to the Peeping Tom he has cohabitated with a fat "ole" skunk, also hiding under the shrubbery near that window. Apparently the Peeping Tom was not the only one frightened by the shrieking sounds. Shocked by the piercing screams, the skunk let loose with a spray; momentarily blinding the Peeping Tom. As the Peeper rolls around on the ground, choking and gagging and crying out, the skunk let's him have a second dose. Just in case he wants to run away again. A short time later he is apprehended without resisting and transported in the back of the prisoner wagon to the hospital decontamination room. The skunk escaped.

Where are you?

DISPATCH (0320 hours): **"Unit 11- Adam-One." "Respond to a burglar alarm at... "**

PATROL UNIT: - **No response**

DISPATCH: **"Unit 11-Adam-One. "**

PATROL UNIT: - **No response.**

DISPATCH: **"12-Bravo-Two respond to 11 District reference burglar alarm..."**

PATROL UNIT: **"Be advised, it's a false alarm." "An apparent accidental trip."**

Meanwhile – (*Where is 11-Adam-One?)*

DISPATCH: - (*Alert alarm is sounded several times.)* **"Unit 11 - Adam-One."**

PATROL UNIT –**Still no response.**

DISPATCH: (*The supervisor orders a Radio Roll Call. Units announce their location.)*

(*Still no reply from 11-Adam-One - last assigned.)*

Other police units start towards the last known location of 11-Adam-One.

DISPATCH: **"Unit 11-Adam-One."**

Finally - at 0410 hours.

PATROL UNIT: (An obviously sleepy voice is heard.) **"Eleven-Adam-One - ten three?"** *(Go ahead with message)*

DISPATCH: **"11 Adam-One, are you 10-1?"** *(OK)*.

PATROL UNIT: **"I'm 10-1"** (Sleepily) **"I've been up in "the Valley"** *(A sparsely populated area out of radio reception.)*

(Correct translation - **zzzzz, zzzzz, zzzzzz.**)

After a long silence, an officer from another sector keys his microphone and the soft, soothing notes of a harmonica playing "Brahms's Lullaby" can be heard.

Followed by a 3 minute encore of microphones banging on the dashboards – *(A police-applause)*

11-Adam-One – (***BUSTED)***

Had again.

The plainclothes detective pulls up to the sally-port gate (Entrance to the police headquarters holding facility) and taps the horn on his unmarked Crown-Vic. The Turn-Key (Officer on duty) in charge of the cell-block and processing area looks at the TV monitor and recognizes the detective, and also notices that he has a prisoner in the back seat of his car who is shaking his head back and forth and can hear him almost pleading: **"I sold everything that I owned and moved to this country to open the store." "I do not understand your customs and rules." "I just do not understand."** The detective has enough and shouts: **"SHUT UP!"** The "Turn-Key" is flabbergasted by the detective's angry demeanor because he is usually calm and collected. Sounding like a continuous recording the prisoner, slunk with his back against the wall, is still shaking his head from side to side and lamenting: **"I do not understand." "I do not understand."**

Apparently tired of listening to the wining any longer, the detective suddenly rushed across room and in a threatening posture screams in the prisoner's face: **"SHUT UP!" "Just shut up, Dot-head!"** In an almost pleading voice the prisoner says: **"Please don't address me in that way."** The "Turn-Key" can't believe what he has just witnessed and refuses to remain silent any longer. Suddenly raising his voice to the detective, for whom he had a lot of respect up till now, demands to know what the prisoner is being charged with. The detective turns abruptly and snarls:

> "I stopped at the 7-11 for a snack. While I was in there I spotted a sign in the window that advertised a hot dog and a cold drink for 99 cents. So I got a hot dog, fixed it the way I like it, poured myself a drink, and went to the register to pay for the stuff and placed a dollar bill on the counter. When this dirtball then claimed that my purchase was $1.99 not 99 cents, I got pissed off. I said, 'What the hell are you talking about?' I then pointed to the sign in the window and said, 'The sign there says 99 cents for a hot dog and a Coke!' The punk then told me that the sale was for last week and that he forgot to take the sign down. I just lost it completely then and jerked him over the counter, cuffed him and here we are. He is going to be charged with ah -Theft!"

After a very long silence the barely audible muttering is heard: **"I do not understand." "I do not understand".** The "Turn-Key" steps away from the booking desk, keys his way out of the processing area and proceeds post-haste to the House Sergeant's office. Seeing the genuine concern on the Turn-Key's face when he reports that the detective has obviously been overworked and has flipped his lid, the Sergeant and Lieutenant decide to investigate. As they approach the processing area, they look up at the TV monitors and see the detective and the prisoner, no longer cuffed, howling with laughter and slapping their knees hysterically.

The Lt looks at the "Turn-Key" and says: **"You've been had ... again."** It turns out that the alleged "prisoner", a naturalized citizen from India, had a scheduled appointment at the police facilities to be fingerprinted. The whole scene had been staged to entertain the "Turn-Key". It was an opportune moment for the detective to play a prank on another friend of his, the "Turn-Key".

She crossed the signal with the seeing-eye dog.

Maintaining a professional posture, the State trooper asks the irate lady who just walked into the troop to take a seat. With her composure somewhat restored she tells him:

> "I just found out that the state is indicting me for my accident that happened over six months ago. Well, 6 witnesses and my daughter all said that the accident was definitely not my fault and I could not have avoided it. With tears rolling down her face and a pretty severe concussion when I was slowing down to stop. My 13 year old daughter said: 'Not here!' 'I don't want to stay here.' So I went to R...... just down the road so my daughter could feel safe. I did not flee the scene. I tried to call the police from there; after I went to talk to the guy tailing me whom I figured called the police anyway. When he pulled away, I went to call the police on my own. I really need the state to stop treating me like a criminal. I need you to tell the state to stop. You are the State Police."

Somewhat annoyed by the trooper's question she corrects him and says:

"No I did not run into the back of anyone!"

"The person crossed the road against her signal with a seeing-eye dog!"
(Signal with a seeing-eye dog?)

"She ran out in front of me!"

"She (Daughter) **had a pretty severe concussion when I slowed down."**
(Did she mean to say – slam on the brakes?)

"She (Daughter) **didn't want to stay there so I drove to R.....just down the road so she could feel save."**

"I just didn't think she was safe at the scene." *(A certified doctor's opinion?)*

"So I didn't leave the scene like they say."

The trooper has heard enough of her expert testimony picks up the phone and calls the local Town police department. Apparently her personal expert assessment is needed by the Local PD to complete their accident investigation. Tighten the noose?

Priceless memories.

Sitting in his squad car and taking a sip of his usual morning coffee the County officer begins to feel his age and remembers a time when his joints didn't creak and he was still fleet of foot. His first foot pursuit...May 1988, when he was working the West Side. In those days on dayshift you could actually get a meal break. He and his sector partner Cpl. John had just finished eating at the old HoJo's (Howard Johnson's). He probably ate more than he should have but Hell, he was still a growing boy; full and happy on a cheeseburger, large order of fries; finished off with a vanilla milkshake. As they left the area, a call goes out from a neighboring PD of a burglary that has just occurred with three suspects on the loose. One of the neighboring PD's officers was in a foot chase with one of the suspects and requested assistance. Apparently an area resident had come home to find three teen-aged burglars in her residence.

He remembers his heart pumping like mad when he flew to the area; lights and sirens ablaze. Back then he was young and full of piss and vinegar and able to run like a white Jesse Owens. Heck, lean and mean and almost 6'03" he had the stride. As he got closer to the area, HQ dispatched a description of the other two suspects. As luck would have it, one of the miscreants emerged from between two houses and ran down the street near his squad car. The officer's predator instinct kicked in as he bails out of the squad car, grabs his nightstick and gives chase. With his feet pumping up and down like a Cheetah against a Gazelle on the great Serengeti he got closer and closer, which wasn't easy in Corfam dress shoes. He managed to get close enough to reach out and shove the suspect's shoulder, throwing him all out of kilter. With his arms and legs flailed lands with a sickening thud, face first onto the asphalt roadway. While straddling him and quickly applying his handcuffs, the officer felt a sudden pain in the right side of his ribcage...a combination of adrenaline and cramps from food. Then it happened…the "Technicolor Yawn"; a second unwanted encore. He will never forget when his entire lunch came up and landed all over the back, head and shoulders of the young suspect but not a drop on himself. Unable to stop laughing, he watched the suspect covered with puke screaming and still feels to this day that that was more justice than the punk would probably have gotten in court that day. The best part...it was an "Away Game" (Assisting another department without having to do paperwork.). He remembers the disgusting WTF look on the other officer's face when he asked: **"What the Hell happened to him?"** He just quickly switched handcuffs with the other department's officer and replied: **"He's all yours!"** and hurried back to his squad car.

Already punished enough.

A Delaware police officer on patrol notices the car ahead of him stop at a red light and then proceed through it. Since it is late and no other cars are coming, he still feels that he should stop the car and check it out and pulls up behind it. When he approaches the car he notices that it displays Delaware plates and that the operator has a New Jersey driver's license. Anticipating the officer's question, the female passenger explains that it is her car and the driver is her boyfriend.

After completing a check with DMV (Dep. of Motor Vehicles) the officer goes back to the car to explain to the operator the reason why he is getting a written warning and is surprised by the operator's ecstatic reaction. Smiling from ear to ear the operator sputters: **"You're not giving me a ticket?"** The officer leans down a little closer and replies: **"Sir, you're from New Jersey; I can't punish you any worse than that!"**

Butterball Caper.

It's a cold night and a City officer driving his squad car working the midnight shift is conducting a security check through a large strip mall. While making a turn to drive through a specific area of the shopping center, he suddenly hears a very loud boom of what appears to be a shotgun blast. Believing that someone is shooting at him the officer instantly flattens his body across the front seat of his cruiser and accelerates out of the immediate area. Anxiously looking through his rear view mirror he is surprised to see a frozen turkey slide down the street; the spot he just vacated. At 3:30 in the morning he feels that he is the only dumb SOB out there and makes a U-turn to retrieve the frozen turkey. He is fairly certain that the frozen turkey has something to do with the loud bang. But was it? The most logical place the lost turkey could have come from is the supermarket, located just around the corner. He recalls stockers (Personnel stocking the store shelves) working inside as he drove past just a few seconds earlier. As a precaution, the officer keeps the car lights off and carefully edges towards the back of the store's delivery and loading area.

Reconnoitering the loading area from his hiding place he spots some people on the roof of the store, throwing stuff into one of the dumpsters below. The subjects on the roof were most likely some of the stockers who were locked inside the store. Since he is not in a position to do anything but watch until the store opens, the officer advises dispatch of the situation and patiently waits until morning. In the morning several suspects are taken into custody and interrogated at central.

According to the culprits arrested and the evidence gathered by the officer during the early hours of the morning, the investigation shows a rather unusual, if not bizarre twist in a criminal act. Full confessions by the suspects reveal the following.

Last night's theft was only one of many previous ones and well planned in advance. Their usual Modus Operandi is to wait a few hours after the group has been locked in the store and then gather the items they steal near the trap door leading to the roof of the super market. After the alarm system has been deactivated, access to the roof will be undetected. Once the articles are in place on the roof the suspects toss the loot into the dumpsters located down below. The trash in the dumpsters not only deadens the sound but also cushions the articles when thrown from a total distance of about 35 ft. Unfortunately for one of the criminal self proclaimed quarterback "wannabee's" butterballs missed the open dumpster crashing on the closed lid of the other; the shotgun blast heard by the officer in the passing police cruiser.

Further investigation revealed that the participants in the crime stole over $150,000 in merchandise over a 6 months period. The question is - when are the next quarterback tryouts?

It's grandma.

A police officer stops at the local Donut shop early in the morning; there is nothing like a hot cup of coffee to get started for dayshift. As he walks in, he holds the door open for a very old woman. Grandma, he's certain - grey hair, purse, long wool coat; the whole nine yards. While waiting at the counter to be served, he suddenly feels a hand pat him on the ass. Shocked, he looks over his shoulder - it's grandma", who smiling from ear to ear says: **"Hey there handsome!"**

Too embarrassed to respond he just grabs his coffee and hurries out of the door; praying all the way that no one saw what just happened.

What about if she had been young and pretty, would he have asked her for a date?

Defense against negative rays.

The police officer is responding to an apartment complex in reference to a neighbor dispute with no further details and arrives at the 2nd floor apartment. When he knocks on the door he is greeted by a seemingly ordinary gentleman who says: "**Oh, hello sir; come on in please.**" Everything appears to be normal to the officer until he enters the apartment and sees the apartment dweller's extremely unique decorating style. The entire apartment interior is wallpapered in aluminum foil, including the furniture. Anywhere paint or drywall had previously been exposed is also covered in foil; resembling a metal cube.

After a short recovery from his initial shock the officer asks the man: **"What's the problem sir?"** Glad to have the officer there replies: **"Well officer, my neighbors are shooting negative rays into my apartment and I want them to stop."** Maintaining a professional posture the officer replies: **"OK sir, I'll get right on that."** The officer gets out of Dodge as fast as his squad car can take him.

The special book.

A couple of State troopers, a Cpl (Corporal) and a trooper responding to a "Domestic in Progress", hear loud screams coming through an open window of the house and pull into the driveway. As they approach the house, the front door suddenly flies open and a very corpulent female, advanced in age, greets them yelling: **"I want that no good son of a bitch oudda' ma' house!" "Get him ouuudda here!"** After the Cpl quickly reconnoiters the interior and makes sure that he can see the subject the female is apparently referring to and is sure that the subject isn't armed, they enter. It is immediately apparent to the Cpl that he has to separate the two hotheaded antagonists. In a very stern and authoritative voice he tells them to be quiet and orders the man to remain seated on the couch and orders the female to sit on the chair opposite him. Before either one of the verbal fencers can start in again, the Cpl raises his hands with the palms facing in opposite directions and says: **"One at a time"**. The man immediately yells: **"That bitch has no right to throw me out of my own house!" "This is my house too."** The Cpl remarks: **"Why don't you two just get a divorce?"** To which the man replies: **"We can't because it costs too damn much money." "Besides that, we are catholics." "An' neither of us wants to have the other one arrested and get a criminal record."** When the two of them begin screaming at each other again, the Cpl realizes that he isn't getting anywhere raises his voice and says: **"All right, both of you just be quiet and you better listen to me or I will arrest both of you."**

When the elderly couple finally remains silent, he walks over to the telephone and picks up the receiver. Sneakily depressing the "on" button on the phone, he dials and speaks:

> "Yes, this Cpl… of the State Police, I would like to speak to Father …***(made up name)***. No problem, thank you very much. Yes your reverence I desperately need your help and advice with a matter of great urgency. We are responding to a "Domestic Violence in Progress" call and we want to avoid a physical confrontation that could easily erupt between this couple here. I suggested a divorce but was told that they couldn't, because they are catholic and it would cost too much money. You may be able to shed some light on this. I heard, very recently, that under very special circumstances the church could allow a temporary emergency separation. Can you possibly tell me how to get that? Oh that's great, I just happened to have a copy of that in my car. All right! Thank you ever so much for your help. Good bye."

Maintaining a professional posture the Cpl turns to the trooper and says: **"Go and get my special emergency law book *(code word for Motor Vehicle Code)*; the one with the black plastic binder on the front**

seat of our vehicle". Mumbling under his breath: "**Special, huh**?" the trooper leaves to get the book. Surprised to see him return so quickly, the Cpl says: **"Boy." "That was fast."** Smirking, the trooper whispers through partially closed lips: **"I just didn't want to miss a beat on this drum."**

Frowning, the couple asks: **"Is this for real?" "Can you really do that?"** Holding up his copy of the special book, the Cpl assures them in the affirmative on both counts. Surprised by his own ability to keep a straight face the Cpl begins his spiel:

> "According to a most recently passed church ruling you can get a temporary separation or temporary divorce under special circumstances. Provided, of course, you have the specific ruling in writing with you. Well, you are very fortunate because I just happened to acquire a copy of it today. However, I need to remind you that it is not valid if you violate **any** part of this specific law. So let me tell you what the two of you have to do. Again, let me remind you that you **must** follow everything exactly the way I tell you. Do you understand me so far?"

When the Cpl sees them nodding their heads, he looks at the lady, the most vocal of the couple, and continues:

> "All right 'Ma'am', I want you to stand up and place your right hand on this special book and repeat after me. According to this special law, I Wanda temporarily divorce thee, Howard, for tonight. *(Wanda repeats)* Ok, Wanda, your oath is binding and you are now required to go upstairs and stay up there for the rest of the night. I warn you. You are not allowed to come back down again until tomorrow morning. Do you understand that?"

Satisfied that Wanda will remain upstairs, he turns his attention to Howard and addresses him:

> "Ok Howard, since I'm certain you are used to sleeping on the couch, it will be easier for you to sleep there. I am going to tell you to remain down here for the rest of

> the night. So don't you dare go upstairs and try to make up. Not tonight! Do you understand me? Remember the special law!"

> Howard – "I know, I know. Why the Hell would I be going up there tonight? I'm just glad I was able to divorce her ass for tonight an' not having to listen to her damn hollering all night again."

Before the Cpl leaves, he takes another very stern look at Howard who obediently remains seated on the couch and decides that it is safe to leave. He wishes Howard a good night and says to his partner: **"Let's go."** As soon as they are outside both of them hold their stomach and burst out in laughter. The trooper turns to the Cpl and says:

> "Man, I wasn't sure if I was able to hold my laughter back much longer. You are f*cking crazy. Nah', f*cking insane. Where do even come up with such crazy shit? How much are you going to charge for legal fees?"

While climbing back into the cruiser and still laughing, the Cpl replies: **"That was too damn funny, so I did that one pro bono." "The most important thing is that our mission was accomplished." "Have you ever heard of Machiavelli?"**

Connie, who?

The page is heard throughout Police Headquarters:

"Officer Connie Lingus, dial 812."

"Officer Connie Lingus dial 812."

"Lieutenant ______, call the Captain's office 10-18." *(That means right away.)*

A handy gadget.

Just before members of the squad assemble for "Roll Call" the Lieutenant sneaks into the room and tapes the receiver under one of the chairs to the rear (operative verb) of the room. Satisfied with the hiding place of the remote controlled "Fart" box (small device that emits various sounds of healthy flatulence) and closes his hand around the "transmitter" (button that signals the receiver to fart) and walks out of the room. 28-30 officers snap to attention and wait for the El-Tee" (Lieutenant) along with two Sgts (Sergeants) who just entered to take their place behind the long desk in the front of the room and on command, sit down. As routine departmental memos are read aloud by one of the Sgts, the Lt "squeezes one off". The room freezes. Several senior officers suppress grins while a stern looking Lt glances around the room, as if to discover the windy culprit. After a short pause, the Sgt resumes reading the memo and the Lt "cranks" out another one. Now, the senior Sgt angrily admonishes the officers assembled to maintain a professional decorum in the presence of the Lt and Sgts. There are obviously more, barely suppressed, grins than frowns. As the Sgt continues with his rant, the Lt "cranks" several more in a row; this time holding up the button for all to see. Momentary uncontrolled laughter erupts. Needless to say, it's the end of "Roll-Call". The cops hit the street with grins instead of frowns.

Look in the mirror.

The courtroom is in session and the complainant has been sworn in. Also present are the defendant and a State trooper. After the judge has the complainant verify the charges of "Sexual Misconduct" and "Defamation of Character", she has filed against the defendant Tyrone.......are correct, he begins.

Slightly turning his head, the judge looks at the complainant and says: **"Here is your opportunity to tell the court what transpired between you two on ....."** The complainant replies: **"Well maybe we got a little warm when we got into it." "But it wasn't hot or anything like that for us to transpire."** Slamming his gavel on the bench and covering his eyes the judge says: **"Hold it!"** It is followed almost immediately by: **"Go on."** The sudden look on the judge's face is priceless. Apparently it took the judge a couple of seconds before he realized that for some people "transpire" and "perspire" are interchangeable.

> "Well after he and I met we got a little cozy on the couch. I had no idea that we was going to be intimated (intimate); but all of a sudden he was into me. I really didn't have a chance to say anything. You unnerstan'? When he was done he just got up and went to the bathroom. After he got dressed again he just said that he would see me around. With the way he treated me, I felt like I was sexually abused by his conduct. Then a couple of weeks later, actually a couple of days ago now, I saw him again. I thought that maybe we had something so I axed him about that. That's when he got really nasty and all that and did nothing but downgrade me. Especially when he said to me that he only did it with me cuz' he hadn't any booty for a few days. Then he told me I wasn't all that for him to be able to get it on with me again. He took full advantage of me and was all into himself. He also told me that I should be glad that he stooped that low. That's when he really, really desecrated (?) my character and should be punished badly."

It is quite noticeable that the judge appears to have an issue with his eyes because he frequently takes his glasses off and rubs his eyes. Suddenly the defendant jumps to his feet and screams: **"Man, that "bitch" is lying her ass off."** Totally ignoring the judge banging his gavel he continues: **"Yoh', your honor, why don't you ask her to look in a mirror?" "Then she can see for herself and prove my point." "She ain' nothing but stone cold ugly."** The repeated loud noise of judge's gavel finally brings the court back to order. With an expression of total disbelief the judge takes off his glasses and wipes his face and in a loud voice says: **"The court will take a short recess"** and rushes out of the room and returns about five minutes later.

As he re-enters the courtroom he glances at the trooper and notices him fidgeting and covering his mouth with his right hand, fighting back the desire to laugh. The judge's stern look seems to telegraph the message – **"Don't you dare!"** is enough for the trooper to correct his posture and portray a stoic face. Before he sits down, the judge takes another quick glance at the trooper, who could swear that he saw a smirk on the judge's face. Assuming his professional posture, the judge turns to the complainant and defendant and says: **"After thorough analyses of this case it is the court's opinion that the complainant was unable to prove her case beyond a reasonable doubt and, therefore, both cases are dismissed.** Without another glance towards the trooper the judge hurries out of the courtroom and the trooper can't wait to return to his troop.

It's the actual contents that count.

Claiming that there is never enough time, a State Police Admin Lt (Lieutenant) frequently orders a Friday staff meeting during lunch time that habitually carries over the allotted time. Not only does he seem to have little regard for his personnel or their need to accomplish their own job-related affairs, but he also expects them to gulp down their food during the conduct of the meeting. A Sgt's (Sergeant) valid request made two days prior to be excused is outright denied. The Sgt easily detects the Lt's spiteful tone in his voice and decides right then to get even with him the coming meeting.

As usual, when it is his turn to eat, the Sgt quickly unpacks his lunch bag and places the contents on the table in front of him. He then reaches into his pocket takes out his key ring and selects his trusty P-38 ("C" ration can opener and memento of his previous active military service) that he has attached to it and grabs the can of tuna fish. Holding the can in his hand he suddenly freezes. Making sure that all eyes are fixed on him he stares at the label and with deliberate drama utters: **"Oh my God, I can't believe this!" "Man, look at what the damn label says!"** Feigning to be upset, he shakes his head and makes certain that the rest of the staff is able to read the label, he laments: **"I just can't believe this has happened to me." "My wife must**

have accidentally grabbed a can of cat food, thinking it was tuna." Claiming to be too damn hungry, the Sgt takes his P-38, firmly holding the can and opens it.

For a very brief moment everyone is in total shock; all eyes are fixed on him in absolute disbelief and their opened mouths are unable to utter a tone. The Sgt looks at the contents of the opened can and grimaces. Somewhat hesitating, he stabs a chunk of cat food and sticks it in his mouth and starts chewing. The spell-bound silence is suddenly shattered when the Sgt claims that even though the cat food isn't really his taste, but is really not all that bad. Noticing the disgust in their stare, he adds: **"Besides, it hasn't killed my cat yet; so it must be safe to eat."** Holding his hands to his mouth, the Lt abruptly jumps off his chair and runs out of the room. Pretending to be surprised, the Sgt just shrugs his shoulders and continues eating and then realizes that the others have stopped eating and are staring at him in amazement. Finally, one of them manages to speak: **"I can't believe that you are actually eating that shit." "I think that you have lost your mind."** The Sgt replies, mumbling: **"Eh, if you're hungry you do what you have to do." "Hell, I ate "C" rats from WWII and I'm still here."** Burps and wipes his lips. The meeting room door suddenly swings open and the Lt reenters, glares at the Sgt and with a distinct threat in his voice says: **"You are damned lucky that there are no departmental charges for the sick bullshit you just pulled." "This meeting is terminated."** The Sgt is able to keep his other appointment in a timely fashion after all and can't wait until he gets home.

Sitting at the dinner table that evening, the Sgt begins to laugh. His wife looks at him with a puzzled look on her face and asks: **"What's going on?"** Laughing even harder, the Sgt turns to his wife and begins: **"Remember when I very carefully removed the label from the can of cat food and pasted it over the tuna can label?"** Displaying a partial smile, laced with a detectable hint of alarm, she hesitantly asks: **"Oh my God!" "You didn't really do it!" "What happened?"** The Sgt assures her that he is not in trouble and still has a job and then continues.

"Man I got the best of him and even made him barf when he saw the cat food label that I had pasted on the can and started to eat my tuna. He actually ran out of the meeting. Then when he came back into the room, you could see that he was really pissed off at me and told me that the only thing that saved me was the fact that there was nothing in departmental rules that covered the bullshit I pulled. You should have seen the other guys. A couple of them looked like they barely avoided keeping the Lt company. By the way, I also made it to my other appointment on time."

Can a "brotha" get a sandwich?

A young County officer, relatively new on the job, is assigned to relieve another officer on perimeter security; his first homicide scene. When he arrives and walks towards the officer he was sent to relieve, he spots a Sgt (Sergeant) sitting in another patrol vehicle. The Sgt calls him over and informs him that the owner of the nearby sub shop (Well known for delicious food) heard about the homicide on the news and was so kind and had a large box of subs for the officers delivered. When the Sgt feels that the bait has been swallowed, he continues: **"Look, there are quite a few left over and it would be a shame to see them go to waste." "It just wouldn't be right since he brought them over, especially for us." "So why don't you go up to the door and ask the officers inside to give you a sub."** Excited to get a free and delicious Italian sub the young officer hurries up the steps and knocks on the door leading into the crime scene. After repeated knocks the door is opened by an evidence technician dressed in a blood splattered Tyvek suit and wearing goggles and a mask; additional blood smears are noticed on the walls. Smiling and rubbing his hands and too excited with expectation the young officer ignores the blood and asks: **"Can a 'brotha' get a sandwich?"** Totally unexpected, the detective replies: **"Get the f*ck 'outta' here"**, and slams the door in his face. Confused and disappointed the young officer walks back to the Sgt and the officer whom he is to relieve and finds them laughing hysterically; clapping their hands and patting each other on the shoulder. The prank was just too good. For the remainder of the year someone would walk up to him and ask: **"Can a 'brotha' get a sandwich?"**

No help needed.

A male officer and a female officer "Darla" arrive at police HQ, and enter the Turnkey (Police holding facilities.) each with a prisoner in custody. Her prisoner is extremely unruly and acts like a complete ass. Judging from his verbiage he does not appreciate women; especially those with a badge.

"Darla", the female officer, proceeds to take the handcuffs off of her prisoner first. As she does, he yells: **"I'll kick your ass bitch!"** Just as the cuffs come off, the suspect swings at her but misses. A male officer close by and ready to jump in and help her quickly realizes that "Darla" really doesn't need his help. Unfortunately for the suspect, "Darla" is a former power lifter. As the suspect struggles with her she snatches him up by his belt and collar, holds him sideways in the air and tosses him against the wall. "Darla" then calmly tells him: **"Now you can tell all of your friends that you got your ass kicked by a bitch!"** and casually returns to logging him in to the prisoner book!

Pizza robbery.

It is evening and a County officer is dispatched to a local housing development, reference a robbery of a pizza delivery driver. Upon his arrival he is approached by another officer who already has a suspicious suspect in custody. When initially questioned by the officer, the potential suspect denied the robbery or any other involvement and claimed to be in the neighborhood to visit a friend. The new officer who just arrived is especially fond of pizza and has a particularly fetish and washes his hands as soon as he can after eating pizza. Recalling how the aroma of pizza will remain on unwashed hands, he orders the suspect to hold up his hands. The officer grabs the suspect's hands and takes a big sniff and immediately detects the familiar and undeniable scent and tells his buddy: **"He ate the pizza."**

"He is your man." Totally taken by surprise, the suspect holds both of his hands to his nose and takes a big whiff. Still glancing at his fingers, the suspect shrugs his shoulders, lowers his head and says: **"Yeah, I did it."** The following days, officers walking past him say: **"Smell my fingers."**

Check on her wellbeing.

A couple County officers are responding to a welfare complaint. The reporting person, a visiting nurse, claims that she has been unable to make contact at the residence of her 80 plus year old female patient. According to the caller, the woman's car is still in the driveway and the doors to her residence are locked. Upon their arrival the officers check the dwelling and find the interior of the house dark, despite the fact that it is a bright and sunny day. Unable to find an open window or unlocked door, one of them pries open the storm door leading to the kitchen. Once inside they announce, **"Police"** and carefully begin to look around; it is deadly silent and dark. With their weapons drawn they quietly creep through the house. When one of them peeks into a bedroom he observes an old lady on a bed, dressed in a nightgown lying on top of a blanket with her arms folded at peace. The officer carefully walks up closer to inspect the body and when he cannot find any injuries or signs of a struggle yells to his partner:"**Hey, I found her." "She's in here and she's dead."** Suddenly the lady sits up like a vampire in a coffin and says: **"No I'm not."** The officer jumps back in shock and screams and is glad that he didn't shoot her.

Macaroni?

A Local police officer approaches the scene of a "Hit and Run" accident and spots the suspect vehicle abandoned on the side of the road. When he arrives at the scene he notifies Central that the suspects are G.O.A. (Gone on arrival) and that he will be out of his unit to investigate. A check of the interior reveals a bunch of cassette tapes, pom-poms hanging from the window frames and a figurine of the Virgin Mary attached to the top of the dash. Several minutes later he comes back on the radio: **"Unit…to Central, be advised that the possible suspects are Hispanic because I found pom-poms hanging from the windows and a figurine of the Virgin Mary on the dash and a bunch of Macaroni, I mean 'Macarena' cassette tapes on the front seat."** Then another voice (Disguised) crackles: **"Why don't you put some cheese into the trap and catch the rat?"** Suddenly the airwaves erupt with the sound of microphones hitting dashboards. A few moments later another voice with a pretend Spanish accent is heard, **"Gracias senior, de cheeze was mighty good." "Ha, ha, ha."**

A glorious day for a "Motor Head" cop.

Two senior County officers along with a much younger officer visiting the capital city are on a break from training and are enjoying lunch at a nice restaurant in the wild. As they sit there chatting and eating one of the senior officers, an old "Motor Head" looking through the large glass window spies her; moving gracefully through the parking lot. He hasn't seen one in almost thirty years. Oh sure, there have been tales of a carcass here or there in some far flung location but nothing confirmed, and yet, there she was alive. An honest to God, light blue, tagged and RUNNING Yugo! Flabbergasted and excited by the sight, the older officers exclaims: **"Holy Sh*t! A YUGO!"** and points to it as it pulls out of the parking lot. Left dumbfounded by their remarks, the younger officer kills their moment of joy and discovery when he asks: **"What's a Yugo?"** Will they have enough time and attempt trying to explain the mystery of Yugoslavian engineering to him? - Well. ***(They need to call the Smithsonian!)***

Who won?

A State trooper operating an unmarked unit pulls up behind two relatively new "Mustang" cars and cannot believe what he is witnessing when the light changes to green. Suddenly the roar of revved motors and a cloud of smoke explode in the air as both Mustangs peel off from the intersection and fishtail down the highway. After quickly jotting down the tag numbers of both vehicles he chases after them and manages to stop both of them a short distance later. As he approaches the vehicles he is somewhat taken back when he sees that both operators are young females. Neither of the young ladies appears anxious as he approaches them; but instead seem to be waiting for him in anticipation. Cautiously, the trooper walks up to the first car and is immediately greeted by a sheepish looking grin on the drivers' face who blurts: **"Trooper, before you do anything to us we absolutely need to know who won." "That's the reason why we did it in front of you." "We needed someone to judge who would be unbiased." "That's the reason we waited for you." "It was just the perfect opportunity for us to settle an argument."**

The trooper does his utmost to maintain a professional edge and needs a few seconds to regroup his thoughts. Then without mentioning anything about the drag racing he calmly asks for their license and vehicle registration. When he turns to walk back to his cruiser to check their credentials, one of the girls runs after him and has the audacity and asks: **"Well, are you going to tell us who won?"** Picking up the mike, the trooper smiles at her and replies: **"I'll be with you shortly".** In the process of writing the tickets (According to the DMV, both female drivers have a clean record), he notices that the young ladies have gathered at the driver's side door of one of their cars.

Although he knows which of the girls won the "Drag race", he chooses not to tell them and includes it as a part of the punishment and also wipe the smiles off their faces. Maintaining a very professional demeanor says:

> "Well, young ladies since you have waited just for the ideal time and place to conduct your race and have elected me to be your judge; I have decided to oblige you. After taking everything into consideration, I have rendered an unbiased opinion that you asked for. It was too close to call because you forgot to give me advance notice. I, therefore, have decided to reward both of you. Here are the official results that I'm going to ask you to sign for. Holding back a desire to laugh; he hands each of them an arrest ticket for "Speed Exhibition".

The smiles suddenly disappear and are replaced with angry frowns as they reluctantly sign their arrest tickets. Tickets are signed solely as an acknowledgement of having received the ticket. As he walks back to his cruiser, he hears one of them say: **"You really aren't going to tell us who won, are you?" "You could at least tell us that since you arrested us."** He just replies **"Have a nice day ladies". "See you in court."** Turns and walks back to his car.

Just because...

Motorist: **"The only reason you stopped me is because I'm Black!"**

Trooper: **"You don't need to apologize for that." "Because I stopped you because you were speeding."**

"I must have missed that because I was just concentrating clocking the speed of your car."

"I stopped you for speeding." "So I don't know what the color of your skin has to do with it?"

"No, the only color that I am concerned about is the red light that you went through."

"Wow, pulling someone over is harassment?" "Oh wait a minute, but only if the person is Black?"

"Oh gee, wasn't I supposed to do that?"

"Man, I forgot to pick up your special 'Free-bee' again."

Motorist: **"Why does it always have to be Black People you all pick on and never White Folk?"**

Trooper: **"Not always." "Only those who break the law, just like you did by speeding."**
"You mean White Folk break the law also?" "Wow, I have to remember that."

Motorist: **"A Black man just can't get a break from the law."**

Trooper: **"Of course you can, just like everyone else." "Except you just broke the law back there."**

Unusual joyride.

In pursuit of a hijacked bus, State troopers and County officers request assistance from City police officers as the bus enters the city. City police officers responding to the radio call spot the hijacked bus and manage to get behind it as the hijacker fails to negotiate a turn. When the city unit slows down more than a dozen other police units also in the chase come to an abrupt halt; officers exit their patrol cars and commence firing on the bus.

With shots directed towards the bus and bullets flying from every direction, the City officers of the initial stop are left with no other choice but to stay in their vehicle and somehow succeed to squeeze their bodies under the dash of their patrol vehicle to temporarily find shelter. When bullets stop flying they run to the bus with handguns drawn and yank the bus door open.

Expecting to find possible black "PJ" clad terrorists, the officers are shocked to find a mental patient sitting behind the wheel of the bus and two small children holding onto the front seat screaming hysterically. Rather than wait for another volley of gunshots to erupt, the officers scoop up the children and run towards the nearby liquor store for safety. A drunk who fails to move quick enough is pushed out of the way first before they kick open the store door.

Finally everything has died down and relative normalcy is established, it turns out that only police officers exchanged shots. Apparently when officers on the left side of the bus heard shots coming from the right side, their blind side, they returned fire; not knowing that the shots were fired by police officers. Miraculously no one was hurt; just a bus full of bullet holes.

Oh well, no terrorists, just a mental patient who wanted to take a bus for a joyride and two small tikes happy to be reunited with their parents. Is there enough room for two cops to squeeze under the dashboard of today's cruisers? ***(Just an afterthought.)***

Do you want your pen back?

A State trooper clocking (measuring) the speed of a vehicle ahead of him; at a speed of 15 plus miles over the posted speed limit is sufficient to warrant an arrest. He activates his lights and siren, indicating for the operator to pull over and the vehicle pulls over and stops on the shoulder. The trooper walks up to the driver's side, introduces himself and states the reason why the driver has been stopped. In a polite but firm manner he asks the driver for her license and vehicle registration and then tells the lady to stand by and that he will be right back. When finished writing the ticket he walks back to her car and informs her that she is being charged for speeding and asks her to sign the arrest ticket and hands her a pen. The operator's signature is not an admittance of guilt, it verifies that the operator understands the charges and acknowledges the receipt of the ticket. When the female is finished signing the ticket, she smiles at him and proceeds to lift her dress and stick the pen between her thighs. With a big smile on her face she looks at him and asks: **"Do you want your pen back?" "If you do, you have to reach and get it."** Although dumbfounded he smiles at her and calmly replies: **"Looks like you got a new pen." "Well, you can just tell the proctologist, when you see him, that he can keep my pen." "Here is a copy of your ticket." "It's a good thing though that you signed it before you had your unfortunate accident with my pen." "I hope that you are not too uncomfortable."** Before he drives off he reaches into his shirt pocket and takes out another pen.

Talk about a fish story…

A Local police officer calls off sick; he wants to enjoy the wonderful day and go fishing. After numerous failed attempts the angler cop casts his lines into a deep spot of the creek. Suddenly his hook snags onto something pretty big. Excited that he may have hooked a trophy fish he carefully starts reeling it in. Afraid that his line may snap he stops pulling, adjusts his waders and slowly inches forward.

He grabs the line and slides his thumb and index finger towards whatever it is the hook is stuck on. Since nothing is flipping or flopping he realized that the large object can't be a trophy fish, he is only able to make out a cast off shirt caught on some sort of tree stump. As he attempts to remove the hook from the garment he finds it extremely odd that the tree stump feels sort of soft and squishy and almost faints.

Horror struck he drops his rod and reel and at the moment doesn't know whether to puke or scream but doesn't dare to do either. After all, he is a hard-core cop and only civilians do that. All he knows is that he needs to get out of the water fast and back to his car. It isn't until he reaches his car and begins removing his waders that he notices he is standing in ankle deep water.

The gas station attendant watches in amazement as the man barges through the door and is leaving wet footprints on the pavement. Holding up a police officer's badge the highly excited man demands to use the telephone. *(Cell phones do not exist yet.)* Unable to utter a sound the attendant merely points to the office door and then hears it slam shut. A short time later a marked police unit arrives at the gas station. On their way out of the door the attendant hears the still somewhat ruffled wet-footed officer practically scream: **"Yes, I hooked a dead body with my fishing line." "Of course I knew it was too big for a fish."**

The question remains should the officer be punished for playing hooky or be paid for working overtime? Regardless, he definitely has the fish story of the year and the fish that he wishes had gotten away.

Is that you George?

A County patrolman relatively new on the job responds to a "Breach of Peace" complaint at a local apartment complex. The complainant alleges that he has broken up with his lady friend and wants her out of his apartment.

The officer is momentarily left totally speechless by what appears when the door opens. There, right in front of him, stands a spitting image of George Jefferson from the TV show "The Jeffersons"; even in stature. A man about 5'04" tall and weighing approximately 100 lbs greets him and says: **"Sir, I just want this woman out of my house and fast!"**

When the officer enters the apartment he is surprised for a second time. Standing in the living room, calmly folding her clothes and placing them in a suitcase, is a woman weighing about 350 lbs; that is being **very** conservative. Now that the officer is present, the "little man" suddenly becomes brave and tries to provoke the woman by calling her every filthy name in the book; cunt, tramp, whore and slut just to name a few. Hoping to prevent the tense situation from escalating, the officer says: **"Why don't you stay quiet and let her finish?"** The officer is genuinely shocked by the woman's amazing ability to just blow off the filthy insults and in particular when she says: **"That don't confront me none!"**

The gentleman then slowly saunters over towards the patrolman and yells: **"Bitch!"** She instantly stops what she is doing and yelling, like a wounded animal, charges at the man. In obvious fear for his safety the man jumps behind the officer. Afraid of being trampled by the 350 plus pounds fireball the little 100 lbs "Smartass" cowers behind the officer. Puzzled by what just happened, the officer thinks: ***"Of all the horrible things he called her, and 'Bitch' is the one that set her off?"***

(Go figure...good times.)

"Sew this SOB up!"

A State trooper assigned to investigate a personal injury accident arrives at the ER to interview the injured driver. As he enters the front door a man, the apparent injured driver, attempts to force his way out. Realizing that the trooper will attempt to stop him, he runs full force against him and head-butts him. After a few rounds tussling on the floor the trooper manages to subdue the subject and cuff him. Totally ignoring the doctor's request to have the laceration to his head treated, the injured driver refuses treatment and continues to struggle and verbally insults the hospital staff. Rather than allow a possible stand-off to develop the trooper takes quick unusual but necessary action, swiftly grabs the suspect and drags him back to the operating room and throws him on the gurney and then orders the ER personnel to strap him down. While the doctor and nurses are busy he ties a sheet around the handcuffs and then around the bar at the foot of the gurney; securing the suspect's hands. When the combative driver is finally securely strapped down and no longer able to resist the trooper tells the doctor: **"Sew this 'Son of a Bitch' up."** Smiling back at him the doctor replies: **"Yes sir!"** Blocking out the screams, the doctor begins with deft precision.

In addition to a traffic violation the suspect is also arrested for resisting arrest.

Just another day on patrol. #5

How come no one is an upstanding member of the community until after they get shot in a drug deal? Then they are a pillar of it.

Subject: **"Officer, how can I be guilty?" "I called the police first!"**

Subject: **"Why are you towing my car?"**

Officer: **"Because you are revoked and the registration on your car is expired."**

Subject: **"How can I get home in the rain?"**

Officer: **"I'm towing your car, not your feet, and I'm not Yellow Cab."**
("Smartass, another service I provide free of charge.")

Officer: **"Sir, how do you spell your name?"**

Subject: **"I don't know officer; my mom done gave it to me."** *(Yeah, the future looks bright ahead..)*

Subject: **"Officer, just because you're taking me to prison doesn't mean you have to cuff me like an animal."** ***(Say what?)***

When you get pulled over for driving revoked and no insurance, the correct response should **NOT** be: ***"Don't you cops have anything better to do?"***

Officer: **"Ok, let me get this straight." "You saw 8 people wearing masks and dressed in black, creeping through your neighbor's yard carrying spray paint AND you didn't think that was suspicious???"** ***(Oh Mr. Darwin----a little help please!)***

How much snow?

It started snowing during night and is still snowing. According to the latest weather report, well over a foot is expected. Nothing was stirring, not even on the major highways; except at the State Police Troop. The D/Sgt (Desk Sergeant) has already responded to countless phone calls, answering basically the same question each time. When he hears the phone ring again he huffs and mutters: ***"What makes these people think I'm the damn weather bureau?" "I wasn't trained to be a meteorologist, I'm a trained trooper." "Maybe these idiots think that I am better at guessing than the weatherman."*** The D/Sgt picks up the phone and the same basic question is asked again. **"Can you tell me how the roads are and how many inches of snow we're going to get?"** This is absolutely the last straw for him and in a very professional tone responds: **"Still and clear." "Still snowing and clear up to your ass."** When he hears a click on the other end he hangs up. It continued snowing for the rest of the day.

Stay there...

Daylight is fading and a couple on their way home spot something in the water as they pass a small lake. When they get closer to inspect, they are horrified to see a car slowly sinking and realize that the accident just happened. Note: *(It was a time before the cell phone.)* They have no other choice but to drive to the nearest State Police Troop to report the accident. As they prepare to leave the scene, the passenger suddenly screams: **"Oh my God, I think there is someone coming out of that car"**. Then both of them see a man struggling and climb on top of the submerged car.

Realizing that neither of them is in a position to help him they holler: **"Stay where you are and don't get off the car!" "We are going to get help."** When they receive a slurred and somewhat incoherent reply, they know that they need to hurry before the unfortunate victim decides to swim to shore.

The local Town police officer sent to the scene arrives at the lake but can't find the subject. It never seems to fail there is always a nosy onlooker intent on asking stupid questions. **"Yeah offica', what'ya' all lookin' fer'?" "Somun' takin' a late night swim or sumptn'?" "Ya' all need some help to find em'?"** Before replying, the officer gives him a stern look and makes sure that he doesn't see any water dripping off him.

When he is certain that it's not the same man he is looking for says: **"Nah', unfortunately I can't find him and don't know where he is." "I tell you what though." "Can I borrow a bottle of your favorite wine?" "Boones Farm."** Frowning at the officer, the drunk asks: **"What ya' need dat' fer'?" "What ya' goin' to do wit' it?" "Ya' ain't allowed to drink no how' wit' dat' uniform on."** Holding in his desire to laugh the officer replies: **"Well since I can't find him I was going to stick the bottle of wine at the edge here and flush him out." "It's like putting some bait on the hook." "Don't you do something like that when you want to catch a fish?"** Staring at the officer and momentarily lost for words, the flabbergasted drunk finally says: **"Ya' might have a point dare' an' all dat' but I still aint' givn' ya' none of my stuff here." "Ya'll' gotta' git your alls' own bait for dat'."**

An hour or so later the Town officer responds to the frantic call of a woman reporting a black man sleeping on her chaise lounge in her back yard. After a brief struggle the officer manages to cuff the belligerent drunk and transport him to the hospital to make sure that he isn't injured. Because his crumpled up wet clothing had been stuck in a plastic bag the doctor allows the trespasser to keep the hospital gown on and says to the officer: **"Other than being drunk and bare assed he is all right and you can have him back." "Since he already took a bath and is all dry you can tuck him in at your hotel."** The officer manages to get a blanked for his new lodger to cover his bare essentials and returns it to the hospital the next day.

I want to file a complaint!

Responding to the request for assistance by a local small City police department, the State Police "Quick Response" team arrives at the scene. The team is immediately confronted by a large group of black people causing a major disturbance at a private pool party. Led by a very level-headed and capable lieutenant the unit succeeds in quickly deescalating the situation and prevent possible racial violence. Despite numerous attempts by several loudmouths to incite the group, team members maintain their professional composure. While clicking handcuffs on him the protester yells that he wasn't even trying to get locked up, the State trooper calmly replies: **"Well, you shouldn't have tried so hard".**

When things have returned to normal and only a few arrests have been made, the team returns to the marshalling area for an AAR (After Action Report) and an assessment of how the situation was handled. During the discussion with his men, the LT (Lieutenant) is interrupted by one of his black team members: **"Hey LT, I want to lodge a protest against Trooper ….."** Obviously caught off guard by the black trooper's remark, the LT gives him a concerned look and carefully asks: **"What is wrong?" "What the Hell happened?" "What are you complaining about?"** The still angry black trooper replies:

> "I just don't think its right what happened here. As you can see (pointing at himself), I'm a pretty good looking guy and pretty jacked. But guess what? All dem' black chicks dare' *(deliberately talking in a guttural manner)* don' see me. Nah! All day' see is that white dude over dare; pointing at a white trooper. Man, what de Hell is

> wrong wit' dem'. Day done acted like I wasn' even dare'. I guts' to admit dough' he ain't bad looking either. Even dough' he don't got dat' pretty tan like mines. An' I have ta' admit, he jacked pretty good too. But day' pose' to look at me not at him! Man, I'm one of da' brothas' an' he white."

Relieved that it was said in absolute fun and extremely pleased with how well his men get along; like a finely tuned machine, the LT replies:

> "You should look at it realistically. Not all people who eat steak like to have it prepared the same way. Some like to have it well done, nice and brown through and through. Then there are those who prefer to have it cooked medium or even tartar. I personally met a waiter in one of those fancy steak houses where you can cook your own steak who absolutely abhors a steak cooked well done. He actually berated me for cooking mine too long. In his mind it drains the juices and ruins the flavor. Maybe those chicks thought that a lighter prepared steak is juicier and know something that we men don't know."

Like being spellbound, the black trooper looks at the LT and then slowly turns and looks at his team member and says: **"With all due respect LT, you not only look pretty good yourself, but you are even crazier than I am."** Everybody then looses it and give each other "high fives; a definite sign of excellent leadership and true camaraderie.

Mobile mayhem. (In the officer's own words.)

It is just another morning, another shift, another cup of DD coffee for the small Town police department Sgt sitting in his "office" looking at the marvel of modern police technology, the police radio. How it has become a double edged sword that is both a gift and a curse to every LEO (Law Enforcement Officer) from the time of its creation. He admires the mobile unit bolted beneath the dash of his cruiser and sits in awe of its 50+ channels, digital-cell signal and for the most part, the crystal clarity of its dispatch. His mind goes back in time and thinks - we sure have come a long way. Now the only thing that may happen is the system may crash or the signal may go "digital" for a second.

There was a period however when this was not so, traveling back in the "Time Machine". To a time when Police Mobile Communication equipment was not quite up to the standards that it is now. Back then the radios were equipped for 12 channels although not all were installed and your portable was also your mobile unit. I even remember old-timers telling me of radios with only two channels, high and low and no mobile phone. Before the handset they had a regular telephone receiver attached to a twelve inch spiral electric chord cradled on a rubber half-cup mounted to the lower dash of the patrol car. Once you stepped out of your car, you were on your own. Computers were still a thing in the distant future. When you got in or out of your squad car, you pulled the portable off of your duty belt and pushed it into the mobile unit. There is a vast difference between "Idiot Proof" and "Cop Proof" and it wasn't unusual for some of us "trained monkeys" to slam the portables into the mobile unit with such force that they blew through the bottom of the unit! There is actually a reason they call it '**SOFTWARE**'.

The new officers will never know the joy of working in a Radio Free area where you could be in the parking lot of an apartment complex and not pick up your sector partner's signal on the 2nd floor of a nearby building, yet you would be able to hear a unit in 25 miles away with crystal clarity. You could always rest assured that on night shift if you called for help the signal would be a garbled mass of white noise. However, if you chose to speak ill of your Sergeant during a car to car meet and your knee inadvertently pressed the mike button you could rest assured that you calling him a "Cigarette smoking, coffee drinking, non-investigating Mo----ker", would go out over the airwaves with a clarity that would make Marconi himself smile! That's why I learned on FTO when you are car to car the mike got draped over the rear view mirror.

I will not forget the bleed over from other agencies. I remember one night everyone overheard a pursuit on Main Ave. with the same call sign as one of our Southern Patrol Units) unbeknown to us, a Washington DC police unit using the same call sign was in pursuit on Delaware Ave....In D.C.! It took a few minutes for everyone to discover that an SPU unit was not 20 miles out of its sector! And of course not to be outdone..the charming strains of hearing Tuna trawlers in the Gulf Of Mexico yelling: **"Tuna, Tuna, Tuna!"** Then drop their nets! I also remember a retired trooper telling me that when he was on patrol one midnight shift he freely conversed with another trooper for 15 minutes; a Louisiana State trooper..in Louisiana!!!" Yup General Electric you sure brought some good things to life. I also have a photograph of one of the old General Electric Mobile/Portable units...I'm sure they aren't missing it by now.

Oh, the good old past. (In his own words.)

Perhaps all of us remember our firsts; first love, first job etc. Usually seconds not so much. For those old enough may not even remember the second guy to walk on the Moon? It is highly unlikely that a police officer does not remember even the intricate details of his/her first day on the job as a lawman and wakes up earlier than usual. Hell, who are we kidding? Most new appointees are hardly able to sleep the night before. They are too excited and can't wait to get dressed in their uniform, strap on their gun belt and proceeded to drive to work. No "Take-Home" cars in those days, so they have to drive their own. For many, driving felt kind of surreal driving a jacked-up, mag-wheeled 1970 Chevelle SS while in full police uniform! Of course for the old-timers it was the mid 60's and early 70's; when the 440 Plymouth ruled the roost. Many of the old police stations and Troops were converted residences, old school buildings or other public buildings that were full of Asbestos, lead paint and mold which may possibly explain the mental attitudes of some of the officers. The new buildings gradually took on the appearances of police stations; some of them even resembled palatial looking structures. Some people went so far as to call the predecessors "shitholes" but those who worked within these abodes lovingly referred to them as having "character".

Anyway, it is 0655hrs and the new police officer walks up to the "Roll Call" room door and does a quick once over of his uniform, checks the gig line, tie bar etc.; first impressions and all. With sweaty hands and a racing heart pulls the door handle and enters. That must have been how Dante felt when he entered Purgatory. As the "Newbe" enters the room his/her senses are overcome by a strong mixture of aromas, coffee and tobacco smoke. In the rear a few old salty Corporals are typing reports, on ACTUAL TYPEWRITERS; some even manual. When there were not enough typewriters available, seniority ruled who was first. The new member notices that no one in the room looks less than fifteen years older than him and ALL have revolvers on. Probably 95% of those in the room are smoking; cigarettes, cigars and a few lighting up pipes. The cloud of smoke in the air was so thick that it would do London Fog proud. Since the "Newbe" is not expected to have anything to report when roll call begins he/she just sits there and watches vet officer correcting reports. He reached into his Speed-loader pouch on his gun belt and withdraws a bottle of "Whiteout" (Correction medicine for typing mistakes). Whiteout in those days was like gold. There were three things that an officer never left lying around; Cross pens, Whiteout and any issue gear. All were fair game for the finders. A wallet could lay there and gather dust...but the other three? Forget it! As roll call progresses, the newcomer is introduced as the "Rookie" and is asked to stand up and tell a little about himself. Somewhat panic struck the "Rookie's" thoughts race through his mind. ***"What do I say?" "How do I say it?' "How long should I talk?"*** Before he even has a chance to utter a word, a sea of voices yells in unison: **"Sit down!" "No one gives a F*CK what you have to say!"** Followed by laughter throughout the room! At last the agony of roll call has ended and he and his FTO go to the House Sgt. to be assigned a car. Since none are available they end up waiting 45 minutes for a squad car. Then, there she was, a Dodge Diplomat with only 136,000 miles on her and no AM/FM radio. The Rookie doesn't care, another first...his first time in an active squad car as a sworn lawman. So that was day one; as he takes another drink from his coffee cup.

I'm special.

A County police officer operating Radar on the side of the road is talking to his police retiree "ride along" when a car passes by their position. Although the vehicle wasn't speeding, they observe that the entire rear of the car is lit up with light blue lights. It literally looks like the "Millennium Falcon" hitting light speed.

The County officer pulls the car over and approaches the driver and asks him for his license and vehicle registration. Slightly frowning, the driver asks: **"I wasn't speeding, was I?"** In a calm and polite manner the officer replies: **"No sir, however, all those blue lights you have on the rear of your vehicle are illegal by state law."**

With a sarcastic tone and a disgusted look on his face the operator replies: **"Wow! You must be slow!"** Being somewhat of a smartass himself, the officer can't pass up the opportunity. Without thinking the officer spontaneously replies in a retarded voice: **"My mom says to me all the time that I'm special."** Then he catches himself. He did really well until he looks at his ride along and sees him double over laughing trying to walk back to the squad car.

I have to work late again.

The wife of a police detective, seriously questioning her husband's excuses of having to work late, has her suspicions verified by reliable sources and decides to get even. To discuss a possible strategy she engages the help of her best friend who lives only a couple of houses down from her. A few days later the detective is working the late shift again and his wife waits.

The tension increases when she picks up the receiver on the third ring and hears the expected excuse: **"I'm sorry but I will probably be late and there is no need for you to wait up for me."** She tells him that she is sorry to hear that he has to work late again and immediately springs into action and calls her girlfriends. Moments later she hurriedly drives her girlfriend's car to the police station and arrives just in time to see her husband pulling out of the parking lot. Recalling what she has seen on police shows she follows him at a safe distance and observes her husband enter the parking lot of a shopping center and park next to another car. Moments later a female exits the other vehicle and jumps into the passenger side of his. After exchanging a few kisses her husband's car exits the parking lot. A few blocks later she spots her husband's car enter another shopping center, douse the lights and slowly drive into the loading area behind the stores.

Figuring that she has given the couple enough time to be fully engaged in their clandestine tryst she quietly climbs out of her car and stealthily approaches her husband's car. When the couple is too busy in the back seat and oblivious to anything else, she slithers under the car and anxiously waits. When she detects the slight rhythmic rocking of the car she jabs the ice pick several times into the side of both rear tires and crawls back out from under the car and sneaks back to hers.

Daylight has not broken yet when she hears her husband come up the stairs. Pretending to have just been awakened she pleasantly asks: **"Oh honey, I bet you're beat." "I think that's the longest you've ever had stay over."** Almost grunting at her he replies: **"Yeah it was a night from Hell." "I need to borrow your car first thing in the morning because I have to go to the garage."** She could swear that he was giving her the "evil eye". Feigning concern she asks: **"What's wrong with your car dear?" "Did you have an accident, or something?"** Practically snapping at her he says: **"Just let me have the damn keys!" "Will ya'?"**

When her husband returns he mutters: **"The guy at the garage said he'll have someone bring my car here after it is fixed"** and throws her car keys on the kitchen counter. Pretending to show pity, she gently asks: **"What is wrong with your car?" "What happened?" "Are you alright?"** Just staring at her momentarily, he finally replies: **"The whole damn deal cost me a pair of new tires."** Fearing that any further questioning might expose her, she merely replies: **"The main thing is that you are all right." "You look beat." "You ought to go back to bed and try to get some sleep."** It wasn't too long before the story is the talk of the garage and quickly spreading. Several weeks later the self-trained detective files for divorce from her husband who also learns what really happened that night.

It should be noted that it was a time before cell phones. When her husband and his girlfriend had finished their amorous encounter and he was ready to drive his clandestine partner back to her car he discovered that he had mysteriously developed two flat rear tires. Since neither had the means to readily communicate with anyone, they had no other choice but to walk a considerable distance back to her car. Then his girlfriend had to transport him back to the police station where he was finally able to make arrangements to have his car towed to the garage. One of his fellow police officers brought him home in the early morning hours. It is highly likely that the husband suspected that his wife was behind the whole incident from the beginning.

Well, it's Halloween.

Only on Halloween are we allowed to grant certain "mistakes". You know, the one where you tell a guy: **"Wow!, you really captured the look of Sigmund Freud!" "Great costume!"** Only to find out that it's not a costume and he's a hipster walking his kids around for Halloween. **"My bad sir, my bad."** In the officer's defense, he was wearing a plaid a sport coat, black horn rims and wearing a bow tie while sporting a goatee!!

Just a friendly observation.

> "Now ma'am, I'm just a simple lawman, not an interior decorator but the Lord did bless me with a pretty good sense of decorum. I'm going to say that a 65inch flat-screen TV throws off the Feng Shui of your mobile home, not to mention the tipping hazard it presents.

> Putting a mobile home back on cinder blocks can be a real bitch. However I was aghast in wonder, much akin to the first time my dad took me to a particular cinema and I saw that wondrous two story movie screen... thank you ma'am for the flashback....oh and the possible radiation damage!"

At the shooting range.

It's yearly qualification time and a group of City officers assembled on line is waiting for instructions from the range officer. When the order to "Commence fire!" is given, a volley of gunfire erupts. Suddenly a Sgt (Sergeant) down the line screams in agony and falls to his knees. Shooting seizes immediately and all the officers put their guns on safe and rush to the Sgt's aid. A few seconds later the worried looks turned to grins and then vocalized with chuckles. Some of the shooters drop to their knees and join the Sgt scouring the range floor for greenish looking pieces of paper.

It turns out that the Sgt had a $100 bill hidden in the barrel of his revolver; the only place his wife never checks. The bill was now confetti on the range. Fortunately the Evidence Detection Unit was kind enough to assist and actually recovered enough for the Sgt to be able to have the bank give him a new one. Yes, he was indeed very lucky that the barrel of his revolver didn't split.

The accent apparently did it.

Thinking back to a St. Patrick's Day long ago when the officer was working 3x11 in a rather run-down neighborhood that encompassed his patrol area and was dispatched to respond to a fight in the roadway. When he arrived on the scene he saw several locals arguing and getting ready to fight. Instead of immediately confronting the subjects he decided to put some levity into the situation, picked up the mike and in his cheesiest Irish accent stated: **"I have arrived at**

the scene and have a bit of a donnybrook in the street!" (Maybe Central thought that they had a rookie Irishman?)

What blood test?

A driver in Germany, suspected of being intoxicated is brought to the local City police station. In order for the police officers to justify an arrest for DUI (Driving under the Influence), they request a blood test and call the local hospital. The hospital receptionist regrettably tells the officer that the regular phlebotomist is on vacation but that she will make an effort to get a hold of someone to draw blood. A short time later the hospital reports back and advises the officer that she has found a doctor who just returned from his dinner is willing to respond to the station. She tells the officer, that although the doctor is not familiar with the police procedure; he assured her that he is certainly able to draw blood.

When the doctor arrives at the station the officers notice that he is quite fidgety and consider it somewhat odd for a doctor to be so nervous for simply drawing blood. Overlooking the doctor's slight speech impediment and keeping with professional courtesy they guide him to the suspected drunk driver. While in the process of giving the doctor detailed instructions of what is needed and standing closer to him, the officers find the sudden rise in odor of an alcoholic beverage rather peculiar. Satisfied that the doctor is able to administer the test, one of the officers tells the suspect to roll up one of his shirt sleeves and hands the doctor his leather case.

The doctor slowly binds a small rubber band around the suspect's arm; then gropes through his case. After considerable deliberation he finds a needle and removes the plastic tip. Apparently ready to inject the needle, the doctor grabs the suspect's arm and for a fleeting moment appears to stare at the needle as if in a trance and collapses and falls to the floor. Panic-stricken, both officers immediately rush to his aid. As one of the officer quickly drops to his knees to administer first aid by giving the prone doctor mouth to mouth resuscitation, the other positions himself to give chest compressions. Several other officers present at the station run in to possibly help.

Prepared to give the doctor the first life saving breath, the kneeling officer rears back with a repulsive look on his face and yells: **"The disgusting 'Schwein' is drunk." "No wonder he was so damned frazzled." "He is drunker than the guy we brought in."** The other officer replies: **"It would be kinda' difficult to arrest him." "How is he going to take his own blood test?" "Na', that would be self incrimination." "Since he got here on his own and is ready to walk out of here, there is no need to call for an ambulance." "Don't forget, we invited him to come here." "It would only be fit and proper to find suitable accommodations for him." "He can boast about his success story to the hospital administrator tomorrow and explain why he decided to stay at our fine hotel."**

The laughter of the group dies down when they notice the suspect whose blood was to have been drawn by the doctor staring at them. Wide-eyed and appearing to be somewhat sobered up he stammers:**"Man, what's going on here?" "What are you going to do to me?" "I didn't do anything."** Grinning from ear to ear, one of the arresting officers walks over to him and pats him on the shoulder and says: **"Look that was just a test case to show you what can happen to you the next time you drink too much and then drive."** Totally confused, the suspect asks: **"What do you mean by test case?"** The officer replies: **"God only knows where the doctor is going to stick a needle the next time." "Man, you were indeed lucky." "Don't you think so too?" "So as a reward we will allow you to use our phone; free of charge." "You may call your home to have someone pick you up; or a taxi if you have the money." "You just can't drive tonight." "In other words, you're free to go."**

Wonders never cease.

When driving down the highway the officer sees it. There in the wild, genuine and alive..in all its prehistoric greatness. He remembers seeing them when he was a rookie cop, mostly on their side in a ditch or upside down on their back like a turtle. He thought that they were all gone by now. Sure, now and then a story would surface that one had been seen but they were all unconfirmed rumors, urban legends if you will. But there she was; witnessed by the eyes of a trained observer. She was traveling down the interstate without a care, the world was her oyster. The veritable "Bigfoot" of the auto world....a genuine mint green, 1980's, Suzuki Samurai!!! All that the driver needed to make it complete was a mullet.

You better safe some of that.

A contingency of State troopers, assigned to assist the City police curtail the violence of a large group of demonstrators, is ordered to secure and protect a sensitive area close by. Since it is crucial that the police cordon stands firm, the majority of them assigned to the front line have prior active duty military police experience. It becomes quickly apparent to the unruly crowd that their extremely verbal insults, threats and menacing gestures do not seem to intimidate the troopers; who resemble a wall of robots. Maintaining a stern and very professional posture they visually reconnoiter the crowd hoping to defuse any potential danger before it has a chance to explode; as the atmosphere grows tense and louder. They are somewhat puzzled when the momentum seems to slow down; definitely a time to be on the qui vive.

As a path in the front ranks of the crowd slightly splits open, they immediately recognize the man squeezing his way to the front. For some unknown reason the well-known activist fixes his hateful gaze on one particular trooper and then walks up close to him. When the display of his arrogance towards the trooper still fails to dislodge him, the scum ball starts hacking, snorting and coughing in an obvious attempt to get a sufficient mouthful of sputum; raising the anger of some in the crowd to a fever pitch. Then, while intensely glaring at the trooper, the creep stands in front of him and gets ready to deliver the grotesque salvo into the trooper's face. Without showing an inkling of emotion, the trooper gives him a dangerously stern look and in an even tone says: **"You better save some of that in your**

mouth to help you swallow your teeth that I'm going to knock down your throat."

Shocked by the trooper's ability to maintain control of what could have been a very explosive situation, the well-known activist turns and disappears into the crowd. Gradually some in the group of demonstrators thin out and join another segment still going strong. Although tension remains high, no one dares to take a chance and encroach on the state Praetorian guard.

I wonder how much this is going to hurt.

A couple of County police officers ordered to execute an arrest warrant arrive at the house of the suspect. Prior to their arrival the senior officer who is very familiar with the suspect volatile behavior advises his partner, fairly new on the job, that it is very likely that the suspect will not go peacefully. Apparently having spotted the marked patrol unit pull in front of his house, the suspect meets them at the front door and snarls: **"What the f*ck are you doing here?" "Get the f*ck off my damn property!"** Without even giving the officers an opportunity to explain why they came, the suspect continues to unleash his foul verbal barrage of insults on them.

Expecting a violent attack at any moment, the junior officer grabs a tight grip on his night stick; ready to strike. When he glances at his senior partner he notices that he doesn't even bother looking at the suspect but is instead squinting at his large mile light (Large metal cased flashlight) and caressing it. Although the senior officer appears to be very calm, the junior officer is getting concerned about his partner's inaction. Even the suspect stops his rant when he also sees the senior officer stroking his flashlight and tapping it against the palm of his left hand. After a few tense moments of total silence he looks at the suspect and still tapping his flashlight says: **"I wonder how much this is going to hurt when I plant this flashlight between your f*cking eyes?"** Obviously totally shocked and seemingly lost for words for a second or so, the suspect slowly turns around and meekly mutters: **"OK, put'm" on me."** A couple of clicks are heard and then the patrol car heads for jail.

A flight without wings.

It is a rather windy day that could victimize things not tied down securely when the officer experiences a rare treat. What he sees reminds him how Marlon Perkins must have felt on Mutual of Omaha's Wild Kingdom. As he patrols the roadway of the sparsely populated area, he spies her. Gracefully galloping across an open cornfield for several hundred feet; desperately trying to lift her 15ft diameter brown and black bulk into the heavens. Lifting her elegantly10 to 15 feet into the air several times it arches across the roadway and flashes past his cruiser; only to come to an ungainly thud into the adjacent shrubbery. ***(The rarely seen and exotic St. Georges Flying Trampoline.)***

Turkey Drive.

It's that time of year again when, as usual, some of the State troopers volunteer to participate in the yearly Thanksgiving "Turkey Drive"; collecting food for needy families. A group of three troopers is assigned to solicit in a specific district and then drop the donations off at the high school located in that district. Prior to starting the day trooper "Paul" asks trooper "Mike" to play along with him and play a joke on trooper "Ed".

Trooper "Paul" who decided to drive his personal vehicle pulls up to a pump at a local gas station. He tells trooper "Mike" to give him the mileage of his car because he was going to use the State Police credit card instead of his own. In reality he was using his personal credit card. Trooper "Ed" immediately protests and stammers that he cannot be a part of any unethical situation and sticks his fingers in his ears to avoid hearing trooper "Mike" giving trooper "Paul" the mileage.

Sometime later the president of the State Trooper Association calls and tells trooper" Paul" that the Assoc. will donate six frozen turkeys for the "Turkey Drive". When the turkeys are picket up trooper "Paul" hands one to trooper "Mike" and places one in the back of his pick truck for himself. He then asks trooper "Ed" if would like one also. At this point trooper "Ed" can't take it anymore and yells at trooper "Paul": **"This is crazy." "You can't do this!" "I want no part of it." "You should also put yours back."** Before they drive to the high school to drop off the donations, trooper "Paul" grabs a bag of canned vegetables and hands it to trooper "Mike" and keeps one for himself. Both of them are barely able to hold back their laugh as they watch trooper "Ed" shaking his head and the displeasure on his face.

When the three of them arrive at the high school, trooper "Ed" immediately rushes over to trooper "David", the collection agent, and tells him what the two other troopers are doing. Out of trooper "Ed's" earshot trooper "David" says to the accused troopers: **"I know that you two are screwing with him." "But he claims that both of you took a bag of canned food and a turkey each."** The two alleged culprits smile and hand trooper "David" all of the cans, including the six turkeys. Trooper "David", now in on the gag, tells trooper "Ed" to report what has transpired to the Troop Commander. Prior to arriving at the troop, trooper "Paul" contacts the captain and fills him in on what is going on and also asks him to play along. The captain agrees.

As soon as the three enter the troop, trooper "Ed" reports to the captain and tells him that he personally witnessed some unethical and inappropriate acts committed by trooper "Paul" and trooper "Mike" and gives a detailed account. Maintaining a serious composure, the captain orders troopers "Paul" and "Mike" into his office and asks trooper "Paul": **"What went on out there today?"** Still able to keep a smile off his face, trooper "Paul" replies: **"Captain, I admit that I put gas in my pickup truck and billed the State Police." "I also admit trooper Mike and I took some canned food and a frozen turkey each."** The captain jumps up from his chair and says: **"What did I tell you guys?" "I said, take only canned food." "NO TURKEYS!"** Pretending to be on the defense, trooper "Paul" responds: **"Well captain, the gas**

and canned food was my idea; as usual." "But the turkeys were trooper Ed's idea."

Trooper "Ed" jumps up, wraps his hands around his red face and explodes: **"I can't take this."** Preempting a possible serious tirade, the captain quickly intervenes and says: **"'Ed', it's just a joke." "They didn't take anything." "I would never authorize unethical behavior."** Trooper "Ed" gives all of them a disgusted look, turns around and storms out of the office. The pranksters decide that it is prudent to leave trooper "Ed" alone for a few days.

The voices told me.

A suspect, interviewed by a Det. (Detective) at the State Police Troop, replies: **"Look you don't understand!" "I can't be really guilty because the voices in my head ordered me to do so."** Suddenly the Det. flashes his left palm in front of the suspect's face and says: **"Hold it!" "Hold it!"** Frowning, he presses his right index finger against his lips indicating for the suspect to be quiet and then appears to become deeply engrossed into listening to something. A faint **"Hmm"** and **"Well, I'll try"** mumbled by the Det. finally breaks the silence when he says:

> "Wow what an experience. I just had voices telling me the whole story. It seems as though your voices and my voices talked to each other. An intelligent man like you may possibly understands the reason why we can't hear them. They probably communicate at a much higher Audio frequency than when they talk to us. That must be the case because you are the only one who can hear your voices and I'm the only one who can hear mine. Since we now know what's what, why don't you just clear your mind and tell me the truth? Remember, your voices told mine that you should tell the truth."

Staring at the Det. in amazement the suspect asks: **"You actually heard voices?"** The Det., still keeping a straight face replies: **"I was shocked when I heard voices telling me that your voices told them to**

have you tell me the truth." "That's the first time in my life I ever heard voices talking to me." "Well, what do you say?"

Left totally puzzled the suspects agrees to tell the truth.

Where are you?

Several State troopers sent to execute a warrant on a dangerous individual are met by a group of protesters attempting to block the entry to the property; yelling: **"False arrest"**. Recognizing the gravity of the situation the troopers know that they must act fast to avoid a potential serious takedown. A couple of them gather around one of the cruisers and quickly discuss a plan of action. Solely as a show of force, the senior trooper opens the trunk of his cruiser and removes his shotgun; he knows that the safety is on. He closes the lid and places the gun on the trunk; suddenly a loud "boom".

Shocked, the trooper calls for his buddy who had been standing next to him and is panic struck when he can't find him. Thinking that he has shot and possibly killed him, he is relieved when he sees his friend slowly getting up from behind the cruiser; without a trace of blood on him. Busy brushing off his uniform his buddy stammers: **"Who the Hell is shooting at us?" "Man when I heard that shot I dove for cover and grabbed my weapon." "Then when I heard you calling out my name, I knew everything was all right." "What the hell happened?"** Totally flabbergasted, the senior trooper replies:

> "I don't know. I just laid my shotgun on the trunk lid and the next thing I hear is a loud boom. At least we no longer have to worry about the crowd anymore. You should have seen them haul ass out of here. They practically fell over each other. Apparently the other unit had no trouble at all making the arrest. One of them told me that the guy couldn't wait to be arrested and out of here. Maybe he thought that we were going to shoot his ass."

A thorough investigation by the gun manufacturer revealed that the shotgun did indeed malfunction; even with the safety engaged.

Although the shotgun was replaced, a different manufacturer supplied the next weapons shortly thereafter. The only casualty was the rear side panel of a cruiser sporting several buckshot imprints and a little missing paint.

Turn the key off!

A State trooper assigned to a specialized DUI (Driving under the Influence) unit heard about the story and thought about doing the same thing if he ever had the opportunity. Many months later when he pulls his cruiser behind a car stopped on the shoulder of the road; with the motor still running he has the chance to try it. He exits his vehicle to check on the welfare of the operator who is slumped over the wheel of his car. A very strong odor of an alcoholic beverage emanating through the open driver's side window leaves no doubt in his mind that the subject is drunk and passed out. He makes sure that the suspect's car is in park and that the operator did not just put his foot on the brake and simply pulled over. He gently shakes the drunk until a pair of bloodshot eyes stares back at him and a slurred voice wants to know what is going on. There is no more time to think about it. It's now or never.

Suddenly the trooper starts running in place and pretending to be breathing hard yells at the drunk: **"Slow the hell down!" "I can barely keep up with you."** A pair of saucer-like eyeballs gaze back at him in total amazement, as the befuddled drunk momentarily gawks at him in total disbelief puts his foot on the gas; hoping to get away. Pretending to run even faster, he screams: **"Turn the damn key off!" "Do hear me?" "Turn the damn key off." "If you don't I'll shoot your damn ass."** When the trooper pretends to reach for his gun the drunk takes his foot off the gas and turns the car off.

Unable to comprehend what he just witnessed, the mesmerized drunk continues to stare at the trooper and mumbles: **"I might be drunk, but I know what I just saw you do." "You some kinda' Super Trooper?"** Holding back the desire to laugh the trooper responds: **"Nah, we are superbly trained troopers and all of us can that." "But**

it depends on how the person is driving." "Of course we can't go over 55 mph." Apparently still awestruck, the drunk says: **"Man, wait till I tell that judge what I seen." "When he hears that, then he'll know that I wasn't all that drunk tonight."** The trooper smiles and replies: **"You do that." "Now don't forget to tell that to the judge."** At trial, several months later, the drunk either forgot to tell the judge or had sobered up a lot.

A turnkey's morning.

In the delightful smell of the cellblock on an early morning day work...the heady bouquet that can only be described as akin to a dead skunk wrapped in old fish with just a hint of an alcohol beverage for balance...........

A close call.

A uniformed County officer in is in the big city while on duty is relaying a package to a government agency. As he prepares to leave the building, he decides to answer nature's call before the ride back to HQ. The officer proceeds into the men's room and strolls up to the urinal. As he begins to relieve himself, he hears the guy at the urinal next to him say: **"Hey there",** which every guy knows is a breach of men's room etiquette. He pauses momentarily and then the officer hears him say: **"It's going to cost you twenty bucks."** The officer startled and thinks: **"Holy crap!" "I'm in uniform and this guy is propositioning me!"** His mind screams: *"Pee faster!!!"* because he doesn't want to get into a fight with this dude while his junk is hanging out. When the guy suddenly turns and walks away, the officer breathes a sigh of extreme relief as he observes the "Blue Tooth" in the guy's ear and has NEVER been so happy to see a "Blue Tooth".

(Gentleman..please..NEVER talk on your Blue Tooth in the men's room.. this is how misunderstandings start!!) ***(LOLOL)***

Cops and Donuts. (As told by the officer.)

No offense to my larger friends but as I got my morning coffee this AM, there was a pair of rather robust women in line ahead of me getting a dozen donuts..**(Yeah, I know cops in donut shops but allow me to continue.)** As the clerk behind the counter is loading up the box, one lady says: **"Don't put any with sprinkles or frosting on them in there." "They are too fattening!" (Ladies, I think that is the least of your worries.)** What was priceless was the wide-eyed look the Indian lady behind the counter shot at me.

Words of wisdom?

Murphy's Law of police work...the discovery of a deceased person, dead for some time, will be immediately after you've received your morning coffee and breakfast sandwich. It will also be a very hot day and of course the A/C will be off in the house and all the windows closed. **Murphy you Irish bastard - I'm thinking you were a cop.**

Perception.

One of the most important things that young police officers learn from their FTOs (Field Training Officers) is that perception is everything. Everyone's view is different as experienced by a seasoned, 38 year old officer interviewing a witness; when he asked her to describe the suspect. It went something like this: **"Well it was a female, with long dirty blond hair and she was old, really old, like in her 40's!"** Wow, just wow......he felt REALLY OLD the rest of the day.

Words sometimes verify who you are. ***(In the officer's own words.)***

As I walked into the Donut shop to buy my morning coffee I saw her there, standing at the counter. I hadn't seen her in years and the last time I saw her, our hands were intimately entwined because I was fingerprinting her on a criminal charge. There she was again. Of all the Dunkin Donuts in the world she had to walk into mine; and she was just as I remembered her. Her ample bosoms barely restrained by her spaghetti strap tank top and emblazoned across her chest in beautiful cursive calligraphy were the words "Classy Bitch"; just as I remember her. A few words eradicate any lingering doubt. No folks, you NEVER forget a "lady" like that. Did I say lady? What's that old adage - "Truth in advertising?"

A flurry of motion.

As he is driving down the highway the officer sees a truck approaching his police car and observes the operator waving frantically. The officer's mind begins to ponder...*"Does he know me?" "Does he require police assistance?"* Then the truck driver quickly pulls over, both hands a flurry of motion. **"Oh I see sir, just the usual Death Match with an angry wasp in your truck."** ***(Guess he won't need coffee to get started this AM!)***

Peanut Butta Ball.

After a lengthy session without any progress and believing that he has reached an impasse, the City police detective prepares to terminate the interrogation. Suddenly the suspects blurts out: **"Yoh' man, might as well tell you de' truth." "Yeah, I been taken some Peanut Butta Ball'." "But I want ya' to know that stuff is legal; for real." "Cuz' it's my persciption'." "Yo' know what I'm sayn'?** He then reaches into his pants' pocket and pulls out a plastic prescription bottle and hands it to the detective. Curious to see the suspect's Peanutbutterball', the detective is anxious to read the label. Left momentarily speechless and suppressing the desire to laugh, he reads the word "Phenobarbital" printed on the label. Unable to resist, the detective grunts: **"Well, at least now I know what Peanut Butta Balls are."**

Why not use the door.

In an attempt to be handcuffed, the criminal breaks loose and is quickly managing to create considerable distance between him and the State trooper. Realizing that he will not be able to recapture the fleeing culprit by normally practiced methods, the determined trooper suddenly has a brainstorm and decides to apply his own unique technique.

The contour of the roadway forces the escapee to run along the road edge; just what the trooper needs to execute his unorthodox plan. When the opportunity presents itself, he suddenly flings open the driver's side door of his cruiser and smacks the suspect with the center part of it in the butt. Contrary to the anticipated results of the impact the suspect is knocked over and in Ninja-like fashion takes a couple of rolls and stands back up. Before he has a chance to recover from the unpredicted results, the suspect gives him a defiant look and takes off again. His luck seems to hold. A short distance away he finds a spot to escape the restrictive confines of the highway; and he is gone.

On his return to the troop his mind races trying to figure out how to justify the dent in the driver's side door; the imprint left by the one that got away. Several weeks later the trooper is charged for violating departmental protocol and is suspended for a couple of days. He will also be required to pay for the repair of the damage caused by his inappropriate procedure. He did wonder though, what would have been the results if he had affected an arrest afterwards? What about a reassignment as a qualified instructor; specializing in a new take-down technique?

Helping with the arrival of a baby.

Realistically speaking, all human beings have some pre-conceived anxiety or even fear anticipating how they will react when having to deal with circumstances out of the ordinary. For some it may even be a phobia of being dispatched to an emergency maternity and having to deliver a baby. A State trooper has been dispatched to a personal injury accident; a woman complains of having been injured.

When the trooper arrives at the scene of the accident and begins to assess the situation, he hears moaning and sees an obviously pregnant woman holding her stomach. It is quite apparent to him that the woman's stomach made contact with the steering wheel on impact and thus the most likely cause of her injuries. The trooper immediately notifies dispatch and requests an ambulance. It is imperative that proper EMS personnel respond to the scene in the event of an emergency delivery.

Hoping and praying that she can hold on until the arrival of the ambulance, he returns to the injured woman and tries to comfort her and keep her calm. In a gentle tone he tells her: **"An ambulance is in route and will be here very soon and you and your unborn child will be fine."** The sudden unforgiving look on the woman's face is one that he will remember for a long time as she turns towards him and snarls: **"I'm <u>not</u> pregnant."** It seems that the large stomach was due large amounts of food impregnation. The trooper's fear of delivering a baby ended at that accident scene.

A PUBLIC SERVANT

As a young man I had the ambition;
To be a policeman became my decision.
A uniform, gun and badge I wear,
Along with responsibilities I must bear.
I'm a cop doing my feat,
Many strangers I do meet.
I spend many long day and night
In pursuit of a culprit in flight.
I arrested the man for the deed he did wrong,
Only to see him set free, like a bird with a song.

I stand alone with no one beside me,
Only common sense and the Good Lord to guide me.
Quite often I feel so damn forlorn,
Cursing the day that I was born.
I keep the oath which I took,
And enforce the law straight by the book.
Many years have come and passed,
Several times I thought to be my last.

I'm known by all as a public servant,
Protecting all, even the non-deservan'.
For many I'm required to be
Father, confessor and referee.
I'm cursed by many and loved by few,
Seldom given the credit that is due.
Some call me "pig", "cop" or fuzz",
But when in trouble, guess who they buzz?

Cpl Rolf J. Wysock
DSP Troop 6

A matter of discretion.

When taking the oath, a State trooper swears to enforce the law without favor or prejudice; with limited discretion regarding that enforcement. The senior trooper running the radar unit, supervising the selective enforcement team is known to be very strict. He certainly would have an issue with a younger and inexperienced trooper using discretion in an arrest without consulting him first. According to him, there are no acceptable excuses for deliberately violating the law.

With that said, the young trooper operates one of the two pick-up cars assigned to flag a specific speeding vehicle over called out by the senior trooper operating the radar unit. Since only speed violators are called out, all operators are issues an arrest ticket. To keep everything fair, each trooper shares equally in the issuance of speeding tickets, including the senior trooper who has every third arrest logged in his ticket book; in the possession of one of the junior troopers.

Approximately thirty minutes into the operation the radar operator calls out the speed and description of the speeding vehicle which is ordered to pull over by one of the junior troopers. The driver of the vehicle identifies himself as a doctor and asks the trooper if he knew trooper so and so. The junior trooper certainly does know the trooper very well; the radar operator. Knowing how the senior trooper feels about discretion used by inexperienced junior troopers, the doctor is handed a summons and allowed to go on his way.

At the end of the shift, the senior trooper's ticket book is returned to him by the junior trooper. Suddenly the senior trooper stares at him and blurts out: **"You gave my doctor a ticket?"** Smiling from ear to ear, the junior trooper says: **"No I didn't." "You did." "I used your ticket book." "It was your turn to take credit for an arrest."** Almost in shock, the senior trooper stammers: **"Oh, my God." "He is doing my vasectomy next week."** Barely able to hold back his desire to laugh, the junior trooper replies: **"I hope he performs his surgery without favor or prejudice."** To this day, both are still good friends.

Three to five seconds rule.

A highly aggravated lady, pulled over for failing to stop for a stop sign, verbalizes her displeasure to the State trooper. Despite her temper tantrum, he remains surprisingly calm and diplomatically continues to make every effort to explain the circumstances of the stop to her. Displaying an "I don't care" attitude, the lady claims that she simply doesn't have the time to listen to him. Then, continuing with her irrational rant, she tells him that as far as she can recall she is pretty sure that she did stop. Wondering if she is perhaps more upset with herself because she got caught going through the stop sign, he decides on a different approach.

Rather than reciprocating in like manner he speaks to her in a fatherly tone: **"Well 'Ma'am', when you become more experienced in driving you may want to apply the 'Three to five seconds rule'.** Glaring back at him she cuts him off before he is able to continue and screams: **"What in the hell are you talking about?"** Without missing a step he replies:

> "Since you seem to experience some difficulty remembering whether you stopped or not, I am concerned about your safety. You may recall how you warn a small child not to touch the hot plate. Well, I want you to be able to take the guess-work out of it the next time you approach a stop sign and apply the 'The three to five seconds rule'. It's relatively easy to

> remember. All you have to do is count either just up to three, or even better yet, count to five. It may even help if you to say it out loud. But don't forget to look both ways before you go. By the way, here is your ticket. At least now you can be sure. Please drive carefully. Others are depending on it."

Without allowing her a chance to rebut, he hands the flabbergasted woman her ticket and walks back to his cruiser.

Just another day on patrol. #6

"Thank you Ma'am, not only were you awaiting your arrest dressed in a Violet Teddy allowing me to revel in the splendor of your Rubenesque frame." "You were also kind enough to inform me that it was hot out, and that you hadn't had a shower yet." "You also wanted to let me know that you might not be fresh "down there?". "Apparently not realizing that even as a Lawman there are things I DON'T NEED TO KNOW."......and now a trip to the mini mart for eye bleach.... yes folks..Law Enforcement..a front row seat to the greatest show on Earth....

With almost 28 years of service as a lawman, the officer has come to the following conclusion – **"My ears have been accosted by every excuse known to man by miscreants attempting to avoid an arrest."**

Some of the classics.

"Don't you know who I am?"

"You don't know who you are F*cking with!"

"I know (insert name dropping here) wait till he/she hears about this!"

"I'll have your job!"

Then one day the officer's "Piece De Resistance"....A female lawbreaker explains to him:

"You can't arrest me! I'm not wearing any panties!"

(*Yes, she was fully dressed at the time! Apparently, you can't go to jail without underwear.)

Halloween.

A State trooper on special assignment on mischief night is advised by radio dispatch to be on the lookout for a teenager throwing raw eggs at houses. He makes a mental note of the suspect's description and heads for the area where the teen was last seen.

As he turns the corner his car headlights shine on some shrubbery, although barely noticeable, he catches a glimpse of what looks like an egg carton. When he finds that the carton is missing some of the eggs, he knows that he is hot on the trail. He can't believe his luck when he spots a young teen wearing a "Starter" jacket matching the suspect's description and finds it rather odd that the subject is holding his jacket away from his body to avoid contact. He stops his cruiser and nonchalantly walks over to the boy; trying not to alarm him. When the teen attempts to walk away, he hollers: **"Yo', what's your hurry?" "Can't you see that I want to talk to you?"** The teenager snarls back: **"What for?" "I ain't done nothing."**

Remaining composed the trooper says:

> "Maybe you can help me. I got a call to be on the lookout for someone who is trying to ruin the night by throwing raw eggs at houses. Can you imagine that? Doesn't the idiot realize that his parents will have to pay for the damages if he is caught? You know kids don't have that kind of dough. I mean the blatant stupidity of that. Hum', that's interesting. Do you know something? You look just like the guy they described. Do you have a twin brother and you two dressed alike? Nah, that's not very likely. So you have no idea?"

Obviously very nervous and still making sure that there is no hard body contact to his jacket pockets the punk replies: **"I just got here and I'm on my way home."** Certainly not expecting the suspect to admit egging the houses, he takes the back of his hand and smacks the left pocket of the suspect's jacket. A barely auditable crack and instant squish reveal his suspicions. Before the shocked suspect has a chance to say anything, the trooper smiles at him and says: **"Looks like you already cracked your eggs." "You just need a pan to fry your omelet." "Just be careful there might be some eggshells mixed in."**

Unable to even utter a sound the egg-thrower just stands there, momentarily frozen in place and watches the trooper drive off. The anticipated call from an irate mother never comes. The rest of the night passes quietly.

Teetotaler.

Several troopers attending a crab and beer party conspire to have some fun with a young trooper who rarely drinks any alcoholic beverages. With the party in full swing, one of the conspirators manages to draw the young trooper into the web and volunteers to get drinks for him. Of course, they are spiked with alcohol. As the evening progresses it becomes quite obvious that the young trooper is getting inebriated. When the party is over the trooper doesn't even know where he is nor has an idea how he is getting home. Fortunately one of the conspirators has not consumed any alcoholic beverages volunteers to drive him home.

When they arrive at the residence, the trooper is too drunk to open the passenger side car door. Concerned about her husband's difficulty opening the door, his wife runs up to the car and opens the door for him. As soon as the door flings open and he attempts to step out he loses his footing and falls to the ground. Unable to walk, he crawls towards the house.

Although it was funny at the time, the conspirators feel some remorse when the trooper has to call off sick for the following three days. It is very likely that in the future he will only drink what he purchases.

I thought you were someone else.

The newly married wife of a trooper is on her way home and notices a State Police cruiser approaching from the opposite direction. As she glances into her side mirror she sees the cruiser suddenly spin around, activate its light and follow her. When she pulls onto the shoulder, she hears a male voice over the outside loudspeaker: **"Get out of your car and stand on your head!"** Before she has recovered from her shock she hears the male voice again: **"Oh my God, I thought that you were someone else."** As he walks up to the car he is relieved when he sees the female laughing hysterically and has to laugh also. Fortunately for the trooper the female driver has a great sense of humor but does not tell him that she is married to a trooper.

Three years later some friends of the young married couple invite them to a crab feast. As the afternoon progresses the couple is introduced to other State trooper guests. During the course of their conversation, one of them begins telling the guests about the time he ordered a lady, whom he thought to be a friend, to stand on her head. Suddenly he recognizes the wife of a trooper who is almost losing it with laughter; the lady he had ordered to stand on her head.

In the manner of "Little Caesar.

Pointing at him a State trooper orders a motorist to pull over and then approaches the car. As soon as he identifies himself the driver immediately blurts out: **"I fully intend to lodge a complaint against you because I object to the manner in which you pulled me over!"** Rather than inquire what the driver meant by that remark he somewhat brashly replies: **"Sir, I need your license and registration."**

Mumbling under his breath the totally irate driver reaches across the seat and literally pounds the glove compartment to open it and rummages through it. Overpowered by anger he practically yanks his license out of his wallet and then jabs the documents at the trooper. As he checks the license the exasperated driver says: **"I have you know that this is the 20th Century United States that we live in and**

not Ancient Rome." He doesn't even bother with a direct reply and simply says: **"Stand by, I'll be back."**

On his return he can't resist to give the "Smartass" driver a parting shot. As he requests the driver to sign the arrest book says: **"Please press hard you are making copies." "So Ancient Rome had posted speed limit signs back then already?" "Who would have thought that?" "Well anyway, thanks for <u>your</u> esoteric history lesson."** Fifteen minutes later dispatch instructs the trooper to return to the troop; obviously the operator drove post haste to the troop.

The trooper smartly reports to the Lt (Lieutenant) who then begins the inquiry: **"Mr. .... claims that you embarrassed him when you pulled him over in the indignant manner of 'Little Caesar' and also verbally insulted him." "Can you explain yourself?** The obvious smirk on the complainant's face seems to say: **"Now I've got you by your ass".** Seemingly left unperturbed by the man's sneer the trooper calmly replies:

> **"Frankly I am somewhat puzzled because that is <u>not</u> how I recall the incident. Mr. ...... became immediately irate with me as soon as I introduced myself and told me that we live in the 20th Century and not Ancient Rome. Then when I asked him to sign the ticket I simply wanted to know if Ancient Rome had speed limit signs back then already. I didn't possess his esoteric knowledge of Roman Law Enforcement or how 'Little Caesar' may have pulled people over. Maybe I should have made further inquiry and asked him if 'Little Caesar' was on horseback or riding in a chariot."**

A sudden outburst: **"That's enough! Trooper!"** abruptly silences any further remarks. Giving him a very stern look the Lt says: **"Trooper!"** Receiving his message loud and clear the trooper musters an apology of sorts and things return to relative norm. Maintaining a professional decorum the Lt continues: **"Alright Mr. ......, I assure you that the matter will be handled appropriately." "Thank you very much for coming here and express your concern."**

When the Lt is finished berating the trooper sends him back on patrol. A written reprimand is filed in the trooper's Personnel Records. It is unfortunate that the trooper forgot it was the 20th Century and needed a civilian to remind him of that; after all, he enforces the law.

The newest Polygraph.

A couple of State troopers riding together find it odd that the car coming towards them suddenly seems to slow down and their curiosity peaks when the car passes them. It is immediately obvious to them that the driver kibitzing them from the corner of his eyes pretended to be looking straight ahead. When the trooper driving notices the car creep through a stop sign, without first stopping, turns on his lights and siren and swings a "U-turn". Moments later they catch up with the car and motion to the driver to pull over and cautiously approach the car.

When the trooper standing at the driver's side asks the male driver for his driver's license and car registration he notices that the driver is visibly nervous. He begins to stutter when the trooper wants to know why he doesn't have his license and doesn't know who owns the car. He just keeps repeating: **"I didn't steal the car!"** In the meantime the other trooper begins searching the passenger side and glove compartment. Dissatisfied with the driver's inability to provide sufficient information, tells him to step out of the car; searches and handcuffs the suspect. By the time the tow truck arrives, the trooper on the passenger side is finished inspecting the car and the car is towed. At the troop the driver is searched again and ushered towards the interview room to give the driver another opportunity to tell them the truth.

Although still denying that he stole the car, the driver now admits that he found the car unlocked and just slept in it and only drove it a little to get closer to where he wanted to go. Aware that they are not getting anywhere with him, the troopers decide to administer a heretofore untried and unconventional method to get the truth and leave the room. When they return they take the suspect to another room and tell him to take a seat next to the Teletype machine and make himself comfortable.

One of them begins: **"Since you don't look like a dummy' to me you probably have heard about a Polygraph and know what it is."** Looking at him somewhat skeptical, the suspect replies: **"Isn't that the thing that says if you are telling the truth?"** The trooper continues: **"See, I just knew that you are no 'Dumkopf'." "So here is your last opportunity to come clean."** Then pointing at the Teletype machine says:

> "Well, I don't know whether or not you have ever seen an actual Polygraph machine, but this is the very latest model. With the old Polygraph there was a bunch of lines that had to be interpreted by a specialist. But this machine; wow! Any trooper can operate it. Instead of a bunch of squiggly lines, this machine prints the answers right out along with a printout called "Tickertape". You can see for yourself. So here, let me hook you up."

One of them rips off a strip of "Tickertape" and begins wrapping it around the suspects head just above the eyebrows and sticks several paperclips around the tape to hold it in place. He then attaches a piece of thin wire that he happened to find, while his partner busies himself with another piece of tape. Anxious to test the newest Polygraph invention one of them says: **"As promised, here is your last chance to clear your name!" "Remember, the machine will tell us right away if you're lying." "So I advise you to tell the truth and nothing but the truth!" "So, are you ready?"** Hesitating slightly, the suspect nods his head and says: **"Yea', I'm ready."**

Mimicking the actions of a genuine Polygraph operator the trooper begins. As expected, the suspect continues denying any wrongdoing. When he is finished questioning the suspect the trooper says: **"Well, I still don't believe you; but let's see what the machine has to say."** Just as his partner hands him the piece of "Tickertape", the Teletype starts clicking; seemingly adding validity to their charade. In very dramatic fashion and frowning, he looks at the piece of perforated strip of paper and says: **"I thought you told us that you were going to tell the truth?" "Well, tell me what the machine says?" "Here, what's written on here?"**

The suspect looks at the piece of paper and gulps and meekly says: **"All right you got me." "I didn't just sleep in it but I stole it first."**

They tell him to sit tight for a moment and quickly rush out of the room far enough away where the suspect can't hear laughter..

You have a coon?

> **(It is strongly emphasized that the following occurred several decades ago, in the absence of PC and the inflammatory connotation now attached to the "N" word).**

The phone at the small Town police department rings and the radio operator, known to occasionally put his foot in his mouth, picks up the receiver. When the caller has the radio operator confirm that it is the police, the voice on the other end yells: **"I got a damn coon in my basement."** Somewhat stunned, the radio operator is unable to reply immediately and has to take a moment to reassess. Unsure whether the caller is being insulting, he hesitantly asks the caller: **"Do you mean there is a "N*gger" in your basement?"** The radio operator is totally flabbergasted when he hears the excited voice on the other end reply: **"No, I'm da N*gger." "An' I have only two legs." "This one has foa' legs an' is a real motha' f*ckin'coon."**

For the next few days the radio operator walks on egg shells. Instead of the anticipated punishment, he is relieved when the responding officer tells him that the caller himself thought that it was funny. The caller also said that in a way he wanted to apologize for making the radio operator feel uncomfortable. Boy how things have changed.

"Cut her down!"

The State trooper just started his mid-night shift patrol when he spots a woman staggering on the shoulder of the highway and stops his cruiser. When he notices that she is drunk he transports her to the holding cell of the small local Town police department. Since the station is not manned during the night-time, the only person present is the cleaning lady. Before he is ready to leave, he has an uneasy feeling and decides to check on the inebriated woman. He is alarmed by what he sees when he looks into the holding cell; the woman is naked from the waist down. She has taken her jeans off and then tied them around her neck in an apparent attempt to commit suicide. Frantic to get to her in time, he yells at the cleaning lady: **"Get the keys!" "Hurry up!" "Get the keys!"** The partially nude woman waits until the trooper is ready to open the door and jumps off the chair. With not a moment to spare, he is able to open the cell door in time and grab the woman by her upper thighs. Since he is a large and strong man, the cleaning lady is shocked to see the trooper's face turn beet red and appears to be ready to throw up.

He desperately holds onto her so she doesn't fall and frantically tries to turn his face sideways; scrunched in her crotch. Panic-stricken and laced with volumes of expletives he screams at the cleaning lady several times: **"Cut her down!"** On the verge of throwing up, he finally manages to lay the woman on the ground and remove the jeans from around her neck and runs into the hallway gulping fresh air. By the time other help arrives he has regained his composure and is able to relate the full impact of the incident to the other newly arrived troopers. **"When I left her here in the cell, I just had an uneasy feeling and had to return to check on her one more time." "Then, when I saw her standing on the chair ready to kill herself I just wanted to save her."** The cleaning lady interjects: "**Was she that heavy?"** Puzzled by her remark, he looks at her and asks: **"What do you mean, heavy?"** She replies: **"Well you turned all kinds of shades of red." "And you looked like you were ready to throw up."** Now fully recovered from his ordeal he starts again:

> "Man all that I could think of was not to let her die. Everything seemed all right until I grabbed her around her waist and her 'cutchie' was right in my face. I have never smelled anything that bad; except maybe a shithouse. It stunk so bad that I was ready to throw up. But I knew that if I let go of her, she was going to die. I tell you, it took every bit of my will power not to throw up."

For the next few nights offers of free smelling salts are broadcasted by ghost radio messages.

I wish I could do that.

A State trooper, known to make occasional crude remarks, walks through the back door of the Troop and comments about the K-9 tied up outside. **"Ha, ha, ha." "You ought to see Trooper ------'s dog outside licking his balls." "Man I wish I could do that."** When hearing that, the Captain turns around and says: **"I don't know." "Why don't you go out there and ask him." "I'm pretty sure he'll let you."** The trooper rushes outside; the laughter was probably too loud for him.

I wants' to buy some of dem' cars.

Pretending to be a black minister from one of the local churches, a black State trooper disguises his voice and calls the troop. **"Ah wants to talk to da capn', capn' ......;** (Deliberately mispronouncing his name). The captain answers the phone and politely inquires how he may help the caller, who without missing a beat says: **"I wants' some of 'dem dare' cars that ya'll' advertise to be sold at da' auction."** The captain proceeds to tell him that he is not able to give him cars and that things are controlled by the state and that his name is not ------, but -----. Pretending to be irritated and grossly mispronouncing the captain's name again, the faux minister says: **"Look whatever that damn name of yours is, we needs' cars for ma' folk here." "We is church-going folk."** The others listening to the exchange are repeatedly reminded to be quiet and are amazed by the captain's cool composure as the conversation continues to go back and forth. Finally, after a barrage of insults, mispronounced last name, the captain has enough and slams the phone down. All are in agreement that the black trooper missed his Sunday calling.

A bear is loose.

At about 4 o'clock in the morning, a civilian operator at the Dispatch Center receives a rather unusual call. The caller claims that he just came off the ferry and when he started driving his car he saw a bear on the highway. Confused, the dispatcher asks the caller to please explain. **"Well I was following a circus truck going through town and when the circus truck stopped at a light the back door flew open and a bear suddenly climbed out of the back and started running away."** The Desk Sergeant at the local State Police troop listening in on the call immediately becomes suspicious. Being quite familiar with people in the area he is pretty sure that he knows who could be responsible for the call and sits back in his chair to enjoy the show. Since "Call Identifier" wasn't even thought of with dial phones and tracing calls was time consuming and required a Court Order.

By the time the D/Sgt goes home at the end of his midnight shift, troopers from the 12-8 and 8-4 shift, local Town PD, the SPCA and the National Guard have volunteered to help search for the bear. A considerable time has passed when the same caller calls the dispatch center again and reports that he saw the circus truck stop on one of the side roads and watched them recapture the bear and load him back onto the truck.

The whole incident remained clouded and under suspicion for many years. Finally, after ten years of repeated denials and with the Statute of Limitation long expired, the culprit breaks his silence and exposes the whole saga. He claims that by the time he wanted to stop the whole thing, it had already gotten totally out of hand. He never thought that it would go that far and it would have been way too risky for him to tell anyone at the time. The people listening to his story almost defecate on themselves laughing.

If he misses any more I have em'.

Wendell, a well known small time thief, frequently contacts a particular State trooper and lets him know what is going on and what he is personally involved in. He even told the trooper whom to look for in case somebody killed him. Leaning out of his car window the trooper says: **"Ok Wendell, what is the reason for you coming here today?" "What is it that you need to tell me?"** In a rather sheepish tone Wendell replies: **"They done told me I done stalled' Alvin's** (A very prominent local farmer) **pigs."** Giving him a stern look the trooper asks: **"Well, did you take them?"** Stuttering slightly, Wendell replies: **"Nah, n'no but if'f he misses any more, I have em' an' jus' h'holdin' em' for him."** Without missing a beat, he smiles at him and says: **"Wendell, why don't you really shock him and return the pigs you are holding for him." "You can also tell him that you were just looking out for him and wanted to make sure that they didn't run away."** After a few seconds of silence Wendell mutters: **"Yeah, I think so too." "An' then he also knows that I ain't n'no real thief."** The puzzled look on Wendell's face is an obvious sign that the double entendre failed to penetrate dense bone matter.

I'm going to kick your ass.

Unable to tolerate it any longer the Desk Sergeant has just about reached his limit listening to the noise coming from the troop holding cell. It has been about two hours of constant loud banging and the man's screaming and cursing: **"Why don't you come in here you no-good bastard." "Cause' I'm going to kick your ass but good you sunna' ma bitch."** As luck would have it, things are about to change when a friend of the D/Sgt walks in. His friend, just finished working out and still dressed in his sweats, decided to stop by the troop to pick up some paper work. When the loud noise from the cell area starts again, the D/Sgt gives his friend a disgusting look and says: **"I'm about sick of that man."** His friend replies: **"I have a plan that will shut him up."**

The two friends start screaming and yelling at each other and throw chairs around the room. Suddenly the D/Sgt's friend yanks the door open and runs outside. The D/Sgt hollers: **"You better stop." "I'm going to get my gun"** and runs after him. He then stands in the doorway and fires a shot into grass and yells: **"You no good son of a bitch." "How do you like that?" "You should have kept your damn**

mouth shut." "Now it's shut for good!" When he is sure that he can hold back laughing he briskly walks towards the cell area and rips the door open and yells: **"So you are the son of a bitch that's going to kick my f*cking ass?" "Well, come on out and do it!"** Pressing his body against the wall and hoping to find an opening to climb through, the criminal slides off the wall cowering to the ground; hugging the toilet and yells: **"Nooo." "That wasn't me." "I don't want to fight."** The rest of the night is quiet as a church-mouse.

This is your lucky day.

A State trooper on patrol activates his lights and siren and orders the speeding motorist to pull over onto the shoulder. He approaches the vehicle and tells the female operator that he is going to charge her for speeding. When he walks back to his marked cruiser he is dismayed to find that he has locked himself out of his car and is left with no other choice. He very humbly walks back to the violator's vehicle and says: **"Ma'am, this is your lucky day, if you drive me back to the troop." "I accidentally locked my car and need to go back to my troop to get another key."** The lady can't believe what she has just heard and tells him to get into her car. Occasionally giving a sheepish glance at his passenger, another trooper drives him back to his locked cruiser. It is quite possible that the woman tells people how to get out of a speeding ticket.

No, it's mine.

A couple of State troopers on patrol spot a cooler at the edge of the median. The trooper riding passenger yells: **"It's mine."** The driver yells back: **"No, it's mine!" "I saw it first."** When the driver stops the car next to the container, he opens the car door and reaches for the lid and carefully opens the cooler and quickly closes it again. Keeping a straight face, he turns to his partner and says: **"I want to be fair about this." "Since you really did see it first, it's yours"** and hands him the cooler. The passenger takes a look inside and screams: **"Yuck"** and heaves it out of the window. Laughing so hard, the driver has to hold onto the steering wheel with both hands and asks: **"What's the matter?" "Don't you like shit?" "You could have used it as manure in your garden."** The cooler went into one door and out of the window on the other side; a surprise package for other motorists.

Look out.

A pair of State troopers is sent on a special assignment to another troop, a couple of hours distance from their troop. About an hour into the drive, the driver notices that his passenger has fallen asleep. When the driver sees a shopping center he carefully drives the cruiser over the sidewalk and stops in front of a large plate glass window. He then flicks on the high-beams, blows the horn and screams: **"Look out." "Look out."** The passenger wakes up frantically swinging his arms looking like he is fighting a ghost. When things have returned to normal and both of them have calmed down from laughing, the passenger says: **"Man, you have no idea what it was like when I saw those lights coming at me." "I almost shit on myself because I thought that it was the end."** He probably didn't hear the car horn.

I've got it right here.

A State trooper tells the motorist, whom he clocked for speeding a 100 mph plus in a 55 mph zone, to follow him to court. The outlandish attire, a pinkish colored fedora hat adorned with a large peacock feather to match his suit and high heeled patent leather boots leave no doubt about the motorist's profession. The motorist's glare at the judge and contemptuous attitude telegraph potential trouble. When the judge asks him how he is going to plead, the pimp sneers at him and says: **"I guess I'm guilty." "At least that's what yo' all trying to tell me."** The judge looks at him and replies: **"For that much over the speed limit I asses a fine of $100.00."** Before the judge is able to say anything else, the pimp smugly replies: **"No problem my man." "I got your damn extortion money right here in my back pocket."** He then reaches into his back pocket and extracts a large bundle of $50 and $100 bills, then picks out a $100 bills and slams it on the bench. Then with a scornful smirk on his face says: **"Here is your blood money for your kangaroo court." "You cross-eyed Baboon."**

To everyone's surprise the judge remains calm and responds in a very judicial manner: **"Sir, can now reach into your other back pocket and pull out three days for contempt of court?"** Puzzled, the pimp looks at the judge and says: **"Say what?" "What the Hell you talken' about?"** He then grabs his roll of money and yells: **"Jus' tell me how much more that shit is going to cost me this time."** The judge smiles and replies: **"I guess your pocket must have sprung a hole in it since you were unable to find those days." "Well, guess what?" "You can't pay for those days anyway." "Those were assessed as 'Contempt of Court' and must be served." "Trooper you may take him to jail as soon as I'm finished with his paperwork." "Have a nice day." "Both of you."**

As he prepares to place the handcuffs on him, the loudmouth pleads: **"Your judgeship, I pay you whatever you want." "I have an important meeting to go to an' I'm already late cuz' a' yo' all."** The judge doesn't even bother to stop writing and replies: **"You should have curtailed your verbose discourse."** Totally dumbfounded by the judge's remarks, the pimp starts crying as he is escorted out of the court. The trooper can't resist smiling at the judge.

Where is my breakfast?

The moment the holding cell at the troop closes behind him the drunk starts his annoying acts; escalating hourly. When the corporal working the midnight shift relieves the 4-12 shift D/Sgt he is appraised about the terrible noise emanating from the holding cell area. He is also told that every attempt to quiet the subject has failed and in fact seems to fortify his unruly behavior. The Cpl grabs a clipboard with a pad and asks the D/Sgt to stand by and walks into the holding cell center. Instead of raising his voice the Cpl hopes to get the subject's attention by speaking to him in a soft voice and says: **"Look, I came in here to help you." "I can tell that you are obviously upset and none of them back there are listening." "Here is what I'm willing to do for you." "If you keep quiet for the rest of the night, I'm going to tell you a little secret." "Are you willing to listen to me?"** In suspense, the drunk eagerly nods his head and says: **"Yeah, I can keep a secret." "What is it?"**

When the fish has swallowed the bait, hook, line and sinker the Cpl continues: **"Now remember what I tell you." "If you break any part of the agreement, all bets are off." "Do you understand that?"** The answer is given with the nodding of the head. The Cpl then says: **"I can arrange to have breakfast served to you right here in your cell." "But only if you keep real quiet for the rest of the night."** With a sparkle in his eyes the drunk excitedly promises: **"I'll be quiet from now on." "Cross my heart." "Can I already give you my order?"** With extreme difficulty holding back the desire to laugh, the Cpl replies: **"Ok, what do you want for breakfast?"** The Cpl pretends to write down the order. Because he is going to be relieved at 7 o'clock in the morning, the Cpl continues spinning his yarn: **"Look, because it's already late placing your order, you cannot get it until after seven."** Certain that the ecstatic drunk has understood he tells him that he is going to see him again in the morning and turns out the light.

It's after seven and the Sergeant prepares to check on the prisoner. Suddenly and for some unknown reason the prisoner yells: **"Where the Hell is my breakfast?" "You promised me a breakfast." "Where the Hell is it?" "I want my damn breakfast." "I'm hungry."** Then he recalls that the Cpl was unusually anxious to get out of the troop. Because the Sgt knows his reputation, he is suspicious and is relatively certain that the Cpl has something to do with the breakfast order. A week later the Sgt corners the Cpl and says: **"You bastard, I'll get even with you"** and busts out laughing.

Neglected by the State Police, the poor prisoner went to arraignment hungry.

I didn't beat anybody up.

In the process to execute an arrest warrant a couple police officers of a small local town enter the dwelling. It is dusk and the light outside has already greatly diminished as they enter the room occupied by close to a dozen people; lying on mattresses thrown all over the floor or flopping on derelict remnants of furniture. One of the officers tells the group that they have an arrest warrant for "Assault and Battery" for Horace who lives here. While the other officer shines his flashlight on the people they spot Horace who looks like he is ready to run. Ignoring his protest of innocence they quickly snatch and handcuff him. Once he is secured in the police cruiser, Horace becomes even more vocal proclaiming his innocence and says: **"Look officers, I recall being in a fight and getting beat up." "It wasn't me that did the beating." "I'm the one that got the beating." "I'm the victim."** The driver flips the car visor down, turns on the dome light and grabs the warrant and takes another look. With a sudden frown on his face he turns to his partner and pointing at Horace's name whispers: **"Hey, take a look at this." "Do you see where his** (Horace) **name is listed?" "Damn, he is the victim."** They know that they could be in trouble; then a State Police unit pulls up behind them to check on their safety.

When the trooper hears of their predicament, he tells the Town officers to come back to his car and bring their prisoner with them. The trooper invites the prisoner to have a seat in his cruiser and says to the man: **"I hear that you claim that you didn't do this and that you didn't beat anybody up."** The man nods his head and replies: **"That's what I have been trying to say all along." "But somebody beat me up."** Adopting a father to son type atmosphere the trooper says: **"You know what?" "I believe you when you say that you didn't beat anybody up."**

Continuing with his charade picks up the phone (At that particular time police microphones closely resembled the slightly u-shaped dial-phones.) and says: **"Since I believe you, I know this judge personally and I'm going to give him a call."** Faking the call he goes into a long spiel. **"Yes your honor I definitely believe this man." "No, I do not think that this man has committed any crime and is innocent this time."** Slightly raising his voice, he continues: **"So judge you say it's OK to let him go and take him back home."** He then turns to the man and tells him: **"The judge said that it was alright and we are allowed to take you back home."** On the way back to his house the man thanks the trooper profusely. The Town officers thank the trooper and want to see the gold on his tongue.

Didn't you see that?

Responding to the locals' request to have the State Police take some action and arrest the drivers that burn through the stop sign, the Troop Commander sends a trooper to the location. When he is finished reconnoitering the area he selects a spot where he can adequately observe the stop sign. After counting the frequent violations, it is apparent to him that immediate action must be taken. He parks his cruiser facing the intersection so that he will not be readily noticed by potential violators and yet have plenty of time to direct them into the parking lot. It is indeed the ideal spot for the operation.

While he is in the process of writing the ticket for a female violator, she suddenly screams: **"Did you see that guy that just went through the stop sign?"** Obviously not realizing that he is still watching the stop sign and has sufficient time to pull the motorist over, he nonchalantly replies: **"Oh really?" "Did you see him go through the sign?" "Yea, I guess you can see it really quite well from here." "Can't you?"** Annoyed because she believes that he failed to see it, she yells: **"You damn right!" "What do you intent to do about it?" "Aren't you going to get him?"** Already in position to direct the motorist into the parking lot he replies: **"I certainly saw it." "Oh by the way, he did exactly what you did." "I'm curious though to see if he at least is man enough to admit that he went through it."** Her hateful glare gives him the expected answer.

She is able to hear the newly stopped driver readily admit that he went through the stop sign and apologizes. Intent on teaching the arrogant woman a lesson he slightly raises his voice and says: **"My compliments to you." "I truly appreciate your honesty." "It is a pleasure to have people like you still around."** Giving her a sideways glance he continues: **"Honesty is indeed the best policy." "Excuse me please." "Let me finish writing the ticket for this lady." "Who incidentally did the same thing you did." "I'll be right back."**

As the trooper hands her the ticket and attempts to explain to her what to do next, she almost snatches the ticket book out of his hand. While grumbling something under her breath she practically scratches her signature on the ticket and says: **"Save me the drama, I already know what to do."** Without losing his composure he replies: **"Oh I'm certain of that." "I saw that when I pulled up your driving record." "Guess what?" "From the looks of things, you may even have accumulated enough points now to qualify."** She pulls off before he has a chance to rub more salt into her wound.

Under the bridge.

The young State trooper helicopter pilot newly assigned to the State Police Aviation unit helps his passenger buckle up. Since his passenger isn't paying close attention to the pilot nor the direction they are flying in; the pilot decides to take advantage of the opportunity. Eager to impress the high-ranking staff officer, sitting next to him, with his flying skills experienced during combat in Nam, he decides to head for the bridge; less than a mile ahead of them. As they approach the bridge and he glances over his right shoulder, he sees a very concerned look on the officer's face. At the last possible moment he dips the nose of the aircraft and flies under the bridge. Instead of being impressed with the pilot's masterful maneuver, the staff officer keeps looking straight ahead. Then shaking a little the officer says: **"I want to see you in my office tomorrow morning." "Now head for our assigned destination!"** The following week the pilot is ordered to take a forced ten days vacation; without a badge. Maybe the pilot had a temporary flashback to Nam.

A day in court. #5

Officer: **"Lady all I'm saying is, if you come into HQ on a "Stalking" charge, you may not want to make the statement."**
Subject: **"He won't let me love him!"** *(It isn't helping your case!!! LOL)*

Most defendants have a "good" excuse why they didn't show up for court on their capiases but this defendant's excuses for each of the handful of court dates that he missed even surprised the judge. ***(No, these are not made up.)***

Defendant:

1. **I missed this one because I changed my address, your Honor.**
2. **I had brain surgery on that date.**
3. **My mom died and I couldn't make it to court that day.**
4. **I was taking care of my sick Aunt.**
5. **I was out looking for a job and forgot the court date.**

(Genius! Pure genius!)

Prisoner quote of the day:

Judge: **"Sir you are being charged with Manufacture of Marijuana."**
Defendant: **"But your Honor, it was all for personal use!"**

Judge: **"You had over sixteen plants!"**
Defendant: **"Damn your Honor, I guess I picked the wrong hobby."**

Defendant: **"Your Honor, I didn't run that stop sign! I stopped then drove onto the road that officers drive off!"** ***(Yeah pal, not much of a defense.)***

Get to church on time.

The D/Sgt (Desk Sergeant) never misses going to church on Sunday. Even after working a midnight shift, he remains at the troop and takes a little nap until it's time to go. In the past there were a few occasion when a new trooper, not familiar with the Sgt's routine, regretted for not waking him up in time and frequently had their intelligence questioned by the grumpy old man. After a similar incident, members of the oncoming shift decide to pay the Sgt back for his unkind verbiage and wait for him to fall asleep. A couple of them grab some super large watermelons and quietly sneak outside and join the group already waiting. After the watermelons are sliced in half, a bunch of them lift the rear end of the Sgt's vehicle and place a melon-half under each rear wheel and gently lower the car. Just in time for wake-up call.

Following his routine, the Sgt unlocks his car and inserts the key into the ignition. Did he see the watermelon under the car tires? Watching from their hiding places, they breathe a sigh of relief when they hear the engine come alive and see the flash of the backup lights. They can hear the noise of the motor getting louder and see the tires spinning; but the car doesn't move. Suddenly pieces of watermelon fly from under the car and the car bolts backwards, instantly followed by the glare of brake lights and then the car abruptly stops. Then the driver's side door flies open and a madman jumps out.

No longer able to refrain from laughing, they emerge from their hiding places. When the Sgt sees them coming towards him he flies into a tirade and words emanating from his lips are certainly unbecoming a churchgoing person. After a thorough inspection of his car and he cannot find any damage, the Sgt also has to laugh. He longer relies on a wakeup call and takes his nap at home; but still keeps a wary eye on the back tires.

A hairy decision.

Rita is a nervous wreck when she sees the State trooper walk up to her car and just about looses it when he tells her that she is under arrest for speeding. She only sees the uniform while feverishly fumbling for her driver's license and car registration. After a brief check of both documents he tells her to stand by and walks back to his cruiser. By the time he returns she is calm enough not only to sign her arrest citation but also take a closer look at the man in uniform. Thanking her politely and in a very professional manner instructs her on what she needs to do next and hands her a copy of the signed ticket. As she steers her car back onto the main travel portion of the highway the image of that rather good looking State trooper comes to her mind and she is determined to get to know him better.

Rita musters enough nerve a few days later and calls the Troop. Although flattered by her request for a date the good looking trooper politely declines and states that it would put him in a compromising situation since her court case is still open and he is the arresting trooper. Despite her disappointment, Rita is still determined to have a date with him.

When she calls him again several days later her determination pays off. Emphasizing the fact that her case has been adjudicated and that he is free to decide; they set a date. Feeling like sitting on a cushion of pins and needles she anxiously awaits the ring of her doorbell and suddenly jumps up and rushes to the door. Thank God her stare was not discernible; of course she realized that he would call on her in civilian attire. Is it really him? It looks a lot like him, but what is it? She can't figure it out immediately. Then, all of a sudden…that's it.

The following day Rita's girlfriend hounds her to tell her about the date. After some back and forth gossip and a reluctance to talk about specific details Rita finally begins.

> "Well, when he came here I still had a mental vision of him looking so debonair in his uniform and his Stetson hat. Of course I realized that he was going to be wearing civilian clothing on our date. So when I opened the door and saw him, I was stunned. It was him but yet he looked somewhat different; it took me about a split second to recover. There he was without his Stetson on and his head covered with patches of what looked like kinky pubic hair; more than I have."

The moment of silence is broken by their laughter. Unable to hold back her curiosity the girlfriend asks: **"So, when are you going out again?"** Rita replies: **"Maybe sometime; when his head is fully covered with hair and it has straightens out."** Laughter erupts again.

The body appears to be unremarkable.

A couple detectives of the State Police "Major Crimes" unit are assigned to investigate the case of a dead man discovered in the bathroom of a convenience store. After a thorough visual examination, the troopers are unable to detect any obvious signs of trauma. Since death cannot be immediately determined, the victim is transported to the mortuary to have the body further examined by the Medical Examiner. The doctor at the facility is a hard-smoking woman in her late 60's or early 70's and a little rough around the edges; she probably has seen it all.

The victim is stripped of his clothing and his naked body is placed on the examination table to be autopsied. Their eyes get as big as saucers when they notice the victim's male member. When they mean large, they mean large. It hangs down close to his knees and is as thick as a soda can. The doctor begins her examination. Following established guidelines, she speaks loudly to make certain that her findings are recorded. She then begins: **"The head is bald." "No signs of trauma." "The face, neck and throat do not appear to have any injuries and appear unremarkable." "The penis and genitalia are also unremarkable."** Surprised, they look at each other and one of them whispers: **"Did she say unremarkable?" "It looks pretty remarkable to me."** They just can't help themselves and burst out laughing. Although the doctor's stern look indicates that she doesn't think it is funny they snicker and still laugh about it today.

I've been doing this for a while.

A young State trooper assigned to investigate the first domestic on his own is met by a young female who claims that her boyfriend hit her in the face. He politely asks her to explain to him what happened. She reluctantly says: **"Aah." "I'm really embarrassed to tell you."** Pretending to be an old salt he replies: **"Ma'am, I have been doing this for awhile and have heard almost everything." "So, it's ok." "Go ahead and tell me."** Then slightly hesitating, she pulls her hair away from her face. He has to force himself to maintain a professional edge when he sees the distinct and unmistakable imprint of a penis on her face. Still holding her hair she says: **"We had a big argument and he hit me with my "dildo". "It broke when he hit me with it and I threw it in the trash can."** Momentarily stumped and unable to find what to say, he grabs a paper towel off the counter and walks over to the trash can. It is the biggest thing he has ever seen.

Psst. Don't talk so loud.

A pair of State troopers is returning to the troop to place their drunken and extremely vocal prisoner into the holding cell. All efforts of diplomacy to quiet him down fail and quite to the contrary, seem to aggravate him even more. Not willing to listen any longer to the verbal profanities the driver glances over at his partner in the passenger side and whispers: **"I'm going to try something." "Watch this."** Then he starts.

"Hey, did you get the scoop on John?" "Man if that comes out; the shit's going to hit the fan." Under the pretext of being concerned to be overheard by the drunk the other trooper replies: **"Psst." "Don't talk so loud." "Man, be careful what you say." "Don't let him overhear it."** The driver smiles and continually gets softer, whispering nonsensical sentences. They suddenly notice that the drunk has stopped with his annoying antics and is totally engrossed trying to listen to them. They can't believe their luck and if they didn't know better would swear that they had practiced this routine beforehand; the drunk remains quiet until they arrive at the troop. The driver says to his partner: **"Whatever you do, don't even talk about it in here." "Nobody knows about ....**(Deliberately said too low for the drunk to hear)**..." "I'll tell you the rest when we are back in the car." "Remember, you don't know anything about it; otherwise it's your head."**

As soon as the trio enters the troop the drunk starts with his boisterous behavior again. Obviously frustrated to have been unable to understand what they were talking about, he is determined that he is somehow going to tell on them and get them in trouble. Before one of them ushers him into the cell, the drunk yells: **"You ought to have heard what I overheard those two talking about." "You better ask them to tell you because they are going to be in deep shit when you find out what they did." "Go ahead and ask them."** Although the Sergeant refuses to engage the drunk he does, however, give them a stern look and asks: **"What the Hell is that all about?"** They just look at him and shrug their shoulders. One of them finally says: **"I have no idea what he is babbling about."** Suddenly the loud commotion coming from the cell area indicates that it's high time that they get back on patrol and hurry out of the back door.

I'm going to follow you.

A northern troop, short on manpower, requests help from another troop. Responding to the call, a nearby troop assigns one of its troopers to assist. Because he is only vaguely familiar with that troop's area, he plans to arrest only those motorists who commit flagrant violations. He doesn't have to wait long. As he approaches the intersection in his fully marked State Police unit, he notices the light cycling to green. When it does, he cannot believe what he just witnessed and is relieved that he does not have to investigate an accident. Fortunately the driver ahead of him waited a second longer to enter the intersection. Just as he lifted his foot off the brake pedal, a car approaching from the right disregards the red traffic light and flies through the intersection.

When the trooper is finished writing the violator's ticket, he realizes that he does not know the precise location of the court and immediately knows that he must come up with a valid sounding excuse to avoid an impending embarrassment. Adopting an air of confidence he walks up to the violator and asks him to sign the ticket, acknowledging the receipt. Then in a stern, yet somewhat friendly tone says: **"You are obviously familiar with the J. P. (Justice of the Peace) court." "Since you pulled that stunt back there at the intersection, I don't want you to get any other hair brainy ideas." "So to make sure that you go to the court, I'm going to follow you; just in case."** They arrive together at the court.

Get out of the car!

A State trooper involved in a high-speed chase of a stolen car successfully forces the car thief off the road. With his weapon drawn he cautiously approaches the vehicle and orders the driver to get out; who instead screams something unintelligible and locks the door.

Just then a State Police K-9 unit also arrives at the scene. Undetected by the thief, the handler and his dog sneak over to the passenger side of the stolen car. Holding his dog on a short leash he rips open the passenger door that the panicked thief forgot to lock and hollers: **"Get'm' boy!"** Screaming at the top of his lungs, the terrified thief yanks the driver's side door open and falls out of the car crying: **"All right, you got me." "I give up." "Jus' don't let him** (dog) **get me."**

For having done such a good job to get the thief out of the car, the K-9 handler's furiously barking partner is allowed to come threatening close to the suspect and bathe him in saliva. In the process of handcuffing his prisoner he notices that the suspect's wet pants also left a distinct mark on the otherwise undamaged car. With his prisoner handcuffed and still under the protection of the watchdog, he reaches into the trunk of his cruiser and pulls out a plastic tarp and walks back to his prisoner. Desperately trying to keep a straight face, he tells the suspect that he couldn't find a diaper big enough for him and had to wrap him in a state police emergency, all purpose one. Of course the slightly aged baby had no recourse but to submit.

Matching wedding bands.

It is almost midnight when a State trooper notices a van on the side of a narrow road. Although it is sparsely traveled the proximity of the van to the road could present a possible problem and stops his cruiser behind the van and cautiously approaches. When he shines his light through the back window he observes a couple having sex and taps on the glass. Despite his presence, they do not disengage their act but instead hold up their left hand; exposing matching wedding bands. Determining that the female is not in duress and an obvious willing participant, he casually walks over to the driver's side of the slowly rocking van.

Curious to find out what is going on he patiently waits. A moment later he hears a masculine moan of ecstasy and then the driver's side window slides down exposing two embarrassing looking faces staring back at him. Somehow managing not to laugh and maintain a professional edge he breaks the ice and says: **"The reason I stopped is because your van is parked at a rather precarious location." "I also wanted to make sure that everything is all right." "I hope that by the sounds of things, everything went well and both of you got it out of your system."** The responding smiles on the couple's face results in laughter by all three. With his curiosity still on edge he asks: **"Look, I know that everything is obviously copasetic but I still would like to know what the hell is going on." "The flashing of the wedding bands?"**

The partially clad driver grabs the pile of clothing crumpled up on the passenger side and extracts his driver's license and the female, now wearing her underwear, hands him her license. A quick glance at matching last names reveals that the couple is married. Lost for words he blurts out: **"Now I definitely have to know what you two are up to."** The driver replies: **"I know that you will find this hard to believe what I am going to tell you."** Somewhat impatient the trooper interrupts him and encourages him to go on and the driver continues: **"Well, both of our parents are visiting us at the same time and are going to stay with us for three more days." "To be very frank with you, we just couldn't wait another day to have sex." "But we just couldn't find a way to do it at the house." "So we decided to have it here."** Shocked, he shakes his head and replies: **"Don't you think a short pause at a motel would have been much more comfortable." "Yeah, it would have cost you a few bucks but would have saved you some embarrassment." "Besides that, you could have enjoyed your tryst in a much more leisurely fashion." "If you feel the urge again, please consider a motel alternative."** On his way back to his car he turns and says: **"It was a pleasure meeting you two; even under the very unusual circumstances." "Good night."**

Gung ho.

A prominent individual in the state, threatened by a foreign organization, turns to the State Police for help. When an investigation by the State Police legitimizes the threat a unit is created to provide 24 hour security. Unforeseen circumstances several days later, caused by a temporary "one-man" shortage to the security team has to be filled immediately. Due to the critical time restraints, a regular road trooper with a relatively short time on the job is assigned to fill the gap. Although the young trooper's impetuous behavior on a couple previous occasions was frowned upon, it was excused as "gung ho" since he is new to the job and wants to make his mark,.

When the regularly assigned senior trooper arrives to relief the young trooper he is unable to find him at the preselected location. Getting somewhat concerned about the young trooper and not wishing to cause an alarm, he softly calls out the young trooper's name. His heart almost stops beating when he suddenly notices a distinctive red dot on his chest and then hears a voice telling him to look up. Hovering between fear and curiosity he looks up and spots the smiling face of the young trooper hiding in the tree above him; still pointing the rifle at him.

Relieved that the threat is not real, the trooper's greatest desire at that moment is to kick the young trooper's ass; especially when he brags about his superb concealment ability. Perhaps fortunately for both, professional conduct prevails. When he is finished with his barrage of expletives, the senior trooper relieves the "wannabe" secret agent.

According to informed sources appropriate disciplinary action was taken. Already skating on thin ice it took one more lame-brain stunt for the young trooper to realize that the ice isn't going to hold again after his final coup de grace. While assigned as part of a security detail he attempted to sell 'Amway' products to attendees at a country club function; wearing his State Police uniform. The subsequent punishment must have sunk through his dimwitted head because he never had another brain laps. The fact that he is basically a quite capable trooper may have saved him from being dismissed from the division.

Say what?

Responding to the judge's sentencing a defendant says:

"Say what?" "Man, dat' shit ain' right."

"No f*ckin' way."

"Yo' all f*cked up."

"No wunna' yo' wearing a black nightgown inna' daytime."

"Na, fow' real, I'm sorry judge fow' what I jus' said."

"But I want you to unnerstan' that I'm trying all da' time to reframe (refrain) from using expearlatives' (expletives) like dat'."

"I was jus' pissed an' had to let off some of my steam." "Yo' know what I'm saying?"

I found him. He is mine!

A City patrol unit, responding to a possible abduction, arrives at the scene. As soon as the two officers emerge from their patrol vehicle they are met by an irate midget; a very concerned elderly man and standing next to him a large, boyish appearing and confused younger man. In an effort to deescalate the brewing temper, the officers begin their investigation with the most vocal of the trio; the midget.

The little person begins to relate what transpired and why the police was called. **"Mr. ... here** (pointing) **called my company and asked them to repair an electrical problem."** The officers then realize the reason for the electric company truck parked in front of the house and listen to what the little electrician has to say.

> "I walked up to the front door and rang the door bell. After about a minute or so, the door opened and this guy (pointing at the boyish appearing man) stood at the door. When he saw me his mouth fell open and he suddenly had a big surprised grin on his face. Before I had a chance to say anything, he just grabbed me and lifted me up like a bundle of rags and carried me inside. Once we were inside he stuck me in a closet and locked the door. I screamed and pounded on the closet door but no one heard me. A few minutes later he came back and still had that big smile on

> his face and offered me something to eat. Although he was nice to me and it was quite obvious that he wasn't really going to hurt me; I wanted to get the hell out of there. He acted like I was his play puppet. It wasn't until quite some time later that Mr. …, his father, unlocked the closet door and set me free and brought me back into the living room where his son was, who had grabbed me. Well, he can tell you rest of the story. But I want his son charged for kidnapping me."

Hoping to get to the truth of a very delicate issue as quickly as possible, the officers turn their attention to Mr. …; the father of the big young man who appears to be deeply concerned. Displaying obvious embarrassment he begins his story.

> "Although my son here (pointing at him) is somewhat slow, he is harmless and can function quite well on his own. I was busy in the back yard and told him that when the electrician comes to let him in and then call me. When I hadn't heard anything from the electric company after quite some time, I went inside the house to make another call. While I was standing by the phone, I noticed my son sneak into my bedroom; so I followed him. I watched him opening the closet door and talk to someone inside the closet. It was then that I heard a voice pleading with him to let them out. I immediately pushed my son aside and was shocked to find Mr.… (Electrician) cowering on the closet floor and allowed him to come out immediately. I honestly did not know just how infatuated my son was with the "Travelocity" gnome. Apparently when he saw this small man (Electrician); in his childish mind he thought that he had found his own gnome and wanted to keep him. You can see, he meant no harm and only wanted him as a play pal."

Suddenly the big young man erupts into a tantrum and yells: **"That's not fair to take him away from me." "He is mine." "I found him and I want to keep him." "He is my new friend."** The officers quickly grab the big man before he has another chance at kidnapping.

Although it is getting more difficult to keep a straight face, the officers maintain a professional posture. A call to the electric company by one of them confirms that the midget is employed by the company and they also were concerned about his safety; they hadn't heard from him since he notified them that he had arrived at the residence. When the officer has finished with the full story, the manager of the company goes berserk and tells him that he will prefer charges.

Several months later a kind and considerate judge finds reasonable extenuating circumstances to dismiss the case; a full day's pay for labor and service charges as restitution. Another electric company with a much taller electrician completed the job.

Not a dental extraction.

As he nears the scene of a burglary in progress, the State trooper turns his lights off and coasts into the empty lot. Careful not to make any noise he sneaks towards the back of the Home Improvement Center and spots the burglar stacking items against the fence and orders him to stop and raise his hands. Obviously shocked, the burglar immediately runs away and climbs on top of a pile of wooden pallets conveniently stacked against the opposite side of the fence; possibly to assist in an escape attempt. When the burglar stands on top of the pile of pallets and reaches for the fence, he suddenly stops. Once again he is ordered to stop and raise his hands. When the culprit ignores the command, the trooper becomes more aggressive.

Not willing to take a chance with this guy he yells: **"Put your hands up in the air where I can see them!" "If you're not going to raise your hands you're going to force me to shoot you." "I'm not going to tell you again to put your hands up where I can see them."** When the burglar still doesn't comply, he screams: **"Put em' up, now!"** A few extremely tense seconds pass and the thief hollers back: **"I can't, I'm stuck and I'm holding myself up." "If I do, I'm going to fall through."** Cautiously moving towards him to get a closer look the trooper is able to verify the suspect's predicament. Although he manages not to laugh, he can't resist a parting shot and says: **"Boy, talk about a tight spot." "That's one of the best burglar traps I have ever seen." "I'm sure you've heard of dental extractions." "They usually leave a hole." "Well tonight it's going to be in reverse because this is an anal cavity extraction." "So just hang in there and don't go anywhere."** Relieved that he doesn't have to take drastic action, the trooper returns to his cruiser and requests assistance for an extraction.

OK! You got me!

A State trooper just purchased a fresh cup of coffee, pulls his cruiser onto the shoulder and decides to take advantage of the lull to catch up writing his reports. When he is finished arranging his reports, he reaches for his hot cup of coffee and very carefully proceeds to remove the lid. Suddenly, out of nowhere, a car comes up from his left rear and screeches to an abrupt halt behind him, almost causing him to spill the hot liquid onto his lap and over the paperwork. he is For a very brief moment he is left totally speechless; helplessly at the mercy of the uninvited motorist. Spellbound, he watches the driver's side door fly open and a middle-aged man jump out and rush towards him.

Before he even has a chance to ask a question, the man holds his driver's license in front of the trooper's face and exclaims: **"All right!" "You got me!" "I know." "I was speeding." "So just give me the ticket so I can go." "I've got to go to work."** Although, initially somewhat confused, he quickly realizes what transpired in the upset motorist's mind. Barely able to hold his laughter in check, he manages to rally his professional composure and replies:

> "Well Sir, I thank you for being so honest and straight forward with me. Also, the fact that I didn't have to chase you down and you instead came to me, is something I will take into consideration and not give you a ticket. Furthermore, I'm not even going to give you a written warning but just a verbal warning. Now slow it down a little bit and have a save trip to work. This time it's on me. Next time it's going to be on you. Have I made myself clear?"

Almost bowing down to the trooper, the motorist can't believe his luck; profusely thanks the trooper and shakes his hand and hurries back to his car.

Although he makes several attempts to return to his report writing, he closes the lid on his coffee cup and requests to return to the troop. He is simply unable to do anything else and has to tell the unbelievable story to someone. Besides, coffee tastes better hot.

What ya'll doin' here?

Responding to the residents' request to have the police do something about the large number of speeders, the State trooper parks his cruiser along the curb in the predominantly black neighborhood and adjusts the cone of his radar unit. While waiting for the first violator he notices that a group of young boys, ranging in age from six to ten have gathered a safe distance away from him. His attention is particularly drawn to the oldest appearing of the group and finds it somewhat disturbing to see an angry kibitz on a child so young. Rather than simply ignore the group, he decides to engage the boy with the 'evil eye' and smiling at him says: **"Hi, what are doing out of school?" "Oops, I forgot, it's Saturday".** Without bothering to answer the question the child replies: **"Man what yo' all doin' in ma' hood?"** Slightly flabbergasted, the trooper maintains a fatherly image and says: **"Well, as a matter of fact I was invited by members of your hood to come here to protect you and your friends and stop people from speeding through here."** Apparently surprised by the trooper's mild manner the youngster takes a few seconds before he continues: **"An' how yo' goin' to do all that?" "Shoot em'?" "Ha, ha, ha".** Without losing stride he chuckles and replies: **"Now why would I shoot someone?" "I may be forced to do that, but only if someone tries to really hurt you or me and I have tried everything else first." "I came here to help you." "Isn't that what friends are suppose to do?"** When the boy's menacing look disappears the trooper knows the hook has been swallowed and invites him to come to the patrol car.

"Why don't you come on over here and I'll show you how it's done." Still keeping a safe distance from the trooper and positioning himself in case he feels that he needs to run away, the little boy shakes his head and says: **"Nah, I've seen what you do when you come here." "I ain't' goin' to let you arrest me and put dem' handcuffs on me and take me to jail."** Having boys of his own, the trooper knows that kids at that age are very inquisitive. When he notices a couple of the other boys in the group getting a little fidgety, he very slowly reels the line in a little more and says: **"Here is what I'm going to do to show you that I'm here to help you." "Because I know that all of you are a bunch of good guys I'm going to give all of you a very special treat and allow you sit in my police car and watch me run radar." "Usually only other troopers get that chance." "All right?"**

When the trooper observes that their mental process is engaged but has not quite reached their legs. it is only a matter of time and. He then steps out of his car, opens the front and rear passenger doors of his cruiser, cranks down all the windows and sits back behind the steering wheel. Apparently satisfied that the trooper is on the level, the group cautiously begins to approach. Wishing for the youngsters to experience real policing and walk away with a positive image the trooper says: **"As you can see, I have left the doors open so that any of you who are afraid** (indirectly challenging their bravery) **can leave anytime that you want to." "I will also remain right here behind the wheel?" "So make yourselves comfortable."**

Still keeping a safety grip on the car door with his right hand the self-appointed spokesman finally slides across the seat toward him. Welcoming him the trooper smiles and says: **"Hey you might like what you see and want to become a State trooper some day."** He has hardly finished welcoming the boy when the rest of the little gang suddenly climbs into the back seat. Unable to find adequate place in the back, another squeezes himself against the boy on the front seat. The trooper's presence must have spread like wildfire when a throng of kids surrounds his cruiser. Even the antagonizing taunts, **"Man they finally done got yo'ass; ha, ha, ha"**, falls silent and the hecklers are enticed to join the party.

Realizing community relations is far more important than running radar and catching speeders; he decides to devote the time entertaining an excited crowd of kids. As he finally prepares to close shop an exuberant crowd, intermingled with adults, thank him and virtually beg him to please come back again. Undoubtedly, the operation far exceeded anything that would have been accomplished operating radar.

The new city ordinance.

A couple of City officers notice that the man standing at the street corner appears to grab his crotch; primarily when a car drives past. Not sure whether the man is doing it deliberately or just has a peculiar and unusual habit. Of course there is always the chance that the man is afraid to lose it and has to make sure that it still hanging there. Since grabbing his Johnson is not against the law per say, it could be considered annoying or even obscene by some. Rather than wait for a complaint to be lodged against the man, the officers decide to take some proactive action and call him over to their patrol car.

Still holding his private parts, the man says: **"Wuz'-up, officers?"** In a very kind manner one of them replies:

> "Look, you seem like a real descent dude and all and we don't want to see you get in trouble with the law. We just want to give you a friendly warning. The city just passed a new ordinance that makes it illegal for anyone to hold their private parts in public. It is a double fine if the person is standing on the street corner because so many people can see."

Before the officer is finished, the dude is grabbing himself again. Once again the officer has to reprimand him and the guy immediately removes his hand and apologizes profusely. The officers realize that they will not be able to hold back their laughter too much longer and have to get out of there quickly. They tell the dude that they have to leave because they don't want to arrest him but give him some time to get used to the new ordinance. He thanks them again; still holding his Johnson. One of the officers yells: **"What did we just tell you?"** Howling with laughter, they speed off.

Interfering with business.

A State trooper assigned on a special duty detail to assist the City police parks his marked unit next to the street curb. As he observes the pedestrian traffic he notices several rather provocatively attired females sashaying up and down the street and realizes that he is in the city's "Red-light" district. Engrossed and fascinated by the activities he almost failed to notice the gaudy looking Cadillac with more chrome on it than paint pull up to the curb directly opposite him. When the door of the Cadillac opens he is in total disbelief when he sees the driver exiting; obviously a pimp. Totally flabbergasted he thinks: ***"Even if totally inebriated or at a carnival, I wouldn't dare wear something like that."***

Dressed in his lime-green suit with an extra long jacket, matching socks, green patent leather shoes, sunglasses and a Fedora hat with long feathers; this character probably thinks that he is the cat's meow. Holding back his desire to laugh, the trooper cautiously watches him approach the cruiser. Addressing him in a pompous manner the pimp says: **"Yo' my man." "What's going on?"** Somehow managing to suppress his laugh the trooper replies: **"Oh, I had nothing else to do and just wanted to stop for a moment and enjoy the unusual scenery."** The pimp suddenly blurts out: **"See; now that's what I'm talking about." "That's why I wants to ax' you to move your vehicle a couple of blocks down de' street."** Acting naïve the trooper says: **"You can't be talking about those women."** Nodding his head in the direction of the hookers he deliberately thinks out loud and mutters: **"Man, I wouldn't touch any of them with a ten foot pole; even if they paid me."** He then notices the dirty look on the pimp's face and knows that his remark struck a nerve. Determined to have a little more fun with the green ostrich he continues: **"I appreciate the fact that you wanted to say (Hi) to me." "Or is there anything else that you want to talk to me about?"**

After a brief moment of silence the feathered hat asks: **"Like I sayed' befo', could you maybe move yo' car here, a couple of blocks down from here?" "Or maybe roun' de corna', or even de Parkin' Authority down dare'."** Pretending to be dumfounded by the request he replies: **"Why would I want to move?" "I have already told you that I enjoy the circus parade."** Suddenly, reversing the humorous atmosphere, the pimp glares at him and in an almost demanding tone asks him again to move the cruiser. Maintaining the upper hand, the trooper responds:

> "Look, this is a public street and that means I can park anywhere, except for areas designated where it is not allowed. Even then I might get permission, if on special assignment. Oh, wait a minute, it just dawned on me what the problem is and why you want me to move. Do you, just by chance, know these girls? Why of course you do. What was I thinking? Now I get it. Am I interfering with your business that you are trying to conduct here? Without a business license I may add. Well, since you haven't obtained your license yet, it looks like you are going to be temporarily out of business. You can't possibly expect me, especially as a law enforcement officer, to allow you to continue your illicit operation and partake in your crime. By the way, do you pay them workman's comp?"

Left momentarily speechless the highly agitated pimp glares at him and hatefully snarls at him with a barrage of expletives that would even make his girls blush. Not willing to let him go without a proper send off replies: **"I didn't mean to cause you cerebral pain." "But you ought to seek some help for your speech impediment."** Too angry to fully recover, the pimp just mutters: **"F*ck you!" "Mother f*cker!"** under his breath and storms off. He then makes a motion and several of the hookers come running up to him and stand next to his car. After a brief moment and countless threatening looks the motley group climbs into the chrome mobile and drives off.

You don't want me on your scales.

The State trooper has just pulled his cruiser into position to chase down truckers who attempt to avoid the weigh station. He has just situated himself when he notices a truck lumbering up the road. A strong indicator that the rig could be overloaded, he decides to stop it and conduct an inspection. The truck driver slowly pulls his rig onto the shoulder and glances into his side-mirror and watches the trooper approach. In a firm, yet polite manner the trooper requests the trucker's license and necessary paperwork. Apparently anticipating the trooper's question why he attempted to avoid the weigh station the trucker mutters: **"The reason that I wasn't going to get on yo' scales is because yo' don' want me on yo' scales." "Believe me!" "I'm jus' telling yo' that I don't want to go on dem' scales."**

Caught by surprise and curious the trooper asks: **"Ok sir, why don't you please enlighten me and tell me why you decided to avoid the scales and disobey the law."** The trucker replies: **"I need to know something firs'." "Are yo' orderin' or axkin' me to pull ma' rig onto dem' scales?"** Pointing and nodding his head in the affirmative the trooper tells him to pull into the weigh station. Obviously extremely reluctant to do what he has been ordered to do the trucker mumbles: **"Remember yo' de' once' dat' done tole' me to do so."** Grimacing, the trucker shifts his rig into gear and slowly lumbers towards the station.

Sneeking one last glance at the trooper the trucker pulls onto the platform. A loud thud suddenly overpowers the ambient noise as the truck sinks several inches into the ground. When the trucker hears other troopers screaming and running towards him, he jumps out of the cab and yells: **"I done tole' all of yo' so!" "Now yo' know that's why I didn't want to pull in here." "But yo'all insisset' fo' me to do it."** Shaking his head, the weigh station supervisor walks over to the group and glaring at the trucker shouts:

> "What the hell is wrong with you? Look what you have done! The scales are shot in the ass. Do you even know how much overweight you are? I was only able to get a partial reading before the scale collapsed. You are at least

> 15000 pounds overweight. How in the hell you were able to carry it is way beyond me; but your ass belongs to the state."

Since he is not in a position to argue, the trucker sheepishly replies: **"Das' why I kept telling yo' that I didn't wanna' pull in here."** A final loud thud is the coup de grâce of the weigh station.

No authority to declare him dead.

A State trooper FTO (Field Training Officer) and his new recruit trooper, responding to a body washed ashore, arrive at the scene. To find out what his recruit is made of, the FTO decides to test him and his common sense and briskly walks over to the bloated body lying on the water's edge. As he watches his recruit, the FTO notices the recruit's pale face and struggling to hold back what he had to eat earlier that day and begins his act.

> "Well, to us it appears quite obvious that the poor man is dead. However, according to the law, we are not authorized to pronounce him dead and it is our duty to administer First Aid. In cases like this, only a medical person or someone from the medical examiner's office is allowed to pronounce him dead. Since I am your FTO and have already performed CPR on a few occasions; it's time for you to learn. I suggest that you drag him over onto the dry part of the sand; so you don't mess up your uniform. Remember, there are people watching you, so be professional."

Struggling to hold back the desire to laugh, the FTO squints his eyes as he watches and waits for his young charge's reaction. With a sudden expression of horror on his face the recruit stares momentarily at the corpse and then almost pleading asks: **"Sir, for God's sake, anybody can see that he has been dead for quite some time." "Besides that, he looks like a balloon, ready to explode."** The FTO likes the fact that the recruit has the fortitude to question an unrealistic order and now wants to see up to what point his recruit will stand his ground and starts again: **"Look, I'm only telling what the law requires and you also need some hands on training in CPR." "So what do you intend to do?"**

Totally unexpected, the recruit trooper assumes a ridged posture and firmly looking his FTO in the eyes says: **"Look sir, with all due respect, that is a totally unrealistic order." "I, therefore, respectfully decline to carry it out!" "Furthermore, I will defend my case to the fullest extent necessary." "Is there anything else?" "Sir!"** After a brief moment of silence a broad smile appears on the FTO's face and he replies:

> "That is precisely what I wanted to hear and see. I wanted you to confirm that you have what it takes to be trooper and stick to your guns. You were absolutely right. I tell you right now, if you had not taken a stand on the side of logic and correctness, I would have been very tempted to kick you square in the ass. My defense would have been that you were too weak and incompetent to stand up for what is right; job well done."

Both of them stand next to the cruiser and wait for the medical examiner. Since the FTO knows the medical examiner personally he can't resist telling him what has just transpired. While listening to the FTO's story the medical examiner is unable to keep a straight face and with a hearty laugh bursts out: **"This is the first time ever that I laughed when picking up a stiff." "But I must admit that was a valuable lesson taught and learned."** Nodding in the direction of the recruit he says: **"Looks like he has what it takes to be a trooper."**

Overdrawn account.

A State trooper arriving at the scene of a "Domestic in progress" hears loud commotion coming from inside the residence and cautiously enters the house through the partially ajar front door. The unannounced appearance of the trooper doesn't seem to bother the young couple sitting at the kitchen table from hurling verbal insults at each other. Concerned that the situation could quickly escalate because his presence doesn't seem to make a difference to the verbal combatants, the trooper intervenes with a very firm and authoritative voice and demands: **"Now listen up!" "That is enough!" "So zip it for a moment and tell me what is going on; one at a time."**

Holding a piece of paper in his hand, the man breaks the silence and says: **"That dumb ass really did it this time with our checking account." "I have told her before to be more careful." "But what did she do this time?" "She not only overdrew on the account but now we also have to pay the bank extra, an 'Overdraw-charge' for her stupid mistake."** His wife's protest is intervened by the trooper's polite request to view the document; willingly handed to him. When he is finished reading, it confirms that according to the notice, the bank has assessed a processing fee for her (wife's) mistake for having overdrawn a total of $158.00 on the account. Appearing to be totally frustrated the wife suddenly yells: **"That can't be true!" "I keep telling him** (husband) **that the bank made a mistake; not me." "But hard head here won't let me explain."** Preventing another likely eruption, he turns to the wife and calmly says: **"All right, let's keep it civil." "Why don't you tell me your side of the story Ma'am?" "Then we might be able to sort things out and solve the problem."**

Having been given a chance to tell her side of the story, the wife grabs her check book but is momentarily too excited to speak and is only able to point at the attached checks. Breathing heavily, she finally regains her composure and stammers: **"See, I have two more checks here." "I told you that the bank is wrong."** Somewhat dumbfounded by her actions he placidly asks: **"What do the checks have to do with this issue?"** Obviously unable to understand the question she blurts out: **"My God are you as stupid as he is?" "I just showed you the checks that I have left." "Look!"** Maintaining his professional edge, he asks if she would grant him permission to scrutinize her check book. Hesitating for a moment she asks: **"Do you know anything about accounting?"** Extending his hand towards her just smiles and assures her that he has been able to keep his own checking account in order for quite a few years and that it certainly doesn't require a degree in accounting. The trooper requests a calculator, takes the check book and sits down at the table.

When he is finished, he looks at the couple and says: **"Well, according to my calculations the bank's claims are legitimate and the mistake was made by you; Ma'am."** Furious with the trooper's assessment, she jumps off her chair, snatches the check book out of his hand and yells: **"I thought you knew how to keep a check book."** Totally frustrated she points at her husband and screams: **"I can see that you are just as stupid as he is."** Fervently pointing at the check book she continues screaming: **"Both of you are a bunch of dumb-asses."** Almost loosing it, she violently flashes the checkbook and screams: **"Here, can you see these checks?" "Do you see these?" "That means I can't be overdrawn like the bank and you jerks claim." "How can I?" "I still have two checks left."** Unable to make heads or tails out of her illogical explanation asks her to please be so kind and explain what she means by that.

With an expression of disbelieve on her face she replies: **"What's so difficult to understand?" "OK 'Dumbo' let me see if I can bring it down to <u>your</u> level." "I just showed you the two blank checks in my book." "Right?" "Since I still have checks left, I can't be out of money." "Obviously the bank forgot that I have not written out all of my checks."** The trooper is beyond disbelieve and sees the husband suddenly grab his head and fiercely pulling his hair yells: **"I can't believe what I just heard."** Then turning to his wife he asks: **"You mean to tell me that you believe that you can write a check as long as you have one left?"** Responding meekly says: **"Yes; that's what I thought."** Unable to reply, the husband lowers his face and pounds his fists on the table top. In a rather nonchalant manner the trooper says to the husband, **"From the looks of things, I believe that <u>we</u>** (emphasized) **have solved the problem." "As far as I am concerned, I am finished here." "Maybe you can find a way to clarify it further to your wife." "Remember – for better or worse."** Shaking his head says good bye and closes the door behind him.

Brand new uniform.

The local sheriff hangs up the phone and says to his deputy: **"Looks like 'Buddy' has a bigger problem than he is able to handle by hisself'." "He says that they is really fightin' at his place and is**

afraid that they is going to tear up his place an' all." "I guess we better done mosey on over there and educate dem' boys an' show em' how to behave." Pointing at the young civilian and potential recruit says: **"Ya'll might as well come along with us and learn how to handle a bunch of drunk' rowdies."** A broad smile on the youngster's face indicates his eagerness to join the party.

When they turn the car engine off, they can hear the loud commotion coming from inside the rather neglected looking watering hole. The sheriff steps out of the cruiser and begins to undo his tie and unbutton his shirt and motions to the deputy to do likewise. Totally perplexed by the sheriff's behavior the deputy hesitantly asks: **"Ya' want me to do that too?"** Somewhat annoyed for being questioned by his subordinate the sheriff replies: **"Ya' think that I'm going to let that bunch in there ruin dis' brand new uniform?" "Remember how damn long I done fought with da' mayor to buy em' for this department?" "Dey' ain't cheap, ya' know."** Left with no other choice, the deputy dutifully follows his boss's order and carefully folds his uniform shirt, places the tie and hat on top and sticks it in the trunk of the patrol car. Then copying the sheriff, he straps his gun belt around his waist and grabs a firm hold of his nightstick.

When both half-uniformed officers are properly attired the sheriff says: **"Ok, let's show dem boys how it's done."** Suddenly the potential new prospect blurts: **"Can you really do that what you plan to do?" "Don't you have to somehow identify yourself and show them that you are the police?" "I mean badge an' all?"** As the sheriff turns and glanced at him says: **"Don't ya' worry none son, dem' boys not only know who we are but also know damn well that dey' is going to get their ass beat if they don't stop dare' tom foolery when we walk in." "Com-mon' depty' let's crash de party."** A short time later two T-shirt clad and pistol toting LEOs escort a couple handcuffed scruffies to the waiting patrol car; peace and quiet returns to the hinterland.

A unique skill.

The D/Sgt (Detective Sergeant) sneaks a quick glance at his partner, a silent message that he has reached the end of listening to the stupidity of the suspect's obvious prevarication. Tapping his pen on his writing pad and squinting at the suspect says:

> "This concludes our interview for today. But before you go let me tell you something that I find somewhat remarkable about what you told us. I suppose that we can safely assume that most advanced living things have a specific orifice to defecate and the other to communicate; otherwise it could cause definite problems. It's probably due to the absence of vocal chords in one of them. Don't you agree? Heifers, for instance, are only able to leave gaseous and frequent physical aspects of their expression behind. Occasionally though, there are people who believe that they possess a unique skill and practice vocalizing through both. Fortunately for us though we didn't have to watch where we had to step since our cerebral ears eventually guided us through your pasture though."

Mumbling something incoherent under his breath the suspect doesn't say anything audible and walks out of the interview room. The blank stare, followed by a confused frown apparently reached the limit of the suspect's intellectual level.

Where is your husband?

The State Police RO (Radio Operator) looks out of the troop window and noticed that a particular white late model Cadillac is again parked in an area marked "Troop Personnel Only". Since he doesn't know who owns the car and is curious to find out which trooper got a new vehicle calls the shift supervisor. An inquiry conducted by the Sergeant reveals that no one at the troop owns the vehicle and tells the RO to run a license plate check which reveals that the owner is not a state employee. Not wishing to jump the gun, the Sgt informs the RO to watch who gets into the car and from which direction the person approaches the vehicle. Later that afternoon the RO advises the Sgt that he just saw a man coming from the massage parlor and porn-shop and then squeeze himself through an opening in the hedge and quickly climb into his car. The Sgt says: "**Keep an eye out for that car for the next few days or whenever you are working and let me know right away.**"

Two weeks later when the two of them are working together again, the RO tells the Sgt that he just saw the same man park his car in the troop parking lot again. The Sgt asks the RO if he is certain that the operator has gone to the porn-shop. When the RO confirms his observation, the Sgt is determined to do something about it this time and replies: **"OK." "Let's see what we can do." "Get me a tag number so I can find the owner's phone number."** When the Sgt finds the phone number, he picks up the phone. **"Yes Ma'am, this is Sgt .... of the State Police." "The reason that I am calling is to find out if you still own the 1976 Cadillac." "Oh your husband does." "No, no problem to get alarmed." "We just need to know why his car is parked here in the 'Troop Personnel Only' area of our parking lot." "Oh, never mind." "We have located him." "We just saw him coming out of the massage parlor and porn-shop." "Sorry to have bothered you."** Click.

From that moment on the Cadillac is not seen again. Maybe he found another place and someone to give him a deeper massage; maybe even a better hiding place. At least his wife doesn't have to worry from now on where he goes.

Let's have a shift party.

Members of several small town police departments decided to have an after-work shift party and meet at the rear parking lot of one of the police departments located in a rather rural area. As the party progresses one the officers, annoyed by the bright light of the lamppost illuminating the area, complains to the group and wants to know if there is any way to turn off the damn light. Someone in the group replies: **"No!" "It's controlled by a timer."** The irritated officer, apparently dissatisfied with the answer, retorts: **"Well, guess what?" "Time is up." "So let me reset it."**

Before any of the party goers fully comprehend what is going on a loud '**bang**' is heard; followed by a small, quick flash of lightning and then darkness. Obviously in momentary shock, no one is able to utter a sound through wide open mouths. Suddenly the laughter of the rogue shooter breaks through the silence. As he slowly holsters his handgun and saucer-like eyes stare back at him as if questioning his mental status says: **"Man did you see that?" "I hardly took aim and hit the light bulb." "Damn, I wish I could shoot that good on the range."**

Relieved that no calls of gunshots are reported, some of the attendees manage a slight laugh while others just shake their heads. Talk about stupid having dumb luck.

Let's see if you can outrun a bullet.

A State Police Captain, in close proximity to the area, hears the radio dispatch a trooper to a burglary in progress decides to assist and arrives at the scene simultaneous with the trooper. As they approach the house, they hear the loud slam of a door and get a quick glance of the suspect bolting out of the house. Although he recognized the burglar, he instinctively wants to give chase and asks the captain to notify central that he is pursuit. (In those days a trooper was totally on his own once he exited his patrol unit.) However the dark weather and a quick visual reconnoiter of the terrain reveals a multitude of possible hiding places for a fleeing suspect to lie in wait and afford too much of an advantage for the suspect. The trooper decides to call off the chase, since it is senseless to follow the culprit in the dark through the underbrush and his flashlight telegraphing his exact whereabouts; but not without doing the following first.

The Captain has just caught up with the trooper when he hears him holler: **"Hey Luther, you better come on out before I flush you out with a bang." "You are not going to like what I have in mind." "Well let's see how fast you can really run."** When there is no response from Luther he removes his gun from the holster and fires two shots into the ground. Suddenly the area behind the house comes to live with the cracking of tree branches and a dark silhouette frantically running towards the partially frozen creek. Then the breaking of ice and splashing of water indicate that Luther got away and outran the bullets.

Still laughing, the trooper turns to the captain and says: **"Did you see that son of a bitch run like he had a set of afterburners stuck up his ass?" "Well, he may have gotten away tonight, but his ass is going to be mine tomorrow."** Expecting the Captain to laugh also, he instead sees a stern look on his face and is surprised when he says: **"The reason that I'm not going to prefer charges against you is because you did have sense enough to shoot into the ground."** Unable to let it go at that, he smiles and says: **"Common' Captain, you have to admit that was funny." "Why don't you lighten up just a little?" "And I want you to know that I sincerely mean that with all due respect."** The Captain replies: **"Like I said no charges."** The trooper is positive that the stern look was missing on the Captain's face that time.

I didn't do anything wrong.

A State trooper, following a car speeding excessively and weaving in and out of traffic, orders the motorist to pull over onto the shoulder. He isn't even given a chance to utter a sound when the female operator suddenly flicks her hand in front of his face, as if scolding a child and telling it to shut up and goes into an annoyed tirade.

> "Don't you even start with whatever and tell me that I did something wrong. I'm telling **you** right now that I obeyed the law just like it says here in this book (shaking a small Driver's Manual). Do you see this? Well that's my daughter's and she is studying for her driver's test. I have you know that I did exactly what it says in here to do. Do I need to show you - Mr. Law? It says right in here that you should drive on the right and pass on the left, which I did the entire way. If you paid attention you would have seen that I passed on the left and as soon as I could I went right away back into the right-hand lane. So there you have it."

Fighting the strong desire to verbally retaliate in kind, he somehow manages to remain professional, introduces himself and politely asks her: **"Ma'am, I need to see your license and registration."** As she hands him her license, she snaps: **"Here you can see for yourself that I have a clean record and obey the law." "Instead of picking on me, you ought to catch the criminals." "Isn't that what you are supposed to be doing in the first place and being paid for?"** He politely thanks and tells her that he will be back shortly. While slowly walking back to his cruiser, he is surprised that he was able to stay calm and ponders the thought of getting even; his way.

When he is finished writing the tickets, one for "Speeding" and the other for "Careless Driving" he grabs his Traffic Code book and steps out of his cruiser. On his way back to the lady's car he senses a slight bounce in his gait. Holding the traffic arrest tickets in his hand where she can see them, he begins:

> "I appreciate the fact that you familiarized yourself with a small aspect of your highly abridged version of this book. I guess that's almost similar to having memorized a verse in the Bible and then claim to have read the whole Bible. Unfortunately that little book has only a small part of what this book has and doesn't address speeding and flitzing in and out of traffic lanes. Since you may not be that well acquainted with the law, the specific section numbers of your offenses that you are being charged with are also listed on the tickets. I don't have the time to show them to you in my official book right now, but since the section numbers are listed on the ticket you may peruse them at your leisure. I'm sure you may find a copy of our Traffic Code in the library. If not, a court certainly does. Please sign at the bottom acknowledging the receipt and press hard so you will be able to read your copy."

For a split second it looks as though she is going to start in again as she gruffly snatches it out of his hand. When she is finished signing and waits for her receipt, she glares at him and snarls: **"Is that all?"** He politely replies: **"Yes Ma'am that is all." "Please slow down and don't forget to drive right." "Have a nice day."**

He is not responding.

Somewhat imbibed and in need of travel directions a motorist spots a police cruiser parked off the shoulder on a slightly elevated portion of ground and pulls his car onto the shoulder. Not wishing to alarm the officer the motorist waves his arms in the air and cautiously approaches the officer and is stunned that the officer keeps looking straight ahead and doesn't seem to react to his presence. Reluctant to take the chance to knock on the window and startle the officer and possibly getting shot, he decides to return to his car; flips the top of his cell phone and pushes 911. The call taker asks: **"What is the nature of your emergency?"**

> "Well I don't know if it is a real emergency but there seems to be something wrong with one of your officer's right here. Oh, I'm on the Interstate and ..... an' parked pretty close to him. I tried to get some directions from him but he doesn't react and just keeps staring straight ahead. I was afraid to get any closer and suddenly scare the shit out of him and get shot. I'm kind of in a hurry, but I'll try to wait here for a little while."

When the motorist sees the responding officer he jumps out of his vehicle and frantically points at the cruiser parked off the shoulder. The officer calmly tells the excited motorist to wait and stand by his car while he is going to check on the officer still sitting motionless in his cruiser. When he has finished his pretend cursory investigation the officer walks back to the anxious motorist and begins:

> "Oh, everything is alright. That's just Billy Mannakeen meditating again and slip into one of his trances. At least he is following instructions. We told him to keep his eyes open so that passing motorists don't think he is sleeping on the job. Don't worry he'll be out of it before too long. I also notice that you have been drinking and shouldn't be driving. Apparently you've been lucky so far tonight because there is no damage to your car. To make sure that you stay out of trouble for tonight I'll allow you stay in one of our luxurious rooms overnight. After all, you

> were kind enough to concern yourself about poor Billy. Let me pat you down first and then I'll have to handcuff you. Just following departmental policy when transporting someone in a police cruiser.."

And you thought that you've heard it all.

No thanks; I'm all right.

A pair of police officers on patrol in a city in Germany notices a man struggling pushing a Volkswagen car by himself and pull up behind him. One of the officers asks him if they can help. They are somewhat puzzled by the man's curt reply when he immediately blurts out in an almost annoyed manner: **"Everything is fine." "I don't need any help."** Considering his plight, the officers find the man's response somewhat curious and decide to take a closer look.

A quick glance of the immediate surrounding area indicates that they are in very close proximity of a garage with several cars tightly parked together around the front and right side of the building. While scanning the area closer their eyes are drawn to the vacant spot at the edge of the parking lot next to the street. Recognizing the signs of a possible car theft, they quickly exit their patrol vehicle and position themselves around the suspect car; one at each car door. It is obvious to the officers that the suspect was going to push the car he has stolen downhill to pick up some speed to get it jump-started. A majority of vehicles in Germany are standard shift and if pushed fast enough can be jump-started.

With their quarry greatly hindered, one of the officers begins:

> ""Look, we can't just leave you here and struggle with your car so we'll help you. Why don't you try it again and let's see what's going on with your car. Don't you have to put the key into the ignition or is it automatic start? (No response from the suspect.) Did you hear me? Put the key back in the ignition. Man it's doing nothing; it's not even making a peep."

When the officers begin to push the vehicle they notice that it appears to be very light and relatively easy to push. Suspicious of the lack of weight of the Beatle, one of them lifts the trunk lid (VW have engine in rear). Noticing that the engine is missing, the officer says:

> "Oh, now I see why you didn't need a key. No wonder nothing is happening. What did you do with the motor? Didn't you know that the engine is missing? Someone must have stolen it. Nah wait, you must have known that and just didn't bother with the key. Maybe you just guessed that, huh?"

Having some difficulty holding back his laugh, the other officer chimes in:

> "No he isn't that dumb; that's why he was trying to push his car into the garage here to get it worked on. He probably heard about the special. 'Bring your empty car to us and we'll fill it with an engine.' Well, maybe he is kinda' stupid after all because he is pushing his car in the wrong direction. Nah' maybe he was just looking for a parking place at the garage. Hey 'Dumkopf', didn't you see that open space right next to the street? You just wasted all of your energy and pushed it right past it. However, since we are a bunch of nice guys we are going to help you anyway. So why don't you get out of the car and let me put the handcuffs on you. It's your lucky night though because we are only charging you for trespassing and auto theft. We couldn't find criminal charges for stupidity or pushing a stolen car without an engine on a public street during the hours of darkness."

Criminals do indeed do the dumbest things; even in other countries.

There is a God. *(A County officer's reflection.)*

I'm not one to revel in the misfortunes of others. However, when said about someone who is a douche bag, I say Cheers! And bask in its sweet taste. As I was driving down the road today, I erred on the side of caution and due to inclement weather I drove in a slow, steady pace below the posted speed limit. When I glanced in my rear view mirror I observed a car fast approaching with nary a sign of care. Hey, sport cars must be immune to the wrath of Mother Nature who is apparently on her period. The car came up fast then changed lanes, its operator glaring at me as he passed me; as if I was some idiot for being cautious. Speeding off ahead of me at a fast pace, it changed lanes and this is where it got glorious. The ass end of the car began to argue with itself, debating which lane it preferred; dancing an Argentine Tango between right and left. Suddenly, it changed styles and performed three pirouettes worthy of the finest Swan Lake Ballet before launching itself into a Gran Finale off road snow and grass. I have no doubt that had this been an Olympic event, the operator would have taken the gold. As I slowly drove by, I tooted my horn and waved....yes....there is a God!

Just another day on patrol. # 6

Officer: **"Yes sir, you are absolutely right....this is a speed trap." "I trapped you doing 58 mph in a 25 mph zone by sitting in broad daylight on the side of the road; in a neighborhood."**

(From the –(*"I Think I Just Threw Up in My Mouth."*) (A small Police Department.)

Officer: **"Sir, you really need to call it quits with your girlfriend." "This is like the fourth time I've dealt with you over her!"**

Subject: **"I tried!" "I just can't!" "The sex is so good with her!"**

Officer: **"Yeah but she's sleeping with all those other guys too." "It can't be all that good or worth it!"**

Subject: **"Sergeant, you don't understand!" "She's my Fifty Shades Of Grey!"**

(Uhmmmm, yeah..........Fifty Shades Of Grey in a trailer. Fifty Shades of Filth is more like it! LOL)

Just a little peck on the cheek.

The nasty disposition of the K-9 handler's dog is well known, especially to the personnel assigned to this particular troop and have been warned to stay clear of the animal and give it a wide berth. A senior trooper and seasoned detective, stationed at the troop for at least a couple of years, apparently thought that he had developed a special rapport with the unpredictable hound.

On this certain evening the K-9 handler just sat down to write a report and commanded the shepherd to stay in the corner of the assembly room. When the detective enters the troop and spots the dog he decides to walks over to him. Before the shocked K-9 handler is able to interfere; lightning strikes and it is all over. While recuperating in the hospital emergency later that evening, he is not able to fully explain what made him do such a foolish thing.

Sporting a large menacing scar on the right side of his face, the detective returns to the troop a few weeks later and rejoins the fold. Although he is still at a loss to explain the reason for his actions, he begins to describe his harrowing ordeal to his fellow troopers.

> "Hell, I still don't know what possessed me to do something that stupid. I just thought that the damn dog wouldn't really do anything unless he was seriously provoked or ordered to attack. I guess I also wanted to prove that he is really not all that bad as he is made out to be. So I bent down and told the dog to kiss me. Well, thirty stitches and almost losing my eye; the son-of-a-bitch proved that he is a genuine badass."

Determined not to let it go with just a simple welcome back, they first make sure that their friend has fully recovered and is doing well. Exploding in laughter, their verbal punishment starts:

> "I bet you were surprises when he gave you a French-kiss instead of just a peck on the cheek."

> "Did you tongue him back or did he have bad breath?"

"Nah', he flunked his first exam on how to dog-kiss."

"I tell you what; I would have bit him back an' right on his ass."

"I wonder if there is something in our Rules and Regulations that addresses how and when to kiss a police dog?"

"No, just on stupidity."

"You are definitely lucky not to have lost your eye; someone could have snuck up on you on your blind side."

"Seriously, welcome back and very glad that you are all right."

Shortly thereafter it is decided to get rid of the dog because of his unpredictable nature. Claiming that the dog is nuts, the K-9 handler's recommendation to euthanize the dog is ignored and the animal is donated to a security agency. Frequent requests by the security agency to have the K-9 handler come there and control the dog make it quickly apparent that the security agency is unable to manage the animal. Level heads finally prevail and carry out the K-9 handler's recommendation.

A terrible day playing Golf.

The State trooper glances at the car speedometer verifying that the vehicle he is following is speeding and turns his red lights on and pulls his cruiser onto the curb behind the other vehicle. He has not fully exited his cruiser when the driver of the other car jumps out of his car and approaches him huffing: **"You are delaying me unjustly!" "I wasn't even speeding and running late for work!"** Concerned about the driver's safety, he orders the highly irate driver to walk onto the shoulder and stand behind his vehicle.

Another trooper, well known for his extremely dry sense of humor, happens to drive by and pulls up behind them to check on their safety. Briefly listening to the two and apparently realizing that his shift partner has an issue with the motorist buts in and says: **"Man I have never been so disgusted with my Golf game." "Do you know what I did?"** Totally ignoring the motorist, he begins to lament over the horrible experience with his Golf game.

Flabbergasted by his shift partner's rant the trooper and the motorist just stand there and stare at him in disbelief. Temporarily left speechless, the trooper looks at the motorist he has stopped and shrugs his shoulders, gesturing - what the Hell is going on? Suddenly the motorist blurts out: **"I've had enough of this." "Just give me the damn ticket and let me out of here." "I'm already late."** Without saying another word the trooper with the dry sense of humor smiles at his partner who still stands there numb, wide-eyed and an open mouth; turns and climbs back into his cruiser. As he drives off, neither of them utter a word and just look at each other. Somewhat dumbfounded and obviously unable to explain what just happened, the trooper shakes his head and numbly finishes writing the traffic ticket. Back at the troop the trooper with the dry sense humor asks his shift partner: **"Was that 'par' or a 'Hole in one'?"** Laughing hysterically his shift partner begs him to tell what just happened to the other troopers just walking in.

Best climax.

A four wheel drive with oversized farm tractor tires State Police unit is patrolling the beach of an unincorporated town; looking for illegal burning of dune fencing. The beach is a little rough and has already created many troughs that make it feel like riding on a roller coaster. As the Cpl (Corporal) comes over one of the hills and then into a trough he hears a thump, thump and stops the vehicle. When he looks back he is aghast to discover that he has run over two men having sex on the beach and immediately calls for an ambulance. In the process of closing the door of the ambulance the Cpl says: **"I bet that was the best climax they ever had."**

I just wanted a kiss.

A City police officer assigned to a walking district in a high activity area of burglaries and robberies has been instructed to link up with the officer of the adjacent beat. When the other officer arrives, Central advises them to respond to the train station and relieve the military honor guard standing vigil over the silver caskets from Vietnam so the soldiers have a chance to eat. Despite the somber occasion, it is a welcomed assignment for the two of them on this cold November night.

Since it is a slow night, the officers decide to get something to eat before they return to their respective walking beat. Busy talking and swinging their Hickory sticks they pass a large US Postal mail box prominently placed at the corner of the intersection. Suddenly a person leaps up from behind the mail box grabs one of the officers and kisses him on the cheek. Alarmed, the officer's immediate and instinctive reaction is to protect himself with a well-places baton strike to the forehead of the unknown assailant; whose semiconscious body slumps to the ground. They are shocked when they recognize the profusely bleeding individual, a well known transvestite and immediately call for an ambulance.

Confused by the transvestite's actions the striking officer asks the transvestite what possessed him to do such a foolish thing. As both officers help place him on the stretcher the transvestite turns to the striking officer and says: **"Man, you didn't have to hit me that hard." "I just wanted to grab and kiss you so that you could arrest me and put me in jail."** With a certain amount of compassion, the officer replies: **"I just reacted out of natural reflex."**

When thinking about the transvestite's rather foolish actions, the officers rationalize:

1. Guys like that occasionally want to be incarcerated and get out of the cold.
2. Going to a shelter could cause problems for guys like him trying to have sex with men while staying there.
3. But in prison he would be warm and have sex with the inmates and have the better of two worlds satisfying his desires.

Perhaps he was also upset because the police officer messed up his mascara.

You're outranked.

A City PD wagon crew is dispatched to handle a possible "Involuntary Commitment". When the police officers arrive at the residence, a woman meets them at the front door. Noticeably excited and nervous she states that her brother is exhibiting erratic behavior and is a possible danger to her or himself. As a precaution she has obtained an order to have him committed to the mental hospital for evaluation.

Suddenly a bedroom door flies open and her brother barges out of the room, wearing lapels with six general's stars on each shoulder. Maintaining their composure, the officers calmly tell him that he has to go with them to a doctor for a check-up. Adopting a very indignant manner, the "General" replies: **"I'm not speaking to you Private!"** Not wishing to aggravate the situation, one of the officers activates his mike and requests his supervisor to respond to the scene. The police supervisor, a lieutenant arrives a short time later.

Quickly recognizing the delicacy of the situation, he walks over to the "General" and respectfully says to him: **"You have to go with us and see the doctor."** In a somewhat aggravated tone the little "General" replies: **"Stand down, Captain!" "You're outranked here."** Without missing a beat the police lieutenant turns to his men and says: **"Escort the general to his staff car."** The two police officers snap to attention and salute. The "General" peacefully rides to the mental hospital without incident.

Tales from the Squad Car-Hide and Seek. *(In the officer's own words.)*

My partner Tom and I were working on the west side of town. It was a crappy, early spring evening and we were working the 3x11 shift. It was raining that night along with heavy winds and lightning, the kind of night they used to show in the old Black & White horror movies on late night TV when we were kids. Tom and I received a dispatch for an alarm in a residence just on the outskirts of town. We arrived at the residence and of course, it's a big old house. Again, the kind you see in horror movies! It all added to the atmosphere of the moment. We put on our old school police, knee length rain coats and covers and approached the residence. As we checked the exterior, we discovered a set of French Doors on the side of the residence which was ajar; somewhat unusual for this type of weather. We entered and began checking the interior of the residence. Now most cops will tell you that nine times out of ten alarms are either false or the suspect is long gone. However, you ALWAYS treat each alarm as legit; just in case. Checking the interior of the residence was like a page out of history; large, dark, full of antiques and lots and lots of rooms and closets. The frequent lightning flashes illuminating the interior and the high winds made the house creak eerily. Suddenly the power went out and we reverted to our trusty flashlights. As we entered a large side room, which was apparently being used for storage, our flashlight beams suddenly played on a figure on its stomach, partially hidden behind some boxes! ***Was it a body? A suspect?*** Tom and I slapped gun leather, drawing our side-arms with a speed and dexterity that would have make Wyatt Earp himself proud. We both yelled **"F*ck"** out loud and then began yelling orders: **"POLICE! SHOW ME YOUR HANDS!!!"** The "suspect" did not comply and in the calm that ensued after no gunfire was heard, we circled around both sides of the boxes in a pincer movement to discover that we had drawn down on a mannequin.....Of course my brother Michael, a member of the State Police K9 unit, chose not to be outdone and also responded to the residence. When he arrived on the scene he put his K9 partner on its lead and entered the residence. As they checked the interior, his K9 suddenly went around a corner and began growling, its hair standing on end and then pounced! Mike quickly ran around the corner, his sidearm drawn thinking his K9 had nabbed a burglar. He was amused to see his K9 partner attacking a stuffed and mounted Bear! By the grace of God the dog was called off quickly enough before it was able to tear out a piece of whatever the bear had been stuffed with.

What did you say?

While standing in line waiting for his coffee at a local donut shop, the officer hears a customer place an order. **"Yah, gimme' one of dem' dare' Babarian cream donuts."** (Bavarian?)

When questioning his veracity, the suspect tells the police officer: **"Man, I'm telling you da troof." "If you don't believe me, have da detective gimme a Mameograph test."** (Polygraph?)

I gots' to work in da mornin'.

Unable to have a uniformed unit respond to a disturbance at an apartment building, the City PD dispatch sends a plainclothes team. When the detectives arrive at the apartment they identify themselves to the female dressed in a McDonald's manager uniform and ask her what the problem is. The woman states: **"My mom and aunt are both drunk an' my aunt refuses to leave unless I gave her da' money for bus fare."** Then in an annoyed tone she continues: **"I gots' to work in da' mornin' an my kids got school." "All this fussin' is ridiculous." "My childrens don't need be dramatized like dat'."** Both detectives have to hurry to the nearest bathroom to relief themselves.

So I grabbed a pair of scissors.

A uniformed City police unit is flagged down by a female walking on the highway. When asked about her bleeding hand she replies: **"My boyfriend was beating me, so I grabbed a pair of scissors to defend myself."** She provided the officers with a description of her boyfriend. A short time later a male fitting that description is stopped by other officers and brought in for questioning and possible I.D. When presented before the complainant she says: **"No, that's not him."** Suddenly the male becomes angry and disorderly and starts a fight.

When the aggressive suspect is finally subdued and handcuffed, the officers notice a small pancake looking piece of skin on the hood of the white police car. While waiting for the suspect to be attended to for his facial injury at the hospital, the officers happen to look up at a McDonald's billboard advertising McGriddles. From then on the incident is called "The McGriddle Caper". Later on that day the alleged suspect is apprehended.

Tell the truth.

In an attempt to explain his side of the story to the judge, a subject says the following: **"To tell you the truth your Honor, I didn't want it to escapade (escalade?) into something physical so I defended myself verbally." "But I also want you to know that he was the source of the whole constipation (confrontation?)."**

The same plumbing?

A City police officer working undercover observes a large fight in progress as he drives past one of the local seedy bars and enters to investigate. He is barely able to notify Central Dispatch of the situation when all Hell breaks loose. When other units arrive things calm down enough enabling the officers a chance to investigate the cause of the melee. It is immediately apparent to them that the sailor who went berserk on one person and in the process of beating the tar out of a second when the undercover officer arrived; was with whom they needed to talk. To prevent a possible re-eruption they quickly escort the sailor outside; who is surprisingly left unscathed.

Once seated in the safety of a police car the sailor relates the following story.

> "Look, I'm new in this town and don't know where the action is. So I hailed a cab and asked the driver to take me to some place where I could find some action. I also stressed that I wasn't looking for anything fancy; just a place where I could get something reasonable to eat, drink and possibly a little dancing and whatever else. So here is where he brought me. When I was done eating at the bar this pretty good looking, what I thought was a "chick" asked me to dance. Everything was going pretty

> good while we were dancing and I was making some pretty risqué moves with that, whatever. Then while we were having a drink at the bar and exchanging some spit I reached under the dress of what I thought was a she and found the same plumbing that I have. Then when he tried to kiss me again I almost threw up and lost it and we started fighting. First of all I wasn't about to let a faggot beat my ass. I was just getting started on his faggot buddy when you guys came barging in. Just thinking about kissing him makes me sick."

At the conclusion of the investigation the assaulted victim did not prefer charges against the sailor and was satisfied with his humble apology. The real losers were the police who departed with two damaged police cars that crashed together hurrying to the scene of the fight.

A tough nut.

The State Police troop commander, a captain, is known to be a no-nonsense guy and tough nut. On this particular day a trooper is involved in a high-speed car chase of subjects wanted for an attempted robbery of a liquor store, close to the state line boundary. Firing shots at the trooper the perpetrators, two males and a female, also make several attempts to disable his cruiser. Whenever possible, the trooper responds in like manner and fires back at them to disable their vehicle. In their haste to lose the trooper they run out of luck when turning down a dead-end road. While the female suspect remains in the vehicle the driver runs into the woods and is later caught by State troopers of the neighboring state; the passenger makes the mistake and decides to stay and fight it out. His will to resist is quickly extinguished when his blood spreads over the cruiser's hood. After the prisoner is medically treated, the trooper leaves the hospital and returns to the troop with him.

Since it is only about 0430 hrs the trooper figures that he has ample time to file an After-Action report and wait for the detectives and parks his patrol unit in the captain's spot; a mortal sin. As luck has it the detectives are late and he is still not finished with his necessary paperwork when the captain arrives at 0730. Understandably hot, the captain abruptly storms into the troop and demands to know who has the nerve to violate his parking space. After a cool-headed desk sergeant explains the circumstances of the case, the Captain picks up the extra set of car keys to the trooper's patrol vehicle and washes it. Later that morning when he finds his vehicle parked behind the troop the trooper is told by the desk sergeant what transpired. He is relieved that he didn't have to see the troop commander. Phew! It isn't until sometime later that he is told that the captain was the one who washed his car.

I'm coming out of the closet.

Several years prior to the above incident, the same captain, then a D/Sgt (Desk Sergeant) was the brunt of a joke. A State Police corporal working in the dispatch center located in the same building, well known for playing some terrific pranks, could not resist the temptation to get one on the hardnosed desk sergeant. Due to new construction in process for two other police departments at the time, the three departments temporarily operated their individual departments' assignments out of the same facility.

It is around 0200 hrs and a pretty slow night all the way around when a dispatcher from another department, who happens to know the caller, tells him to hold on because there is someone at the center that would like to talk to him. After quickly relating to him about the male caller, the corporal picks up the phone and goes into action. The word that the corporal is about to pull another stunt somehow spreads like wildfire but yet unbeknown to the Sgt and puts the suspense on edge with every ear listening.

When the Cpl (Corporal) begins, one of the supervisors has extreme difficulty controlling the hysteria of the listeners. The Cpl picks up the phone and listens.

> "I understand that you two know each other. Although he is not a Trans' like you, you two are on friendly terms. Is that right? Well, I might as well come out of the closet. Yeah we can meet; of course, tonight. You can come right here in the lobby and ask for Sgt H..... I'll be sitting at the desk. I'm the desk sergeant."

About 20 minutes later a couple of the call takers almost lose it when they see a yellow cab pull up and a black male wearing high heels and a dress climbs out and walks to the front door of the building. The D/Sgt (Sgt H...), smoking his usual cigar, almost chokes when he looks up and sees the Trans' enter the lobby. Apparently believing that the Sgt sitting behind the desk is the trooper he talked to on the phone makes a dash for him to give him a hug. When the onlookers watch the sergeant clear the desk, total hysteria results causing some of them to almost fall over each other as they hurry down the stairs and back to their work stations.

The poor "Trans" leaves the troop, obviously heartbroken; but not until the sergeant puts him straight (pun intended...). No one dares to talk about it until well beyond the Statue of Limitations; the corporal made coming to work fun for everyone. If the State ever gave an award for entertainer of the year, he should get it.

Improvised traffic control.

Driving down the road an off duty officer sees red and blue lights pulling in and out of traffic at an intersection but not going away and thinks that it must be an accident. As he gets closer, he sees a uniformed police officer from another department directing traffic. When, the off duty officer takes a closer look he is in total disbelieve in what he sees. The other officer is pulling his car in and out of the intersection while remaining seated in his car direct traffic from the open driver's side window!!!! Now, the off duty officer has to admit that he has been guilty of laziness but this is a new low. Before he departs the unbelievable scene, the off duty officer debates whether it is worthwhile to educate the uniformed officer and tell him that is not an effective way to direct traffic. Of course he could tell him that they issue things called RAINCOATS and RAIN COVERS, rubber boots that actually keep the rain off as you direct traffic in the proper way. Yeah he knows, it's new fangled technology but it just may catch on...so put them on, grab a flare and do it right...........rant off....

Look for a red passenger vehicle.

A couple of police officers in a city in Germany are excited having a new patrol vehicle assigned to them; considerably faster than any of the older ones. Interested in finding out what this car can do they decide to put it through the paces a little bit and drive to the outskirts of the city. Since they are not fully acquainted with the vehicle, they did not anticipate the car's quick response and sudden acceleration. As they are rounding a left-hand curve the driver overcompensates causing the vehicle to spin out of control and run off the right side of the road. After flipping over a couple of times the car comes to rest on its side jamming both doors. Only slightly bruised, both officers manage to extricate themselves by forcing the sun roof open. The vehicle is a total loss. Fortunately the communication system of the patrol vehicle is still functioning and they are able to call for help. Realizing that they are in deep trouble they maintain sufficient presence of mind and immediately concoct a plausible story of what happened.

When satisfied that their stories match, the driver radios central and advises dispatch what has happened; claiming that a red colored sedan bearing a Remscheid ID (Identified by first two letters of the license plates in Germany) forced them off the road at high speed. For the next half of an hour all red vehicles are stopped and questioned. Of course since no red vehicle is ever found, no charges are placed and the officers are back on patrol. At least now they are better familiar with the new machines.

You know that you've been a cop too long.

When you and your buddy are driving down the road, and both of you say: **"Wow, dispatch is really quiet today."** Then you realize "A"- you aren't working. "B"- you aren't even in a police vehicle!!!!!! ***(WTF)***

But a good start.

A State Police D/Sgt (Detective sergeant) sitting in the witness stand is obviously and deliberately being badgered by the defense attorney. When asking the sergeant a somewhat confusing question, pretending to be perplexed, the D/Sgt replies: **"Your honor am I required to answer such a stupid question?"** Infuriated by the trooper's question, the defense attorney raises his voice and almost goes into a tirade objecting to that remark. Hardly able to speak the attorney asks the sergeant: **"Did you just call me stupid?"** The sergeant smiles at him and replies: **"No I didn't!" "It's too soon for that." "But you definitely made a good start."** Totally dumbfounded by what he just heard, the attorney mutters that he is going to take further action against the sergeant for insulting him; after this trial is over.

Apparently desirous of keeping order and prevent the present trial from going onto a different and unwanted direction, the judge motions for the defense attorney to approach the bench. When the defense attorney stands before the bench, the judge asks him in a somewhat fatherly manner: **"Did you just claim that the Sergeant called you stupid?"** Happy that the judge is willing to address the insult, the attorney nods his head and replies: **"Yes your Honor he did, and I am so glad that you heard it also."** Assuming a very stern look, the judge lowers his voice and says:

> "Let me clarify something for you, so that we may proceed. He did not call you stupid. Did you hear what I just said? He merely stated his opinion when he said that it was too early to make that judgment. He only said that the question was stupid and that you made a good start. As far as this court is concerned, that is only his opinion. As an attorney, you should know that it is allowed under

> the First Amendment; Freedom of Speech. Your objection has no basis. Therefore, your objection is overruled. You may continue with your line of questioning but be alert how you phrase them."

Even attorneys sometimes lose track of where they are going. They should always be careful not to lose their composure; it interferes with logic.

I may not know how to say …

A State trooper notices the vehicle speed up in an attempt to beat the red light but fails to do so. For some reason the female operator didn't see the second light turn to red, a short distance further down the road and runs through it also. As he flags her over he thinks: ***"Well, one red light certainly is enough reason for a stop." "But two red lights in a row is a definite must."*** When he asks for her driver's license he hears her speaking in German, telling her male passenger to get the registration out of the glove compartment. She looks up at him and with obvious arrogance almost slaps the documents into his hand. He somehow manages to keep his cool and calmly says: **"I see here that you are an out-of-state driver." "Our law requires that non-state residence violators must be taken forthwith to the magistrate court." "I am going to charge you with going through a red light and ask you to follow me to the court."**

The driver huffs and momentarily stares at him and wants to know how long it will take because she doesn't have much time for such nonsense. Furthermore, she demands her license back; claiming that it is not allowed to drive without a license. Surprised by his own ability to keep his temper in check he replies: **"Right now you don't need to have your license in your possession** (tauntingly flipping it in his hand) **because I'm going to hold onto it for safekeeping until we get to court." "Besides that, you are under arrest and have been ordered to follow me."** As he returns to his cruiser he hears her uttering endearing insults about him to the man sitting next to her and then sees them laugh. In route to court he muses: ***"Well, we will see who has the last laugh."*** Several minutes later they pull into the court parking lot and the couple is escorted into the courtroom by the trooper.

While the trooper is occupied typing the specific traffic arrest warrants he can't help but overhear the couple conversing in German and referring to him with frequent barrages of insults. Occasionally the female rudely interrupts him demanding to know how much longer she has to endure the kangaroo court. Smiling at her and in the most polite manner that would be the envy of any actor he answers: **"This is a rather lazy afternoon." "Don't you think so too, Ma'am?" "You must not forget that this is a court and we can't rush to judgment."** Fortunately looks and barely audible expletives don't kill but can hurt your feelings; unless you are hardnosed trooper. Suppressing the urge to verbally engage the couple, he finds the whole thing rather very amusing and finishes typing; then asks the couple to follow him into the courtroom.

Prior to rendering a decision, the judge asks: **"Are there any extenuating circumstances reference this case, trooper?"** Pretending to have been caught off guard he replies: **"Oh dear me I almost forgot, in her case there are two charges." "The defendant went through two red lights; each at a separate intersection." "I was also bothered by the lady's hostile demeanor towards me."** Startled by the sudden outburst by the defense side of words he couldn't understand the judge gives him a disturbed look and murmurs: **"What is going on?" "Do you understand what they are saying?"** Grinning from ear to ear and shaking his head and flaring his hands in the air replies: **"I don't have the foggiest idea." "I don't understand them either your honor." "By the way if it pleases the court, may we have a verdict in the cases before the bench?"** Preceded by a loud bang of the gavel, the judge says: **"Guilty!"** Then with a very stern look tells the couple to report to the clerk for the payment of the adjudicated fines.

On their way out of the courtroom and with absolute disgust in her eyes the female (defendant) says to the trooper: **"I may not know how to say ziss' correctly in English, but..."** and is abruptly cut off by the trooper. Before she has a chance to start again he mockingly says: **"Although I don't like to, I will lower my standards considerably just**

to accommodate yours to make sure that you are able to understand me." Then mimicking her accent he continues: **"So duts' allrite' Dirne** (slang for slut) **you may say ziss' in your usual guttural cherman'."** "Shocked and in disbelief and almost out of breath, she screams: **"I can't believe what you just said." "I'm going to report you."** Smirking at her, slightly shaking his head from side to side replies: **"I really don't know what you are talking about." "However if you feel that you must lodge a complaint, you're in the right place." "Remember, this is a court?" "By the way, do you also desire the governor's telephone number?" "That might be quicker." "Have a nice day."** When no further insults emanate out of her trash mouth he smiles, opens the door and walks out of the office whistling.

You'll need something bigger...

Ted and his girlfriend have found a somewhat secluded place and park the car. He dowses the headlights, cuts the engine and turns his attention to Jane sitting next to him. A few minutes later a thud and the shaking of the car dislodges their amorous embrace. Their puzzled looks instantly freeze into fear that seems to press their body through the backrest of the front seat. The momentary eerie quiet is suddenly shattered by Jane's hysterical and blood curdling screams that only seem to abate when she is taking a breath and yet appear to prevent Ted from going into shock.

Ted somehow retains the presence of mind and realizes that if they want to stay alive, they have only seconds to get out of there and no time to console frenzied Jane. Miraculously, he manages to start the car and slam it into gear. Then squealing tires and burning rubber fishtails it out of there; the envy of some professional stunt drivers. Panic struck, this is probably the only time in his life that he wants a cop to stop him for speeding as he races in the direction of the police station. They finally breathe a sigh of relief when they find someone at the station; this late at night.

After several attempts, the D/Sgt (Desk Sergeant) finally manages to get a coherent account of the couple's life or death encounter from the still shaking Ted.

> "We were just sitting in my car and necking when we felt a bump and the car shook a little and we looked up to see what it was. A real life Gorilla suddenly jumps off the hood of my car. I just froze for a split second and thought we were going to die right then and there; then Jane went hysterical and broke out with an ear piercing scream. I knew that if I didn't get us out of there he was going to kill us and got the hell out of there."

The Sgt picks up the phone and dials and then:

> "Hey Bill, I need you to clear and get back here right away. I also need you to stop by your house and pick up one of your big rifles because that .38 pea-shooter isn't going to do the job. We may have a Gorilla running loose. There is not much else we can do until mornin'. Right now you are our only line of defense."

Cpl Bill immediately rushes home, grabs his M-1 Garand along with some ammo and is ready for his Safari. Despite a lengthy and thorough search "Bwana" has to return to the station empty handed. Just as he enters, the Sgt motions to him to stand-by. As he slowly cradles the receiver of the phone the Sgt turns around and says:

> "Well, we may never know where or who our Gorilla is. But what we **DO** know for certain is that it was **NOT**, a real life Gorilla. I just received a call from a guy, that I just hung up on, who wanted to apologize and tell me the real story. According to him he found a Gorilla suit that looked so real that he couldn't resist the temptation to try it on and when he saw the couple park their car; it was a ready-made opportunity. He said when he saw the fear in their eyes and heard her unbelievable loud screams he almost peed in his pants and couldn't even say anything. Then the way they pealed out of there, he just about lost it completely. Well, he thought that was the end of it until he

> saw a uniformed cop with an army rifle walking around and figured that the whole thing got out of hand. He felt that he had to tell the police before someone got hurt and not to worry because the Gorilla is back in his box. That's it folks."

Last day on the job.

It is the D/Sgt's (Detective Sergeant) last day on the job and several members at the troop decide to give him, along with his wife, a farewell party and an appropriate send-off. When he and his wife arrive at the troop they are greeted by the troop commander and several troopers. After shaking hands with the couple the troop commander says: **"It is my pleasure to escort you to your office for the very last time." "So that you may remember this occasion, all of us had a share in decorating your office specifically according to your personal taste."** When the D/Sgt notices the troopers crowding around the Capt, he realizes that something is going on at his expense. As soon as the troop commander swings open the office door, D/Sgt's wife screams: **"Oh my God"** and covers her face and then the rest of the crowd busts into laughter. The D/Sgt finally manages to get a look at his office and hollers: **"You no good rotten bastards"** and also brakes out in laughter. He knows that he will never be able to retaliate for this prank that has been pulled on him; it's his last day. The now extremely jovial troop commander says: **"Hey, come on now." "The least thing that you can do is show your appreciation for all of the hard work these guys did redecorating your office."**

The D/Sgt gently pushes his wife ahead of him as they enter the office to admire the troopers' esoteric decorating skills. He can't believe his eyes and has difficulty to speak because he is laughing so hard. When he looks at what his friends have done he is at first speechless while his embarrassed wife is still covering her face and laughing hysterically. The office ceiling is totally decorated with pornographic paraphernalia ranging in varying sizes of dildos, provocative looking undergarments, and a large array of sex toys. There is hardly a void place remaining on the walls. Every conceivable space is plastered with pictures of couples engaged in erotic sex acts and the floor is dotted with genuine looking piles of feces.

He finally manages to control himself and catching his breath says: **"This is by far the best that you guys ever got of me." "But you first made sure that I could not return the favor." "You bastards!" "To tell you the truth, I can't think of a way that I could ever have gotten even with you."**

When everyone has calmed down the Captain leads the couple to the small conference room for coffee, cake and snacks. At the conclusion of the festivities, the D/Sgt and his wife thank everyone, bid farewell and walk out of the backdoor. As he turns and takes one last poignant glance, the D/Sgt sees his friends looking out of the troop windows, smiling and waving good bye. What he doesn't know at that moment is that his friends are setting him up for one last prank and want to make sure that he keeps his attention on them and doesn't look at the back of his privately owned vehicle. Feeling somewhat melancholy, he climbs behind the wheel of his car, waves good bye and drives off.

On their way home the D/Sgt and his wife notice that some of the cars passing them are beeping their horn and giving them the high sign. They find it extremely odd that several truck drivers blow their loud truck horn after they passed them and seem to stay unnecessarily long behind them. Then the D/Sgt and his wife are totally flabbergasted when a few truck drivers smile at them and beep their horn again as they pass by. The D/Sgt turns to his wife and says: **"Those bastards did something else to me, but I can't pull over now." "I have to wait until we get home to see what they did." "God only knows." "I just know that they did something."**

Cont'd.

They finally got the best...

When they finally arrive home both of them leap out and run to the rear of the car and are not just shocked but horrified at what they find. Affixed to the rear bumper is a professionally looking sign with bold letters written on it, "I AM GAY and I AM PROUD". The D/Sgt looks at his wife and says: **"I knew it." "Damn, they finally <u>did</u> get the best of me." "This is truly a fantastic pay-back; especially since I can't do anything about it."** Both of them burst out laughing and rip the sign off the bumper. The D/Sgt dials the number of the troop and requests to speak to the Captain; whose voice is almost drowned out by the roar of loud laughter. Hardly able to speak the Captain wants to know if the D/Sgt had a nice ride home and continues laughing. Unable to hold back his own laughter the D/Sgt says: **"I must tell you guys that was by far the best job ever pulled on me." "Even though you finally bested me, I thank all of you for a send-off that I will never forget."** Many, many years have passed since then, but those who were part of it occasionally meet and still laugh about it.

Conclusion

The disintegration of family unity, the lack of proper and adequate parental guidance, as well as teaching obedience to Law and Order are major contributors to the rise in crime. Young unwed mothers, too young to have gained experience in life are required to assume the role of both parents since the males are unwilling to accept their responsibility. Should the adult stepfather, jumping up and down like a trapped animal in a cage (Ferguson) yelling: **"Burn this bitch down!"** be the example we are looking for? No criminal charges for inciting a riot were ever placed against this antagonist. To what extent is today's society willing to tolerate such outrages behavior? Sadly most seriously and negatively impacted by these critical issues is the struggling African American community. Regrettably that volatile bone of contention will not and cannot be resolved until strong and level-headed leaders of the Black community emerge and are willing and brave enough to also point the finger at their own community and put the shoe on the right foot.

> "Everyone wants to live at the expense of the state. They forget that the state wants to live at the expense of everyone."
>
> Frederic Bastiat, *The Law*

It is an absurdity blaming the plight of the so called Ghetto on others or outside sources. Too many fail to realize that such accusations are a direct affront to the countless successful African Americans; who likewise struggled through tremendous adversities. Instead of allowing themselves to be patronized and respond with senseless action and frequent violence, these successful individuals decided to take charge of their own lives and managed to crawl out of the abyss. A closer look at these eminent, frequently referred to as nonconformists, reveals a predominance of a **"can do"** attitude. These men and women, nurtured by **strong guiding hands**, learned early in life to appreciate the importance of a sound education and a way to better selves. Rather than emulate the strong character of these African American achievers who were determined to do it on their own, come under immediate assault by an easily manipulated and exploitable Black community which all too often appears to be reluctant to accept them. Because they readily see through the false façade and dare to deviate or even defy to **"fall in line"** of the "Left" expected norm, they are viewed as **"sell-outs**.

Every stratum of our society is plagued by those who are quick to pass judgment. These misguided persons do not seem to realize, or even care that police officers are also a product of their society. Yet they readily lambaste people who are willing to say **"NO!"** to the often acceptable transgressions by the general public to pursue a career in Law Enforcement; that already makes a difference. Added to that is **legal** authority. Human nature is said to have an innate dislike and an aversion for rules. Already apparent in very early childhood; a child doesn't like to be told what to do. Unless that natural desire to do "whatever" is curtailed and properly channeled, it will manifest and generally progress throughout life. Without meaningful consequences for rule violations, it is very likely that the seriousness of offenses will escalate. This seems to be the accepted norm by vacuous characters that are determined to create unjustifiable senseless havoc of unfounded acts and totally ignore the legal aspect.

> "The mission of law is not to oppress persons and plunder them of their property, even though the law may be acting in a philanthropic spirit."
>
> Frederic Bastiat, *The law*

Regrettably, a tremendous blemish has been created on Law Enforcement by the less than 1% of despicable men and women serving, who somehow managed to weasel their way into the time-honored profession. In comparison to the general citizenry, that is phenomenally low. It is inconceivable how such a large number of inept creatures of the general society exists who unjustly accuse an entire profession by the misdeeds of a very few; yet do not seem to care about the murderous gun violence in their own neighborhoods. Our genuine goal of harmonious coexistence cannot be reached as long as we continue to swerve to avoid the truth.

Despite the absolute lunacy associated with the anti-police segment of our society, the "**Blue Line**" is determined to hold and keep its oath to serve **all citizens**.

> **"No man is above the law and no man is below it; nor do we ask any man's permission when we require of him to obey it. Obedience to the law is demanded as a right; not asked as a favor."** Theodore Roosevelt.

A very thought provoking question may be asked:**"Are Police Officers different?"** The answer is an unequivocal "**YES**". Simply put, it is the nature of the individuals wearing the uniform and an unconventional job demanded of them. The uniform may one day be retired and hang in the closet but the badge is placed in the heart.

WHEN COPS RETIRE

When a good cop leaves the 'job' and retires to a better life,
Many are jealous, some are pleased and yet others,
who may have already retired wonder.
We wonder if he knows what he is leaving behind,
because we already know.
We know, for example, that after a lifetime of camaraderie
that few experience,
it will remain as a longing for those past times.
We know in the law enforcement life there is fellowship
which lasts long after the uniforms are hung up in the back of the closet.
We know even if he throws them away,
they will be on him with every step and breath that remains in his life.
We also know how the very bearing of the man speaks
Of what he was and in his heart still is.

These are the burdens of the job.
You will still look at people suspiciously,
Still see what others do not see or choose to ignore and
Always will look at the rest of the law enforcement world with a respect for what they do; only grown in a lifetime of knowing.
Never think for one moment you are escaping from that life.
You are only escaping the 'job' and merely being allowed to leave active 'duty'.

So what I wish for you is that whenever you ease into retirement,
In your heart you never forget for one moment
That 'Blessed are the Peacemakers for they shall be called children of God,'
And you are still a member of the greatest fraternity the world has ever known.

Author: Unknown

Can you think back that far?

A time for LEO old-timers to be envious of their modern successors in Law Enforcement has long past, they are instead left in wonderment. Those who remember their time are amazed by the technological advances and ask themselves: "What could I have accomplished?" They can't help it but to think back:

Oh yes, the reliable and fast 440 Plymouth.

1. Got you there in a hurry.
2. Didn't lose many high-speed chases.
3. No seat belts; in race cars yes – but these were patrol vehicles.
4. Learned to shift your body when taking corners.

Especially on those ice cold winter days - cold Naugahyde bench seat made your essentials feel like sitting on ice cubes. Grateful to have a functioning heater.

On super hot summer days - hot Naugahyde seats were ready to fry an egg. (Don't forget to place a cloth under your posterior.

1. Hoped there would be a chance to change your sweat-soaked uniform pants.
2. Summer uniform – material not as thick as winter.
3. Headgear had to be worn at all times when in uniform; in and out of patrol vehicle.
4. Windows manually rolled down.

    a. Careful that your paperwork didn't fly out of the window.
    b. If rain, stop vehicle and manually roll up windows.

5. Occasionally stop at a gas station to wipe the dust and grime off your face; ring around your eyes left by sunglasses.
6. Sunglasses were absolutely essential.

Communication.

1. Two bands radio – High and Low.
2. Transmit car to car – permission first.
3. House phone receiver attached to 18" spiral electric cord, cradled in half-moon rubber cup on medal stand affixed to the hump.
4. Once out of car, no communication; you were on your own.
5. Help on the way in 5 minutes often seemed like an eternity.
6. Frequently needed the physical stamina to stay in the game; if a golden tongue failed.
7. "On Call" detective able to be reachable by phone or in person.

    a. No cell phones yet.
    b. Limited use of home phone by family members when on call.

Computers?

1. In some Banks and large businesses, yes.
2. Miles of cable under floors.
3. Large wheels rotating on massive wall computers.

4. IBM cards.
5. Teletype machines and Ticker tape.
6. NCIC (Natl. Crime Information Center) frequently down.

    a. Had no immediate cause to detain suspect if wanted was not confirmed.
    b. If established later and suspect had already been released, not likely to be found bagain.

Essential personal gear and equipment.

1. 38 cal. Revolver (6 rounds); 38 cal Snub nose (5 rounds)
2. Had your trusty Blackjack, Flapjack.
3. Several ballpoint pens, pencils.
4. Nightstick.
5. Adequate notepads.
6. Familiarity with manual typewriter; if lucky and available - electric. Kept seniority in mind.
7. Couldn't leave work until a brief, initial report was submitted.
8. Proficiency in cursive and print.
9. Nav. System.???

    a. Critical to have a detailed map of patrol sector.
    b. Proficient in map reading and Land Navigation.
    c. Helped if able to read True North, Grid North and Magnetic North.
    d. Helped if able to read a compass.

10. Practiced driving at various speeds.

    a. Became familiar with your patrol area like wearing a well fitting glove.
    b. Practiced what speeds corners could be taken.

11. Relied on thorough knowledge of the traffic code – Computers in police cars were not even thought of and came many, many years later.

Issues of another sort.

1. Smoking in patrol cars was frowned upon. A blind eye given if smoking material was held below window; out of public view.
2. Civilian radios were not a part of police vehicles.

    a. PO brought transistor radios.
    b. Installed 8-Tracks and hide them under seat.
    c. All non-issue items were removed prior to formal inspections.
    d. Built car counsel w/ flip lid for writing table.

Speed Enforcement.

1. Radar.

    a. Unit attached on tri-pod and cables attached to car battery.
    b. Used Tuning forks to test apparatus accuracy.
    c. Adjusted cone.
    d. Unit reading Radar and calling out speed remained stationary.

        a. Old units with needle indicator.
        b. Later units with digital readout.

    c. Mobile Pick-up unit ran first test.
    d. Radar Override occasionally created havoc on drivers with Radar Detectors.

2. VASCAR (Visual Average Speed Computer And Recorder) 1966.

    a. Radar Detectors useless against it; no beams.
    b. Able to read car speed a long distance away.
    c. Adjusted with shadows reflected on roadway.

Driving Under the Influence breathalyzers.

1. MOBAT – Field test.

    a. Carried in patrol vehicle.
    b. Subject's breath collected by blowing into a balloon attached to a couple chemical tubes.
    c. Results tested by State Chemist.

2. OMICRON machine stationary at troop or police station..

    a. Tested subject's alveolar air.
    b. Subject's breathed into a tube attached to unit (fresh mouth piece for each test).
    c. Digital readout/paper printout.
    d. Subject received copy and officer retained copy for court.

EPILOGUE

Written for those who are brave and demand the truth and are unafraid to accept it.

It would be unjustifiable and thus inconceivable not to mention the irrational, unreasonable and illogical demands progressively placed upon us today. The deliberate alterations and selected prohibition of true history seizing our schools and academia are systematically molding minds into soft targets. Historical facts that reveal many of today's issues are not new and have in fact threatened the harmony of the human race for hundreds of years; extensively watered down or totally suppressed. It is alarming that not only the disrespect for law and order has become an accepted norm but also the gradual destruction of our pride in this great nation and of being an **AMERICAN**.

Throughout history generations have struggled with critical issues and considered the dilemma they were faced with at a particular moment unique; that is precisely what is happening today. Unfortunately human nature's great disdain for authority advances along with societies; which invariably leads to a conflict with established laws and to physical confrontation with those enforcing them. It is further magnified by the absolute arrogance displayed by many of those in position of leadership. An absurdity of proposals, hinged on the fringes of lunacy, flood our minds in an effort to remedy the Weltschmerz; curing the ills of the world. All of these, solely based on computer generated data, totally disregard the unpredictable power of Nature; an offense to common sense and reason.

> "It is dangerous to be right in matters on which established authorities are wrong. Opinion has caused more trouble on this little earth than plagues and earthquakes." Voltaire (1694-1778)

We choose to ignore the wisdom of great minds and mock their words of caution. Deliberately altering past history to fit the agenda doesn't change the eventual outcome. Let those who possess the wisdom to separate facts and reality from fantasy and fable, discard the pompous attitude of their believed superiority and understand the warnings for the future.

> "The pharisaical catchwords such as on "tolerance" and "racism" actually mean the opposite of any: who do not agree with them. Their agenda requires....to accept the substitution of "discrimination" for "choice". It is not discrimination but choice that decides with whom I associate or whom I employ. I do not discriminate against white wine when I choose red. How I base these judgments is my own business absolutely. But it won't stop.
>
> Not until you and everyone you know have submitted to their terms....By then it will be too late to rid the language of such obvious examples of "Doublespeak", ("Political Correctness" added) and to set the record straight and return genuine meaning to our vocabularies."
>
> "Tolerance is the last virtue of a depraved society. When an immoral society has blatantly and proudly violated all the commandments, it insists upon one last virtue, tolerance for its immorality. It will not tolerate condemnation of its perversions. It creates a whole new world in which only the intolerant critics, of intolerable evil is evil."
>
> *(Hutton Gibson, and thank you, Mel)*
>
> "Democracy extends the sphere of individual freedom, socialism restricts it. Democracy attaches all possible value to each man; socialism makes each man a mere agent, a mere number. Democracy and socialism have nothing in common but one word; equality. **But notice the difference: while democracy seeks equality in**

liberty, socialism seeks equality in restraint and servitude."

A translation of de Tocqueville's Speech on Socialism (1848) from Hayek, The Road to Serfdom):

"Order is not pressure which is imposed on society from without, but an equilibrium which is set up from within."

Jose Ortega y Gasset (1883-1955)

"There is no room in this country for hyphenated Americanism....The one absolutely certain way of bringing this nation to ruin, of preventing all possibility of its continuing to be a nation at all, would be to permit it to become a tangle of squabbling nationalities.

Theodore Roosevelt,
Speech before the Knights of Columbus,
New York [October 12, 1915}

"I studied the Koran a great deal, I came away from that study with the conviction there have been few religions in the world as deadly as that of Mohammad. So far as I can see, it is the principal cause of the decadence so visible today in the Muslim world and, though less absurd than the polytheism of old, its social and political tendencies are in my opinion to be feared, and I therefore regard it as a form of decadence rather than a form of progress in relation to paganism itself.

Letter to Arthur de Gobineau,
22 October 1843, Tocqueville Reader, p.221

"Instead of 'Rose Colored' glasses, acquire the wisdom that helps you uncover the hidden truths of reality." (Author)

CPSIA information can be obtained
at www.ICGtesting.com
Printed in the USA
BVHW031255180222
629333BV00026B/141

9 781733 336659